JEWISH QUESTIONS

To Jackie –
With special thanks
for your advice, support,
and friendship.
Matt Goldish
7/25/08

JEWISH QUESTIONS

RESPONSA ON SEPHARDIC LIFE
IN THE EARLY MODERN PERIOD

Matt Goldish

PRINCETON UNIVERSITY PRESS

PRINCETON AND OXFORD

Copyright © 2008 by Princeton University Press

Published by Princeton University Press,
41 William Street, Princeton, New Jersey 08540
In the United Kingdom: Princeton University Press,
6 Oxford Street, Woodstock, Oxfordshire OX20 1TW

All Rights Reserved

Library of Congress Cataloging-in-Publication Data
Goldish, Matt.
Jewish questions : responsa on Sephardic life in the
early modern period / Matt Goldish.
p.   cm.
Includes bibliographical references and index.
ISBN 978-0-691-12264-9 (hardcover : alk. paper)—
ISBN 978-0-691-12265-6 (pbk. : alk. paper)
1. Jews—Turkey—History—Sources. 2. Sephardim—Turkey—
History—Sources. 3. Turkey—History—Ottoman Empire, 1288–1918—
Sources. 4. Turkey—Ethnic relations—Sources.   I. Title.
DS135.T8G58 2008
305.892′40560903—dc22   2007047195

British Library Cataloging-in-Publication Data is available

This book has been composed in Sabon

Printed on acid-free paper. ∞

press.princeton.edu

Printed in the United States of America

1   3   5   7   9   10   8   6   4   2

This book is dedicated to three generations of great women from the Nahmias family, one of the most illustrious clans in Sephardic history: Simhah Nahmias, Rahel Nahmias, and Betty Goldish.

לכבוד שלש,דורות של נשים מבית נחמיאש
שמחה ,רחלה, ובטי

CONTENTS

Preface   xi

Introduction   xvii

Short Biographies of the Hakhamim   lviii

Part I: Life among Muslims and Christians

1. Caught in the Middle of Ottoman-Italian Wars
   (Greece, 1716)   5
2. The Financial Fallout of a Blood Libel (Ragusa, 1622)   8
3. A Blood Libel among the Sephardim (Ottoman Empire,
   mid-seventeenth century)   13
4. Preparations for Siege (Algiers, 1732)   15
5. The Jew Who Stood Up to the Governor—But Maybe
   Not Enough (Algiers, mid-eighteenth century)   16

Part II: Trade and Other Professions in the Sephardi
   Diaspora

6. An International Loan Gone Awry (Mediterranean,
   late-sixteenth century)   23
7. The Woman with a Steel Welding Monopoly
   (Aleppo, ca. 1559)   26
8. Death of a Salesman in Persia (Bursa and Persia,
   late sixteenth century)   29
9. A Case of Mistaken Identity (Constantinople,
   late seventeenth century)   32
10. The Death of Tall Aslan (Aleppo and Turkey, 1681)   35
11. Egyptian Jews with Civet Cats (Egypt, mid-sixteenth
    century)   38
12. Jewish Trade in a War Zone (Zante and Venice, ca. 1620)   39
13. The Tale of the Clothier and the Vizier
    (Constantinople, 1641)   42

Part III: Life within the Sephardic Community

14. Divorce and an Indian Impostor (Greece, mid-sixteenth
    century)   53
15. The Great Fire of Saloniki (Saloniki and Lepanto, 1620)   58
16. An Apostate Soldier of Fortune (Zante, ca. 1620)   61
17. The Fallout from a Tall Building (Ottoman Empire, early
    seventeenth century)   64
18. Polish Fugitives in Egypt (Egypt, late seventeenth century)   66
19. The Quarantine Colony in Spalato (Spalato, seventeenth
    century)   68
20. Unscrupulous Partners and the Fear of Forced Conversion
    (Rhodes, early seventeenth century)   71
21. A Change of Fortune, an Unwilling Wife, and a City
    in Panic (Morocco, Algeria, and Egypt, 1737)   73
22. The Causes and Consequences of a Denunciation
    (Meknes, Morocco, 1721–1728)   77
23. The Persecution of a Witness to Immorality (Tangier and
    Fez, 1744)   83

Part IV: Ritual Observance and Jewish Faith in Sephardic Communities

24. The Jew Accused of Heresy (Ottoman Empire, early
    sixteenth century)   93
25. Jews Becoming Karaites and Karaites Becoming Jews
    (Egypt, late seventeenth century)   96
26. Bequests of Conversos and Their Status as Jews (Istanbul,
    early sixteenth century)   99
27. The Converso and the Charitable Fraternity (Amsterdam,
    late seventeenth century)   102
28. Monstrous Births and Marvelous Creatures (Venice,
    mid-seventeenth century)   106
29. Protestants Who Send Money to Poor Jews in the Land
    of Israel (Palestine, mid-seventeenth century)   109
30. What May a Jew Do With a Nativity Medallion?
    (Greece, early sixteenth century)   112
31. On Loaning Money to Priests (Jerusalem, ca. 1624)   115
32. The Penitence of the Kastoria Community (Greece,
    late seventeenth century)   120

⸓ V: Marriage, Family, and Private Life

Converso and His Flemish Concubine (Turkey, early
⸱enth century)   127

⸱vert Repudiates Her Marriage (Ottoman Empire,
⸱teenth century)   129

⸱cholic Monogamist (Egypt, late seventeenth
                                                                        131

⸱Bigamist (Morocco, early eighteenth
                                                                        134

⸱nancy (Shekhem [Nablus], Palestine,
                                                                        136

⸱lterer (Western Europe, 1730)   139
⸱s in Belgrade (Belgrade, late
                                                                        143

⸱ttoman Empire, late
                                                                        147

⸱n's Right to Divorce
⸱   150

⸱ade, 1698)   153
⸱2)   155

                                                                        159
                                                                        171

PREFACE

Responsa are collections of questions on Jewish law asked by individuals or groups, and the responses given by rabbis. The genre has existed for well over a thousand years, and it has been used by historians almost since the inception of modern Jewish historiography. Much of the responsa literature has been easily available in print for a long time, and is now available in electronic form as well. At the same time, the responsa are one of many sources shedding light on the history of the Sephardic Jews, the group with which the present volume is concerned. There are Ottoman and European court records, travelers' diaries, municipal records, Hebrew books of all genres, personal correspondence, and more. Several good histories of the Sephardim are already available. What, then, makes this book different and useful?

One answer is that the book includes texts that are usually available only to the Hebrew reader who knows where to look and how to understand specialized legal terminology. This material throws light on every aspect of post-Expulsion Sephardic life, but it also opens vistas into Jewish social, economic, religious, and political history in the early modern era.[1] Even seasoned historians may well discover something new in these documents.

The book has another, more novel goal as well. In the past, historians have generally used responsa in the pursuit of specific historiographic goals reflecting the scholarly concerns of each generation. These texts have been a basis for the study of Jewish communal structures, community histories, rabbinic biographies, histories of specific laws and their application, and, more recently, topics in social history, such as the position of women, gays, converts, and other groups in Jewish society.[2] I am

---

[1] While Jewish political history between 70 C.E. and the modern period has not often been considered a viable topic for research, new scholarship is finding fertile ground in this field. The Jewish community itself had specific political structures (some of which are touched upon in the documents below); but Jewish thinkers also dealt with political questions, and their ideas sometimes related closely to Christian political philosophy. On all this see the writings of Abraham Melamed, the dissertation research of Anne Oravetz Albert (University of Pennsylvania), and the new journal *Hebraic Political Studies*.

[2] The use of responsa for social history, especially in Sephardic contexts, is expanding.

interested in all these topics, but I am also drawn by another facet: the narratives embedded in the questions—the stories people tell about their lives when they come to a rabbi with queries.[3]

Whoever constructed or edited the questions into their current form was constrained to configure ephemeral life experiences into a coherent tale. In some cases the result is a dry, terse Hebrew legal style, but often the story should be recognized as a piece of literature in itself.[4] The authors searched biblical and rabbinic language for expressions that capture both the events under discussion and their emotional impact. Sometimes this exercise is quite creative. If we tune in to the rhythm of lived Jewish experience, we can hear the voices of the past telling their tales in the responsa. Though the texts that have reached us are usually edited, they remain remarkable for their preservation of life stories.

I focus on the Jewish exiles from Spain and Portugal and their progeny, so my sources are limited to Sephardic material from the early modern period (late fifteenth century to middle eighteenth century). If a story was interesting but told little about the specifically Sephardic experience, I might have passed it by, but this was seldom the case. Every tale gives details about life in one or more Sephardic communities. These particulars are woven together into a tapestry of Sephardic life that can only be perceived when the narrative portion of a document is read as a whole.

While I do not completely avoid the very best known collections, I have generally preferred the responsa of figures less familiar today. The type of material in all these collections is substantially the same, but historians have mined the famous works to the extent that these cases may be familiar. The lesser known collections, containing equally interesting cases, often languish in obscurity—especially those from rabbis outside the largest cities.

The parameters of the world I treat in this book may not be the same as those chosen by other historians of the Sephardim. The entire question

---

Excellent work is being done in this field by Yaron Ben-Naeh, Leah Bornstein-Makovetsky, Jane Gerber, Minna Rozen, and others.

[3] In this approach I have been particularly inspired by Goitein's *Mediterranean Society* (whence my general organizational scheme); Kagan and Dyer's *Inquisitorial Inquiries*; and the work of Natalie Zemon Davis, particularly *Fiction in the Archives*. While *Fiction* focuses on the tailoring of testimony to fit witnesses' purposes, which is not generally the situation in the responsa, the book beautifully demonstrates how to exploit narrative fragments buried in archival or legal material.

[4] Students of Hebrew literature might be well advised to study the original documents from this approach. Elchanan Reiner ("An Event") may be the first to recognize the point, though Cecil Roth ("Romance at Urbino") had some sense of it as well.

of who the Sephardim are, especially after 1492, has long been in dispute. Most books about Sephardic history contain some discussion of this issue. A conference at Stanford University in March 2007 broadened and deepened the scope of the question, interrogating not only the term "Sephardi" but also related or alternative concepts as "Edot Mizrah" (Eastern communities) or "Mizrahim" (Eastern Jews).[5] By the end of the conference it was clear that no terminology remains untainted by questions and qualifications.

My essential criterion for the Sephardic diaspora is linguistic. Any country or community where Spanish or Portuguese in some form was generally used by Jews, either for everyday speech, business purposes, or religious discourse, is included in the Sephardic world for this book. Occasionally, however, I impinge on areas (particularly in Morocco) where Spanish was far from the main spoken language among local Jews.

The Sephardim who left Spain and Portugal usually made their way to existing Jewish communities that were predominantly non-Sephardic. In the Ottoman Empire and much of North Africa, despite a good bit of resistance, Sephardic culture, language, and traditions overshadowed the older, local ones after a time.[6] The leading place of Sephardim in trade made Spanish the necessary language for Jewish merchants in the whole region. Thus, our material involves a number of individuals who were not technically Sephardim but who lived in this Sephardic milieu. On the other hand, the book does not incorporate responsa from Persia, Yemen, or other Eastern Jewish communities that did not absorb major influxes of Iberian exiles. A second issue is my inclusion of the Western Sephardim of Amsterdam, London, Hamburg, Livorno, and southern France. As I explain below, these communities were made up of escaped *conversos* and were different from the rest of the Sephardic world in many ways. Nevertheless, they considered themselves Sephardic congregations and their languages were Spanish and Portuguese. The documents show that some important cultural and religious commonalities appear along the same lines as my linguistic borders.

I also make a complicated choice in my temporal parameters. The date of the Spanish Expulsion, 1492, is a natural division. Though Sephardim were leaving the Iberian Peninsula long before, that is when they departed in large numbers. It seems to me that the next two and a half centuries, though obviously full of changes in every area, have a certain co-

[5] "Sephardic Identity on the Margins of Europe," Stanford University, 11–12 March 2007.

[6] On this process see Lehmann, *Ladino*, chap. 1; Benbassa and Rodrigue, *Jews of the Balkans*, chaps. 1–2.

herence in the Sephardic experience. The attachment to Iberian roots was always present. The vast majority of Sephardim observed Jewish law, lived among other Sephardim, spoke Spanish or Portuguese, and identified most essentially as Sephardi Jews (in one sense or the other) rather than as members of another national group. This was the time when there were still identifiable *conversos* in the Iberian Peninsula, among whom were some Judaizers. The flow of those escaping, and of the inquisitional trials that helped fire an outraged Sephardic unity, slowed drastically by the middle of the eighteenth century.[7] I thus feel justified in viewing the interval from the Expulsion until 1750 as one period that can be studied meaningfully as a whole.

Around 1750 I detect a certain shift in the pattern of Sephardic life in both the Mediterranean and European worlds, marked by two trends. One is a general decline in conditions for the Sephardim in economic standing, social relations, educational standards, and treatment at the hands of governments. Oddly, a subtle indication of the educational decline in the East was the appearance of the first great literary work in Ladino: Hakham Jacob Culi's wildly popular *Me'Am Lo'ez* (the first volume of which appeared in Istanbul in 1730). While literature scholars and specialists in modern Sephardic history view this as a great event, it also indicates that the masses of Sephardim were no longer comfortable reading biblical commentaries in Hebrew. At the same time, a financial downturn in many communities may be linked to the larger declines of Mediterranean trade and the cooling of certain Atlantic markets. A second trend in the mid-eighteenth century was an increased level of assimilation and more familiar contact with non-Jewish majorities. The responsa reveal a sharp increase in the incidence of Jews appealing to non-Jewish courts in the eighteenth century, and along with this a decline in respect for rabbinic authority. North African Jews, some of whom had always done extensive business with both Muslim and Christian associates, seemed to be slowly removing many of the social barriers they had previously maintained in these relationships. In western Europe, assimilation and apostasy among the Sephardim, never a rarity, becomes quite marked in the early eighteenth century. Altogether, then, based on both concrete factors and my overall impression of the time, I believe that the middle of the eighteenth century marked the beginning of a new era in Sephardic history.

A final point about my presentation concerns its division into sections

---

[7] The flow did not cease entirely, of course. Eliezer Bashan points to evidence from the end of the eighteenth century showing it was still occurring on an occasional basis. See Bashan, "*Conversos* returning to Judaism."

dealing with Jews' relations with Christians and Muslims, economic activities, communal life, private life, and religious matters. In a sense, this sort of division is antithetical to my emphasis on the stories told and the natural interweaving of all these factors. Almost all the texts in this collection cross boundaries between these artificial categories, and in every instance readers may object to my classification. Nevertheless, the division helps orient the reader to some of the major topics on which to keep an eye when studying the material. Within each category the order is vaguely chronological, but the chronology is broken up in many places to follow a theme between two or more documents.

The genesis of this project was an invitation from Marina Rustow and our friend and colleague Elka Klein, of blessed memory, to participate in a roundtable discussion they organized at the 2003 Association for Jewish Studies conference called "Integrating the Sephardi/Mizrahi Experience." The discussion was designed to consider strategies for bringing Sephardi and Mizrahi Jewries into the curriculum of the Jewish history survey course and other standard classes. My pitch at the roundtable was that one could use primary documents in the classroom when standard textbooks failed to introduce sufficient Sephardi and Mizrahi topics. I took a few volumes down from my shelves to prepare examples, including some responsa I happened to have. Looking through these books reminded me of the treasures to be had there. I also noted that the classic history and text reader on Eastern Jewry, Norman Stillman's *Jews in Arab Lands,* uses almost no rabbinic material and does not deal with all the areas where Sephardim settled, since many were not Arab lands. I handed out some translated texts and was delighted to receive a message shortly afterward from Julia Cohen of Stanford University, who had used them in a class. I was thus encouraged to look further and propose a group of responsa translations as a book. I examined scores of collections, still only a fraction of what is available, and took the stories I found most interesting or instructive.

Perhaps my greatest piece of luck in this little project was the cold call I put in to Brigitta van Rheinberg of Princeton University Press. She not only took on the book but also gave me extremely valuable advice about how to improve it. The original proposal called for a text reader made up of just a small preface and then texts with introductions. Brigitta suggested creating a larger general introduction to make the work more useful in the classroom as an orientation to early modern Sephardic history. She has been helpful at every step of the process, for which I want to express my appreciation. Brigitta also selected readers for the proposal who invested an amazing amount of time and effort and gave me tremendously helpful input. I am deeply grateful to them as well.

I must give profound thanks to Professor Mark Cohen of Princeton University, who read the entire typescript with exemplary care and made extensive, important comments. Numerous passages of the book were improved by his insights. My gratitude also goes to colleagues, friends, and graduate students who led me through the linguistic maze of these texts: Professor Masha Belyavski-Frank for her help with Serbo-Croatian terms; Professors Carter Findley and Jane Hathaway, as well as Okan Çakir, Emre Sencer, and Ufuk Ulutas for their help with Ottoman Turkish; Professor Daniel Frank for his help with Arabic; Rabbi Albert Elbaz and Mrs. Léa Schottenstein for their help with Moroccan Arabic dialect; and William Young Jr. for helping identify the source of a key term. Professor Francesca Trivellato of Yale University corrected several errors concerning issues of trade and currency.

My mother, Dean Dorothy Goldish, my sister, Judith Goldish, and my friend, Marshall Huebner, Esq., read the typescript and gave me very valuable editorial advice. I am also grateful to the Ohio State University's outstanding Judaica librarian, Professor Joseph Galron, to the staff of our Rare Book Room, and to the editors of the more recently published responsa collections, whose work helped me enormously. My good friend Mr. Eric Schramm edited the book with the fine care that characterizes all his undertakings. Finally, I am thankful to my family, friends, and students for listening to endless repetitions of the stories I was finding as I waded through the responsa.

INTRODUCTION

And the captivity of this host of the children of Israel that are
among the Canaanites as far as Tzarphat, and the captivity of
Jerusalem that is in Sepharad will possess the cities of the South.
—Obadiah 1:20

Jewish Life in Spain

The history of the Jews in Spain is a long, important, and well-known
chapter in the annals of the Jewish people.[1] Jews had certainly arrived in
Spain by the period of Jesus; it is likely that some came even earlier. The
Book of Obadiah refers to the "captivity of Jerusalem that is in Sepharad," which the Aramaic translation renders as "Espamia," referring to
Apamea or another location in Mesopotamia. Espamia was easily con-
flated with "Hispania" or "España," so the term Sepharad has been understood since late antiquity to connote Spain.[2] Indeed, the Jews of Spain
referred to their community using the verse from Obadiah.

Jews lived there in organized colonies throughout Roman times. As
the power of the Romans deteriorated, and Christianity became the religion of the Empire in the fourth century, the sense of order and respect
under which Jews had thrived in Spain began to disintegrate. Various
Germanic tribes invaded the region at the beginning of the fifth century.
Spain fell under the power of the Visigoths, who were Arian (that is, non-
Trinitarian) Christians. These were difficult times for the Jews, and matters became even worse after the Visigoth's King Reccared converted to

---

[1] This introduction is based on Gerber, *Jews of Spain*; Baer, *Jews in Christian Spain*;
Beinart, *Sephardi Legacy*; EJ, s.v. "Spain," and others as noted, and additional sources
cited throughout. It is necessarily selective and superficial; the reader should consult the
works in the bibliography for detailed studies of everything discussed here.

[2] On this matter, see Ayaso Martínez, "Tarsis, 'Aspamia.'"

Catholicism in 587. Under Catholic rule the Jews experienced strong persecution, including a decree of forced conversion and attempts to impose their total extermination. The severity of these measures could hardly be matched at any other place or time throughout the period.

The critical change for both Spanish history and the life of Sephardic Jews came early in the eighth century, when armies of the new Muslim religion invaded the Iberian Peninsula from the south. The Muslims marched through Spain in a series of victorious campaigns until they reached far into the northwest, where they were finally halted. For the next seven and a half centuries, Muslims and Catholics faced off in Spain in a war that alternated between active fighting and resigned stalemate. This situation began changing in the eleventh century when the Christians, galvanized by the crusader spirit, made a concerted thrust southward. They captured Toledo, beginning a campaign of Christian reconquest that would come to an end in 1492 with the victory of the Catholics under King Ferdinand and Queen Isabella.

Jewish life in Muslim Spain was distinctly better than it had been under the Christians. Relations between Jews and Christians started off on a very bad footing: the Jews were represented in the New Testament as the people who turned Jesus over to the Roman authorities for crucifixion. Since Rome had become the very center of Catholic Christianity, it hardly made sense to harp on the Romans' role in this event. The Jews, however, who were a minority in Christian lands and widely reviled, became the lone culprits for the death of Christ. Mohammed, the seventh-century prophet and founder of the new faith, oscillated in his stance between positive sentiments and vicious polemics. This ambiguity was generally better for the Jews than their unfortunate position in Christendom. The nature of relationships between Jews and Christians on the one hand, and Jews and Muslims on the other, receives further attention below.

The areas of Spain captured by Muslim armies were called al-Andalus, or Andalusia, and they quickly attracted a new influx of Jews who wished to participate in the unique opportunities there. As Spain became an important center of Muslim politics, culture, religion, and thought over the following centuries, the Jewish community flourished. There were Jewish governors, political advisors, poets, writers, scientists, physicians, and translators, as well as talmudists, biblical exegetes, mystics, and philosophers. Often several of these roles were combined in one person, such as Samuel Ibn Nagrela, vizier of Granada, who was a famed soldier, exegete, talmudist, and poet; Judah ha-Levi, the influential Neoplatonist rabbinic philosopher and poet; or Moses Maimonides, the great twelfth-century physician, philosopher, and legalist (who in fact spent much of his life in Egypt, but came from Spain). Many of the major medieval developments in almost all areas of Jewish culture—law, belles lettres, philosophy, mysticism, preaching, exegesis, and to some degree liturgy—occurred in Muslim Spain. Aside from intellectual luminaries, there were numerous less notable merchants, craftsmen, laborers, and paupers who made up the bulk of the great Sephardic community of the Middle Ages.

The Sephardic Jews created a unique Spanish-Jewish cultural identity. They read and wrote in Arabic, Hebrew, Spanish, and Latin. Their intellectuals believed they were a special class of original thinkers and mediators between the worlds of Islam, Judaism, and the ancient Mediterranean, translating texts and cross-pollinating ideas between these traditions. It was true that they were a minority, and, along with Christians, inhabited an inferior place in the official hierarchy of Muslim society. Sometimes there were periods of rule by more dogmatic Muslims who viciously persecuted Jews. And yet, the Jews were no less Spanish than the Christians and Muslims among whom they lived. They fashioned a self-image as a distinctive class of Spaniards: a royal breed of ancient Hebrews enriching the life of Iberia until such time as God chose to bring the messiah and return them to Jerusalem. This is how they lived and thought for the many centuries of Andalusian Sephardic life under Islam, and often under later Christian rule as well.

Between the eleventh and thirteenth centuries the Christian forces in the north began to prevail in the long process of *Reconquista* (reconquest). There were periods during these centuries, to be sure, when it appeared that a Muslim resurgence would beat back the Christians. Aggressive Almoravid and Almohad forces from North Africa swept northward and threatened to destabilize Andalusia in their campaigns against the Christians. These invaders persecuted Jews as well as Christians, and many Jews fled to the north to avoid their wrath. Over time, however, things got worse for Jews in the Christian north and the trend reversed itself.

As Christian rule slowly flowed southward, the Jews anxiously waited to see what their fate would be under renewed Catholic domination.[3] For a while it looked as if life under the Christians would not be very different than it had been under the Muslims in Spain. As some Muslims fled before the reconquering Christians, Jews were often encouraged to fill vacated government positions and populate towns. Jews were also seen as reliable economic stabilizers who could help to hold the financial

---

[3] On the continuing debate about whether life was indeed better under Islam than it was under Christianity, see Cohen, *Under Crescent and Cross.*

structure intact in the captured cities during these upheavals. From the political standpoint, the continuity of secure Jewish life in Christian Iberia seemed assured.

Relations between Jews and the Catholic faith were less encouraging. The end of the *Reconquista* coincided with an era in which the Church sought to more thoroughly Christianize Europe, a project that included the extirpation of heretics and infidels. In the early thirteenth century the pope created two new religious orders, the Dominican and Franciscan friars, whose task was the execution of the Christianizing mission. The presence of Jews in Europe, and particularly in Spain, was viewed by the Church as an anomaly that needed rectification. The most desirable outcome would be the conversion of the Jews, and the friars took the leading role in this policy. They forced the rabbis to participate in public disputations designed to weaken the faith of the Jewish masses and convince many Jews to convert. They also encouraged royal strategies that would compel Jewish conversions. These efforts met with more success than historians have often been willing to admit. At the same time, the Jews' close cooperation with the crown often aroused anger among the gentry and lower classes. Ordinary people became increasingly willing to believe outlandish accusations alleging Jewish perfidy or religious crimes against Christians.

Despite these growing pressures, the Jewish community remained reasonably stable and amazingly productive until the end of the fourteenth century. This period produced luminaries such as Moses Nahmanides, a profound talmudist, biblical exegete, mystic, and polemicist (he argued the case for Judaism in a forced disputation in 1263); and his student Solomon Ibn Aderet, most famous today for his voluminous legal and talmudic writings. It was also the context in which the *Zohar,* the most influential work of Jewish mysticism, appeared in Spain.

Around 1378, Ferrant Martínez, archdeacon of Ecija, started to preach extremely bitter anti-Jewish sermons to receptive crowds in Seville. As savage as the policies advocated by Martínez were, they might have remained a local matter were it not for the death of King Juan of Castile in 1390, which left only the crown prince, a child at the time, in control. Martínez had meanwhile risen to the rank of diocese administrator, and his message gained a wide following. During the discontent and weakened state of government in 1391, crowds in Seville began to carry out Martínez's appalling program. They physically attacked the Jewish community, burning the gates, killing many, and threatening the rest with the choice to convert or die. Many converted, many died. The community almost disappeared overnight; the synagogues were turned into churches and the Jewish homes taken over by Christians. This angry storm of anti-Jewish violence swept all across Castile, spilling over into Aragon, Catalonia, and Valencia. It caused untold destruction of lives, faith, and property. The message of the Church and the superstitions of the populace exploded together into a campaign of brutality whose impact lasted a century.

While much of the violence against Jews abated after 1391, both the damage and the trend toward high-pressure conversionary methods remained. The campaign of Martínez was followed by a wider conversionary mission by the charismatic preacher Vicente Ferrer. The disputation of Tortosa, from 1412 to 1414, stands out as an event of disguised compulsion: the rabbis were forced to participate in long debates with the friars, while their congregations back home, bereft of leadership, were harangued until large numbers converted. The fact that so many Jews did convert to Catholicism between 1391 and 1492 was particularly disheartening to those who remained steadfast.[4]

Conversos and the Inquisition

These converts, known also as *conversos, marranos* (a derogatory term apparently meaning "pigs"), *Alboraycos, chuetas, nuevos christianos* (New Christians), and other terms, were of diverse types. Some accepted baptism only by physical force and deathly terror. Others did so out of fear of financial ruin if they remained Jewish, or from alarm about the new mood in the country. There were also many who converted simply to gain the advantages of Christian status in business or social life. Finally, there was a group that apparently apostatized out of conviction, having become persuaded of the gospel truth. These conversions, almost unprecedented in their extent in Jewish history (over half of Spanish Jewry may have converted between 1391 and 1492), were all the more distressing because many highly respected rabbis were among those baptized. Some contemporary authors suggested that such men had become so enamored of Greek and Muslim philosophy that they felt more dedication to Aristotelianism than to Judaism. Others blamed the blandishments of courtly life and high office for the apostasy of so many Jewish

---

[4] For detail on this and much of the following discussion, see Roth, *Conversos,* who has a thorough discussion of the history of *conversos* and their reasons for conversion. While Roth says that fifteenth-century Spanish Jewry was almost without leadership, Mark Meyerson (*A Jewish Renaissance*) argues that despite the woes of 1391, the fifteenth century actually saw a revival and rise in the creativity of Spanish Jewry.

leaders. Historians have cited numerous, more complex causes for the widespread conversions among all classes, from Sephardic legal attitudes toward apostasy and the corrosive impact of mysticism to the particularly good relations between Christians and Jews in Spain that helped narrow the conceptual gap between faiths.[5]

The birth of a *converso* class among the Spanish population created a whole new set of complexities. Whereas previously Spain was home to Muslims, Christians, and Jews, it now had Muslims, *moriscos* (baptized Muslims), Christians, Jews, and *conversos*. Among the latter were many crypto-Jews—apostates who continued to feel some attachment to Judaism and often kept in close contact with the Jewish community. Since *conversos* frequently maintained the same homes and neighborhoods as when they were Jews, this contact was not difficult to sustain. It was even easier when some members of the household converted while others remained Jewish, a not uncommon occurrence. Other *conversos* became dedicated (in some cases even bigoted) Catholics and wanted nothing to do with the old religion. The majority probably kept up some Jewish contacts and a few practices out of habit or nostalgia but, if undisturbed, would have assimilated thoroughly into Spanish Catholic society within a generation or two.

In fact, many *conversos* did assimilate. Over the course of the fifteenth century, there were numerous successful businessmen, statesmen, merchants, intellectuals, and even priests. The Christian population, however, did not always welcome former Jews with open arms. They often suspected them—sometimes rightly—of failing to completely embrace Catholicism and of maintaining a secret Jewish identity. Many Spanish Christians also resented the ease with which a Jew, whose economic and social activities were severely limited, could accept baptism and instantly be competitive with "Old Christians" (those with no Jewish or Muslim forebears) in every field. Thus, despite the official church position that every Catholic is as good as any other, the growth of the *converso* group deeply irritated Spanish Old Christians. In 1448–49 in Toledo, this chafing broke out into full-fledged violence against the *conversos* that spread to many parts of the country. One of the results was the development of "purity of blood" statutes, eventually adopted by most institutions in Spain, which barred anyone with Jewish or Muslim ancestors

[5] On this and the following discussion see, among others, Baer, *History*, 2: chaps. 10–15; Netanyahu, *Origins*, 1: III; José Faur, "A Crisis of Categories: Kabbalah and the Rise of Apostasy in Spain," in Lazar and Haliczer, *Jews of Spain and the Expulsion of 1492*, 41–63; Roth, *Conversos*, chap. 1 and throughout.

from participating. While the effects of these statutes might be mitigated by bribing a scribe to forge a family tree, they still did a great deal to make the lives of *conversos* miserable.[6]

Popular agitation against the *conversos* was bolstered by a certain strain of Spanish millenarian fervor. This excitement was stoked by the marriage of Ferdinand of Aragon with Isabella of Castile in 1469 and their ascent to the united throne of Spain in 1479. Ferdinand and Isabella, approaching the critical half-millennium in 1500, engaged in a series of activities designed to make the consolidated Spanish state not only the center of Catholicism but the launching station for the process of the Second Coming of Jesus. A linchpin of this campaign was the purification of Iberian Catholic faith, to which the *conversos* were perceived as a threat. After hearing much from their subjects about the perfidy and false Catholic faith of the former Jews, the Catholic monarchs took action. In 1478–79 they applied to the pope for permission to open a hybrid institution: a national court of inquisition with a mandate to search out and punish bad Catholics.

Inquisitions—courts of ecclesiastical law authorized to interrogate and punish Catholics suspected of heresy—had existed for hundreds of years around Europe. They were conducted under the auspices of the Catholic Church and commonly operated by Dominican friars with a special directive from the pope. Now, Ferdinand and Isabella were asking the pope to create a Spanish Inquisition—an inquisitional court that would be operated by the friars as usual but would be a national institution of the Spanish crown. The pope had little choice but to agree (he was under great military and political pressure), and in 1480–81 the Spanish Inquisition began processing cases in Ciudad Real. Soon it had opened branches in a number of other cities and would continue in operation well into the nineteenth century.

The Inquisition was not empowered to try or punish Jews who were not baptized. Its job was to try heretical Catholics, who might include social deviants, witches, Cathars, and any number of other types; but everyone understood that its first target was the *conversos*. Denunciations would be taken from anyone and the accuser's identity was kept secret from the victim, so the process was often abused for motives of revenge or profit. Once arrested, a victim's goods were confiscated and he or she was held for an indefinite period. The court would assemble evidence and try to convince the victim to confess. If that occurred, and the victim expressed proper remorse, she or he was reconciled with the

[6] See Netanyahu, *Origins*, especially Books 2–3.

church, given various public penances, and released. If the victim refused to confess, she or he was often tortured, a common method in many medieval court proceedings. Few had the fortitude to hold out long. If the victim confessed and expressed remorse there might be clemency; obstinacy simply resulted in more prison and torture. If one had stood trial once and was caught "Judaizing" a second time, the penalty was often death. The Inquisitors would "relax" the victim to its secular arm. At large open-air ceremonies, reconciled victims were ceremonially pardoned while the less fortunate ones were burned at the stake.

Around the time the Inquisition began operations in Spain, Ferdinand and Isabella initiated a policy of forcibly separating Jewish and *converso* populations in major cities. The Catholic monarchs expressed their hopes that fear of the Inquisition and separation of *conversos* from Jews would end crypto-Judaism. In some senses, the purity-of-blood statutes, segregation, and Inquisition actually reversed the process of assimilation among the *conversos* by singling them out for punishment and censure. In any case, the king and queen understood that their measures had failed. The Inquisitors and other advisors urged them to take the next step and eliminate the Jewish community altogether. Without Jews nearby, it was supposed, the *conversos* would lose their lifeline to Jewish practice and all become true Catholics.[7]

Expulsion from Spain and Forced Conversion in Portugal

Between 1478 and 1492, the Catholic monarchs (as Ferdinand and Isabella are often styled) completed the *Reconquista*. The last major stronghold of Iberian Islam, Granada, capitulated in the winter of 1491, ridding Spain of almost all infidels. The last remaining obstacle to a pure Catholic state was of course the Jews, against whom there was plenty of popular animosity. This feeling peaked with the "Holy Child of La Guardia" trial in 1490–91, in which a group of Jews and *conversos* confessed under hideous tortures to having murdered a Christian boy in a macabre Jewish ritual.

In January of 1492 (by current reckoning), while the Spanish celebrated their victory in Granada, rumors circulated that the Jews were also about to be expelled. A group of Jewish courtiers struggled, using every influence and monetary inducement at their disposal, to reverse the coming decree. Various tales about this period have been preserved in the literature. Some see Isabella's religious fervor as the decisive factor, while others say it was both the monarchs who stood adamant. One story re-

[7] See Kamen, *Spanish Inquisition;* Kamen, *Inquisition and Society;* Netanyahu, *Origins;* Netanyahu, *Toward the Inquisition;* Roth, *Conversos;* and footnote 15 below.

lates that Ferdinand was about to give in because of an enormous bribe being offered him by the Jews, when Thomas Torquemada, the chief inquisitor, rushed in and accused the king of selling out Christianity for money like Judas. The monarchs found other ways to make money from the expulsion anyway—by confiscating Jewish property and canceling debts owed to Jews, among other things.

Whatever the machinations and motivations for the expulsion of the Jews, the decree was indeed announced on 31 March 1492 that all Jews in the lands belonging to the Spanish crown must either convert to the Catholic faith or leave the country by the end of July that year.[8] Scholars have argued for centuries about how many Jews there were in Spain to begin with, and of those, how many chose to remain and be baptized and how many chose exile. It might be reasonable to assume that there were between 100,000 and 300,000 Jews in Spain, and that one half or more stayed behind as Christians.[9] Among the most disheartening aspects for the steadfast was the fact that Don Abraham Senior (or Seneor), the court rabbi and chief tax collector, a revered figure over eighty years of age at the time, chose to convert along with his family. On the other hand, the second chief Jewish courtier, Don Isaac Abarbanel, accepted exile along with his Jewish brethren, and has remained a beloved leader and biblical exegete in the eyes of Jews to this day.[10]

The Jews, leaving the land their ancestors had inhabited for over a thousand years, trekked to the sea, past the small fleet of Christopher Columbus (possibly a descendant of *conversos* himself) who was then preparing to leave port, and wondered where they would go. Much of Europe did not allow Jews to settle, and in those lands where there was a Jewish community, there were often strict quotas on population that were already filled. North Africa seemed to beckon from relatively close by, but the hapless Jews knew their defenselessness was an open invitation to every sort of brigand to despoil them on their journey. An independent Spanish state, Navarre, was willing to take them in temporarily. So was Portugal, though only at a steep price that few could afford to pay. No route was safe from highwaymen, pirates, starvation, and the ever-present threat of plague, all of which claimed numerous Jewish lives. Many poorer Jews found themselves sold off as slaves. Ultimately, though they might not have known it, there was grave danger in every di-

---

[8] On the edict of expulsion see Beinart, *Expulsion*, chap. 2; Orfali and Dolader, "Examination"; Suarez Fernandez, *Documentos*.

[9] See the detailed study in Roth, *Conversos*, appendix B.

[10] See Beinart, *Expulsion*, chaps. 8–9; Netanyahu, *Don Isaac Abravanel*; Lawee, *Isaac Abarbanel's Stance*.

rection. Some suffered so much that they eventually returned to Spain and converted.

Perhaps the most insidious situation ensued in Portugal, which definitely looked like the most attractive haven, especially for better-off Castillian Jews. It was directly over an easy terrestrial border, the language was very similar to Spanish, and the culture was Iberian. King João II would let Jews in either for a short time (for a large fee) or longer (for a very large fee). Even this, however, was not enough for the avaricious monarch. When the reprieve period was over, he forced the temporary Jewish residents to make a choice between conversion or slavery. He then kidnapped the children of the unconverted Jews and shipped them to the deserted island of São Tomé, lately discovered by Portuguese explorers off the central African coast and coming into use as a criminal colony. According to contemporary reports, many children not eaten by the great reptiles which inhabited that place soon died from hunger and exposure.

João died in 1495. His son, Manoel, quickly released the enslaved Jews, but other factors soon came into play to the detriment of his Sephardic subjects. He wished to marry Princess Isabella, the daughter of Ferdinand and Isabella of Spain, and thus bring the whole Iberian Peninsula under his own rule. But she and her advisors refused to consider the match while Manoel harbored Jews in his land. Manoel did not wish to see the Jews leave because many had skills and resources he wanted to exploit. His solution was cruel and devious: he declared a general expulsion of unconverted Jews and Muslims for 1497, like the one promulgated in Spain five years earlier. Tremendous conversionary pressure was brought to bear on the Jews, and the chief rabbi died resisting these attempts. All children were seized and forcibly baptized during the Passover holiday, leaving their parents to face the horrible choice to abandon either their faith or their children. When the remaining Jews assembled in Lisbon in March 1497, expecting to find ships that would take them away, they were instead subjected to endless conversionary sermons and coercion of every sort. Some reports speak of Jews being physically dragged to the baptismal font. In the end, by hook or by crook, almost the entire community was baptized.[11]

This forced conversion in Portugal created an interesting new situation. The Portuguese *conversos* were the hard core of Sephardim who had refused to convert under every enticement in Spain and became bap-

---

[11] See, e.g., Gross, *Iberian Jewry,* chap. 1; Tishby, *Messianism,* chap. 2; Usque, *Consolation,* introduction and 200–209.

tized only by the most barbaric and deceitful means in their new land. They did not want to be Catholics. Manoel promised that his *conversos* would not face an inquisition for a period of twenty years, and that they would not abide the discrimination suffered by their Spanish brethren. This, however, was not in the king's power to control, and the *conversos* were attacked by an angry mob of Portuguese Old Christians (led by friars) in 1506. Thousands were murdered in this bloodcurdling episode.[12] It is instructive to note that, despite these horrors, the majority of *conversos* chose to stay as Christians in Portugal rather than risk the perils of travel even when the opportunity was available a decade after their conversion.

Bribes and well-heeled envoys succeeded in delaying the establishment of a Portuguese Inquisition until 1536, but thereafter the Portuguese *conversos* suffered the same fate as their Spanish cohorts. They could not stay in safety, and in most periods it was highly illegal to leave. While they could now participate fully in Iberian society almost on par with Old Christians, the New Christians (as converted Jews were often called) lived in constant fear that they would be arrested with no warning and lose everything in a moment. It is hardly surprising to find, then, that a constant stream of escaping *conversos,* some crypto-Jews and some simply fearful of the Inquisition, made their way to Sephardic communities throughout the Mediterranean and Atlantic worlds, from the sixteenth well into the eighteenth centuries. Many who remained behind moved back and forth between Portugal and Spain as the persecution cooled in one country and warmed in the other.[13]

The Eastern Sephardi Diaspora

What happened to those Spanish Jews who did leave in 1492 and succeeded in establishing themselves in new lands? These were the people at the heart of the Sephardic dispersion, who brought Andalusian Jewish culture to the cities of the Ottoman Empire and North Africa. It is testimony to the strength and tenacity of that culture that the Jews from all these regions are referred to until today as "Sephardim," and that the *lingua franca* of the Jews there generally became Spanish.

[12] See Yerushalmi, *Lisbon Massacre.*

[13] The literature on the expulsion and related matters from the period is enormous. See especially Beinart, *Expulsion;* Lazar and Haliczer, *Jews of Spain and the Expulsion of 1492;* Waddington and Williamson, *Expulsion of the Jews;* Kedourie, *Spain and the Jews;* Assis and Kaplan, *Jews and Conversos;* Raphael, *Expulsion 1492 Chronicles;* Sachar, *Farewell España;* Yerushalmi, *From Spanish Court,* chap. 1.

Despite all the adversity they encountered in their journey to Ottoman lands, and the many who perished or were enslaved on the way, those who made it found a relatively favorable haven. The Ottoman Turks captured Constantinople (renamed Istanbul, but usually called by the former name in Jewish documents) from the Byzantines in 1453, and by the beginning of the sixteenth century were masters of the rest of Turkey, Greece, Palestine, Egypt, Algeria, the Hejaz, many Balkan regions, and much of Central Asia and southeastern Europe. The wars were bloody and often left cities depopulated. The Ottomans used a system called *sürgün* (transfer) to move populations around; but they were also on the lookout for reliable groups from outside the Empire who could help bring order to the chaos left by war. The sultan could especially depend on the Sephardim to support his anti-Habsburg policies, because soon after the Expulsion the Habsburgs had annexed Spain.[14]

Jews were valued as settlers by the Ottomans for a number of reasons. They were perceived as faithful subordinates because they had no nationalist agenda beyond their utopian hopes for the arrival of a messiah. Many had skills that were desperately needed by the Ottomans, including linguistic, commercial, and scribal expertise. In the case of Sephardic Jews, they also tended to come with de facto trading networks that were invaluable to the rebuilding of economic infrastructure. A Spanish Jew might flee Spain in 1492 for religious reasons but leave behind baptized relatives and friends. His family would likely be scattered between central Ottoman cities, Italy, North Africa, and later Amsterdam, London, or Barbados. The ability of such networks to move around credit and goods was an especially valuable resource that gave the stateless Jews a bit of ballast in the sea of adversity.[15]

The Ottomans brought large numbers of Jews to Istanbul in the expulsion period by two means. First, Jews from the former Byzantine provinces in Anatolia and elsewhere were forcibly moved to Istanbul after the Ottoman victory there. (These people were called "Romaniotes" because Byzantium was seen as the remains of the Roman Empire; Greece and Anatolia were often called Lower Romania.) They commonly lamented the Ottoman victory and were very displeased by their summary resettlement.[16] Fleeing Sephardic Jews were brought in as well, but in their ab-

[14] See Hacker, "Jewish Community of Salonica"; Rozen, *History of the Jewish Community.*

[15] See, e.g., Arbel, *Trading Nations;* Bernardini and Fiering, *Jews and the Expansion,* section 4; Rozen, *Days of the Crescent;* Beinart, *Sephardi Legacy,* vol. 2; Yogev, *Diamonds and Coral.*

[16] On the important background of Jews under Byzantine rule before the Ottomans, see Bowman, *Jews of Byzantium.*

ject condition, most felt tremendous gratitude to Sultan Bayezid II for allowing them to settle. In their literature, the Sephardim often contrast the benevolence of Bayezid with the cruelty of Ferdinand and Isabella, though Bayezid was not always so munificent. We get the first inkling of the power exercised by Sephardic culture in the fact that popular history has remembered only the Spanish Jews' positive response and celebration of the Ottomans. This is partly because Sephardim from the generation of the expulsion did a lot of historical writing, so their views were preserved; but even the Romaniote author Elijah Capsali expresses the general pro-Ottoman attitude of Spanish Jews in his histories.[17]

The second great assembly of Jews in the Ottoman Empire, Saloniki, was apparently bereft of any Jewish community before the Spanish exiles arrived. In fact, the city itself had been so greatly depopulated that when the Sephardim arrived they were actually the majority population of the city for a long period. Their centrality in Saloniki's sea trade was so great that the harbor itself was closed on Saturdays, the Jewish Sabbath, as late as the beginning of World War II.[18]

Ottoman Jews enjoyed the status of *dhimmis*—protected minorities—along with Christians. They were allowed a large degree of self-government because, like many regimes ruling over Jews in the Middle Ages, the Ottomans preferred to let the Jewish community deal with its own problems and collect taxes on behalf of the state. To the dismay of the noble classes, the sultan also extended certain tax exemptions and privileges to the Jews and other *dhimmi* who had been settled in Istanbul. This gave them a leg up in commercial success, though it should be noted that only a minority of Jews became at all wealthy there.

Istanbul had the largest Jewish community anywhere in the world during the early modern period, with as many as 10,000 Jewish households, perhaps between 30,000 and 40,000 individuals. Saloniki, a smaller city, topped out at about half that. Istanbul and Saloniki were recognized de facto as the capitals of the Sephardic diaspora. The constant travels of Ottoman Jews and their extensive family networks greatly aided their cultural and religious hegemony. These factors helped bridge geographical separations, keeping the Jews of these central communities in close contact with co-religionists around the Mediterranean rim. Inquiries from all over were directed to their famous rabbinic courts, and their printing presses produced an amazing array of both standard rabbinic works and innovative new volumes read by Jews everywhere.

[17] Rozen, History of the Jewish Community, chaps. 1–5.

[18] See Hacker, "Jewish Community of Salonica"; Joseph Néhama, "The Jews of Salonica in the Ottoman Period," in Barnett and Schwab, *Sephardi Heritage*, 2: 203–42.

One outstanding feature of these two Jewish centers was the structure of their internal divisions, called *kehillah/kehillot* or *kahal/kehalim* (community/communities). The new Jewish populations under the Ottomans came from such a variety of towns that in many cases one or more *kehalim* were organized of Jews from an individual place of origin. Thus there were separate and sometimes multiple *kehalim* of Jews from Aragon, Castile, Sicily, Evora, Lisbon, Catalonia, Italy, Provence, Calabria, Ashkenaz, and others. In Saloniki there may have been over fifty *kehalim* in some periods. Perhaps six of these were quite large, the rest small to middling. The larger *kehalim* had their own neighborhoods or regions in the cities. Within a very short period the ethnic origins of the *kehalim* ceased to be the central determinant of membership, and Sephardim essentially overwhelmed the other groups, though the names often remained in place. The key organizing factor throughout most of the early modern period was, in fact, the *kahal* through which one paid taxes, both internal (to the Jewish community) and external (to the Ottoman government). For a short period around the time of the expulsion there was a chief rabbinate in Constantinople, occupied first by Hakham Moses Capsali, then by Hakham Elijah Mizrahi.[19]

Another important feature of the Constantinople community was the existence of a small group of Jews in court circles, serving one or another vizier or even the sultan himself. Several prominent women, such as Doña Gracia Nasi, and Esther Kyra, who managed the sultan's harem around the turn of the seventeenth century (see introduction to Document #7), were among their number. The best known of these courtiers were the Jewish physicians, some of whom became important royal advisors; and wealthy Sephardic merchants (most notably the Nasi/Migues family), whose money made them objects of interest to the sultan. In these pages we will encounter several minor courtiers, whose names are anonymous in the responsa, but whose identities might be traced some day.

The prestige of both Constantinople and Saloniki declined in the seventeenth and early eighteenth centuries, which had an extensive effect on their Jewish communities as well. While Suleiman the Magnificent and other legendary sultans of the sixteenth century expanded the Empire and challenged Christian Europe, the politics and personalities of the later period often stymied progress. One must not, however, suppose that the fortunes of either these cities or their Jewish communities declined

---

[19] See Benbassa and Rodrigue, *Jews of the Balkans,* chaps. 1–2 (and see p. 202 n. 27 for a population table); Ben-Naeh, "Jewish Society"; Ben-Naeh, "Kehillat Yehudei Istanbul"; Cohen, *Constantinople;* Ankori, *From Lisbon to Salonica;* Hacker, "Jewish Community of Salonica"; Levy, *Jews of the Ottoman Empire;* Rozen, *History of the Jewish Community.*

with anything like the suddenness or extent that older textbooks suggest. One event that did have a powerful negative effect on Istanbul Jewry, and indeed on the entire Jewish world of the period, originated in the third great Jewish community of the central Empire: Izmir (Smyrna).

Until the middle of the sixteenth century, Izmir had been a neglected backwater in Mediterranean trade, partly because the Ottoman government did not want it competing with Istanbul. When the Ottomans eased their economic domination of the city after the death of Suleiman the Magnificent, enterprising local merchants and European agents were quick to move into the vacuum. In short order they turned the sleepy Anatolian port into one to the busiest trade cities in the Mediterranean—so busy, in fact, that it suffered from a plague of piracy. The Ottoman government, contemplating this magnetic new entropôt, sought ways to profit from the competition there between Venetians, French, English, and other national trade interests.

Jews, too, particularly the Sephardim (including a large number of escaping *conversos*) came to Izmir to participate in the boom. When their numbers grew in the early seventeenth century, Izmir displaced Edirne as the third great Jewish center in Turkey. Sources from the period speak of between seven thousand and fifteen thousand Jews there over the course of the seventeenth century, though these numbers may be too high. There appear to have been seven *kehalim* in the middle of the century, but they were not organized according to national origins like those in Istanbul and Saloniki. Part of the rapid growth in Izmir was spurred by a crisis in the textile industry centered in Saloniki and Safed, in which Jews were deeply involved.[20] Another draw was the relatively low tax rate paid in Izmir compared to many other provinces. Jewish artisans and important rabbis arrived to provide services to the burgeoning merchant community.[21]

One of the Izmir Torah scholars was Shabbatai Zvi (1626–76), the son of a Romaniote Jew who served as factor for English merchants in the city. Shabbatai was deeply involved in the study of Jewish mysticism (Kabbalah), but also appears to have been troubled by personal or psy-

---

[20] See Avitsur, "Woolen Textile Industry"; Avitsur, "Safed"; Braude, "Cloth Industry"; Braude, "Rise and Fall"; Simon Schwarzfuchs, "Quand commença le déclin de l'Industrie Textile des Juifs de Salonique?" in Toaff and Schwarzfuchs, *Mediterranean and the Jews*, 1: 215–35.

[21] On Izmir see Goffman, *Izmir;* Jacob Barnai, "Prototypes of Leadership in a Jewish Community: Smyrna in the Seventeenth Century," in Gampel, *Crisis and Creativity,* 146–63; Jacob Barnai, "The Jews of Spain in Egypt," in Levy, *Jews of the Ottoman Empire,* chap. 4.

chological abnormalities. In 1665–66, Shabbatai and his self-proclaimed "prophet," a certain Nathan Ashkenazi of Gaza, declared that Shabbatai was to be the long-awaited Jewish messiah. For a number of complex reasons, this message received wide acceptance in the Jewish world, and the young kabbalist traveled to Istanbul to take the turban of sovereignty from the sultan. He was arrested at once, and, after various further adventures, was hauled up before the Porte a second time, at which point Shabbatai donned quite a different turban—he converted to Islam ("accepted the white turban") and was thus spared his life. This episode deeply affected the entire Jewish world, but the hope and later the dejection it inspired were felt especially keenly among the Empire's three greatest Jewish communities, Istanbul, Saloniki, and Izmir. Very few traces of these events were left in the published responsa, but it is important to know about them to understand certain features of that era.[22]

Several other fair-sized Jewish communities could be found in the central part of the Ottoman Empire during this period, almost all in sea or river ports where they could participate in international trade. These included Bursa, Edirne (Adrianople), Patras, Larissa, and Kastoria. Each was composed of immigrants seeking economic stability and refugees from a variety of countries. Again, however, the Sephardim, with their ancient and deeply rooted culture, usually dominated the scene. Each city's Jewish community had its individual traditions and special relationships with the government, but all essentially looked to Istanbul and Saloniki for guidance. Each city also had outstanding rabbinic figures at one time or another. For example, both Hakham Joseph Karo (author of the authoritative code *Shulhan Arukh*) and his friend Hakham Solomon Alkabetz (author of the famous Sabbath-evening hymn *Lekhah Dodi*), who are best known as part of the Safed mystical circle of the sixteenth century, moved to Palestine after living for a period in Edirne.[23]

Venice was the commercial hub of the Mediterranean world and another major center of Sephardic Jews. It could be equally placed in the western or eastern Sephardi diaspora, for Venice was truly a pivot between worlds. The Veneto had long been home to populations of Ashkenazi, French, and native Italian Jews, but both its "Ponentine" (western, i.e., Iberian) and "Levantine" (eastern, i.e., Ottoman) Sephardic communities became very important in the sixteenth and seventeenth centuries. The Ponentines were mainly former Portuguese *conversos* who had con-

---

[22] On Shabbatai Zvi, see Scholem, *Sabbatai Sevi*; Goldish, *Sabbatean Prophets*.

[23] On the Edirne Jewish community, particularly economic aspects, see Gerber, "Jews of Edirne." On the Patras community see Cohen, *Constantinople*. On Bursa see Gerber, "Jews in the Economic Life"; Gerber, *Economy and Society*.

siderable commercial and religious impact on the community. Venice was
the city where the walled, enforced Jewish ghetto first appeared, in 1516,
but this does not mean Jews were excluded from the life of the city.
Many famous rabbis lived there in the early modern period, and questions were directed to the rabbinic court from both European and Ottoman communities. Christian savants came to ask Venetian rabbis
about the Jewish views on many theological issues. Even King Henry
VIII of England, having no Jews in his own land, sent an agent to consult
with Venetian rabbis about the annulment of his marriage to Catherine
of Aragon on biblical grounds.[24]

Again, trade was the major economic underpinning of the community,
though Jews were also moneylenders and craftsmen. Venice appears innumerable times in the responsa as a commercial center indispensable to
the Sephardic mercantile network. Recent studies on material in the
Venetian archives reveals the complex ways Jews and Venetian Christians arranged their commercial relationships around the Mediterranean.
For example, educated, wealthy Jews (often physicians) with multiple
languages and contacts in many lands could negotiate various arrangements for their Christian neighbors in exchange for the relaxation of certain restrictions on Jewish commercial activities. Although scholarship
has long spoken of the eclipse of Venice by northern ports like London
and Amsterdam in the seventeenth century, and there was certainly some
decline for both the city and its Jews, it was really not until the eighteenth century that one detects the full impact of this shift.[25]

A group of Jewish communities in various Greek and Mediterranean
islands were critical to the all-important maritime trade that stood at the
center of Jewish commercial life. The most important of these, which
turn up constantly in the responsa, were Rhodes, Corfu, and Crete.[26]

Rhodes had a Jewish community since ancient times, and the Jews
helped the Christians fight against the Ottomans when they laid siege to
the city in 1480. The following decades were miserable for the island's
Jewish inhabitants, however. Those who would not convert were expelled in 1498–1500, and thereafter the Knights Hospitalers who ruled
the island brought thousands of captured Jews there as slaves. It is not
surprising, then, that in 1522 these Jews helped the Ottomans overrun
the Rhodes fortress, and they enjoyed much better conditions thereafter.

[24] On this amazing episode see Katz, *Jews*, chap. 1.

[25] On Venice see Arbel, *Trading Nations;* Davis and Ravid, *Jews of Early Modern Venice;* Roth, *Jews in Venice.*

[26] On all these see Marc D. Angel, "Sephardi Communities of the Eastern Mediterranean Islands," in Barnett and Schwab, *Sephardi Heritage,* 1: 115–43.

Several important rabbis served there, and the island was a major en-
trêpot in the Jewish trade networks of the Mediterranean. Jews were also
involved in crafts, tax farming, and other trades.[27]

Corfu, too, had been home to small number of Jews in the Middle
Ages. Unlike Rhodes, Corfu remained in Christian hands—under the
Venetians—throughout the early modern period. As Christians go, they
were relatively benign masters. Jews helped defend the island successfully
against the Ottomans in 1716. Italian and local Romaniote Jews were
the majority on Corfu, but considerable numbers of Sephardim settled
there and left their mark on the culture. The responsa offer extensive evidence for the centrality of Corfu in the Mediterranean trade. The island
was clearly a widely used way station for goods traveling between Europe and the Ottoman Empire, though the Adriatic ports absorbed some
of that traffic in the later part of the period.[28]

Crete was apparently the original home of the biblical Philistines, who
are sometimes called Cherethites. Jews had lived there since at least the
Second Temple period, and there was a small but vigorous community
when the Sephardi exiles arrived in 1492. Like Corfu, Crete was ruled by
the Venetians, who gave the Jews a fair amount of security against the
widespread popular sentiment against them. The Jews of Crete were
deeply involved in moneylending and money changing, and as with
Corfu, the island served as a major stopping place for Jewish, Christian,
and Muslim merchants trading between Ottoman and European markets. Crete produced outstanding rabbinic scholars in this period, mainly
from the Capsali and del Medigo families. After 1669 Crete fell into the
hands of the Ottomans, and (interestingly) Jewish fortunes there began
to decline.

A region whose Sephardic communities are perhaps less familiar to
many is the Balkan states. Among the Balkan cities with Jewish populations were Belgrade, Ragusa (now Dubrovnik), Spalato (now Split), and
Sarajevo.[29] These lands were part of a strange, divided world in the sixteenth and seventeenth centuries that oscillated between Ottoman rule,
European rule, and semi-independence, though each city had its own
complex history. As ports for trade moving between Ottoman and European lands, they offered an alternative route when war or other circumstances made the western Mediterranean routes difficult. On the other

---

[27] For more on Rhodes Jewry see Angel, *Rhodes*.

[28] For more on Corfu Jewry see Benvenisti and Mizrahi, "Sources"; Benvenisti, "Letters."

[29] See Zvi Loker, "Spanish and Portuguese Jews Amongst the Southern Slavs—Their Settlement and Consolidation During the Sixteenth to Eighteenth Centuries," in Barnett and
Schwab, *Sephardi Heritage*, 283–313.

hand, the Adriatic was plagued with pirates, and the constant tension between great powers was another threat to security. Nevertheless, the Jewish communities did reasonably well in peacetime.

Esther Benbassa and Aron Rodrigue emphasize the strength of Sephardic culture in these regions after 1492:

> In the Ottoman lands of the Balkans, from the Adriatic coast, through Bosnia, Serbia, Macedonia, Bulgaria, Greece, Thrace, and in Asia Minor, a new Sephardi *Kulturbereich* (culture area), an Eastern Sephardi heartland, came into being that lasted as a distinct Judeo-Hispanic unit well into the twentieth century. . . . Unlike their counterparts in the West and in North Africa, the Sephardim in these regions overwhelmed local Greek-speaking Romanioteiot ex-Byzantine Jews, as well as the few Ashkenazim that migrated over the centuries from Central and Eastern Europe. While the process lasted well into the seventeenth century, it was the local Romanioteiots who assimilated to the newcomers and not the reverse.[30]

These authors' conception of the Balkans is very broad, embracing Turkey and Greece as well as the eastern Adriatic states, but their thesis is important for understanding Jewish culture in the Balkans proper as well. I would suggest that in all the lands where Sephardim settled they created a significant cultural impact on Jewish life—each community established a unique balance between Sephardic and native traditions. The Balkans was a region where this balance was indeed heavily weighted toward Sephardic influence.

Belgrade was captured by the Ottomans in 1521 and thereafter had a small but well-known and learned Sephardic community living in good circumstances. In 1688, with the Austrians approaching, Turkish troops plundered and burned the Jewish quarter; then the Austrians entered and did it again. The community was essentially destroyed at this point, its members having fled or been sold into slavery. The Austrians held Belgrade until 1739, allowing a small Jewish settlement to return, but the Turks then recaptured it. Some of these reversals of fortune are reflected in the responsa translated below.

---

[30] Benbassa and Rodrigue, *Jews of the Balkans,* xvii. Much of the material below is drawn from this book; Zvi Loker, "Spanish and Portuguese Jews Amongst the Southern Slavs—Their Settlement and Consolidation During the Sixteenth to Eighteenth Centuries," in Barnett and Schwab, *Sephardi Heritage;* Benjamin Ravid, "An Autobiographical Memorandum by Daniel Rodriga, *Inventore* of the *Scala* of Spalato," in Toaff and Schwarzfuchs, *Mediterranean and the Jews,* 1: 189–214; and *EJ,* s.v. "Belgrade," "Dubrovnik," "Split," "Sarvajevo," etc.

Ragusa was an independent seaport, but it operated under the protection of Venice in some periods and the Ottomans in others. The Sephardim came after 1492, and there was a large community of refugees moving through at any given time, as seen in the responsa below. Much about the treatment of the Jews in Ragusa testifies to the Venetian Christian influence. In the early sixteenth century the Jews were blamed for a murder and several were killed. A ritual murder accusation occurred there in 1622, though the much-abused Sephardic victim, Isaac Jeshurun, was released after a few years of imprisonment. The Jews' expulsion was declared on several occasions; the Ottomans' influence, however, prevented it from being carried out. A walled ghetto (a Venetian invention) was established for Jews in 1546. After the 1622 libel, most of the Jews left Ragusa, but they soon returned and the community actually grew until the middle of the eighteenth century.

Spalato was also a Venetian possession in this period. Like Venice, it had two Sephardic communities: the "western" Jews who came from Spain and Portugal, mainly through Italy; and the "eastern" Jews who came from the Ottoman Empire. A Sephardi, Daniel Rodriga, convinced the Venetians in 1592 to make Spalato a free port, which was an extremely successful project. The small Jewish community profited well and enjoyed reduced taxes for their success in promoting international trade. Still, like Jews in Venice and its other territories, they were confined to a ghetto. Spalato was besieged by the Ottomans in 1657, and the Jews helped defend the city. They were involved in trade, of course, but also in textile work and moneylending.

Sarajevo appears to have had the largest Jewish community in the region, made up mostly of Sephardim who arrived in the middle of the sixteenth century. Sarajevo was under Turkish rather than Venetian control until 1679, and conditions were relatively good for the Jews. They lived together in a Jewish quarter, but there was no ghetto. Although trade was a main staple of the Jewish economy, many Sarajevo Jews were artisans or craftsmen, and there were not a few paupers. In 1679 the Austrian army laid siege and captured Sarajevo, destroying the Jewish quarter, but the Jews were able to resettle and live decently under the Austrians as well. By this time, Ashkenazim had begun to arrive in fair numbers. Several important rabbis lived in Sarajevo, including the Hakham Zvi Ashkenazi, still a famous figure today.

One of the most moving opportunities for the Sephardi exiles came in 1516/17, when the Ottomans captured Palestine.[31] There had always

---

[31] See David, *To Come to the Land*; Avraham David, "The Spanish Exiles in the Holy Land," in Beinart, *Sephardi Legacy*, 2: 77–108.

been a Jewish presence in the Holy Land, but conditions under the Ottomans were much more encouraging than they had been for many centuries. Spanish Jews arrived together with Italians, Ashkenazim, and many others to live in Palestine. There was little industry or trade to be found there, so many subsisted on charity. Jerusalem was, of course, a very desirable location because of its sacred history, but avaricious local governors made life quite difficult through much of the period. Instead, many Jews preferred to go to the Galilean town of Safed, known for its textile industry and especially for the many rabbis and mystics who settled there in the late sixteenth century. The Kabbalah (Jewish mystical tradition) was given new impetus and forms by the schools of Hakham Moses Cordovero, the AR"I (Ashkenazi Rabbi Isaac, or Rabbi Isaac Luria), and others. There was a short-lived Hebrew printing press there as well.[32]

Another Galilean city, Tiberias, became the site of a settlement attempt by the great *converso* philanthropists Doña Gracia Nasi (Mendes) and her nephew Don Joseph Nasi (Migues). Tiberias never became self-sustaining and the colony did not thrive for long. Other cities, including Hebron and Gaza, had small Jewish communities. One interesting impact of the Palestinian Jewish congregations on the larger Jewish world, particularly the Sephardim, was that the Jews of larger Palestinian towns would send emissaries all around the Jewish world to collect funds so that the Jewish presence in the Holy Land could be maintained. Some of these emissaries were eminent rabbis who made an impact in places they visited.[33]

In close connection with the Palestinian Jewish communities were those in greater Syria, the most important of which were Aleppo (also called *Aram Tzovah* and *Halab* in rabbinic sources) and Damascus. Aleppo was a city known in biblical times, and its Jewish community dates back at least to the Roman period. Aleppo, too, fell to the Ottomans in 1517, and the Sephardim began arriving in numbers at that time. They established a congregation separate from the *Must'arib* (Arabic-speaking local) Jews, but the Sephardic influence gradually became dominant. Trade with Persia and India supported the community, but there were disputes with the so-called Francos, European Jews who came to participate in this commerce with special tax exemptions. Several very important rabbis served there throughout the period.

Damascus, another biblical city, had a Jewish population in the thou-

---

[32] On Safed see the journal *Sefunot*, vols. 6–7. The literature on mysticism in Safed is enormous, but one might start with Werblowsky, *Joseph Karo.*

[33] See David, *To Come to the Land; EJ,* s.v. "Palestine," "Tiberias," "Safed," "Aleppo," "Damascus."

sands, many of Iraqi origin, before the Ottomans captured it in 1516. Thereafter, numerous Sephardim arrived, and conflicts arose between them and the existing communities. The Sephardim, Iraqis, and Sicilian Jews maintained separate institutions and rabbinic courts for a long period, but they eventually overcame their differences and joined together. The culture of the Sephardim became dominant, as in many places, though in Damascus they eventually ceased speaking Spanish among themselves. The close ties between Damascus, Safed, and Jerusalem in the late sixteenth and seventeenth centuries brought the influence of the Kabbalah to the city, as rabbis moved back and forth. The intellectual and religious life of the community declined somewhat after the beginning of the eighteenth century.

Egypt was conquered by the Ottomans in 1517. There had been a Jewish community of several hundred families living there under the previous Mamluk rulers, and Jewish fugitives from the persecutions in Spain had already been arriving for decades before the Expulsion. The Ottoman period created a complex situation for the growing Jewish community, made up increasingly of Sephardim. On the one hand, the rapidly rotated governors sent by the sultan almost always had Jewish treasurers and physicians, as the responsa in this volume well illustrate. The most famous of these Jewish courtiers was Abraham de Castro, director of the mint in the early sixteenth century.

This situation would seem to speak well of the Jewish position, but in fact it often turned against them. The governors were interested in acquiring power and money during their tenure in Egypt, and they often extorted funds from the Jews; this happened to de Castro himself. At times these court Jews were caught in the middle of intrigues and insurrections that were also turned to their detriment. On at least three occasions—in 1523, 1735, and 1754—the Jewish community suffered terrible persecutions as a result of tensions between local governors and the capital in Istanbul. These pressures from the Ottoman government were exacerbated by the fact that the creation of the office of *nagid,* the speaker or overseer of the Jews since Fatimid times (in the eleventh century), was now appointed by the Ottomans in Istanbul to govern the community in Egypt. The *nagid* sometimes clashed strongly with the local rabbinic leaders, causing the abolition of the official office in 1560. Thereafter the leaders of Egyptian Jewry were called the Çelebi (gentleman). Many in that office got caught in the same trap as other court Jews and were executed by despotic governors. Conditions continued to be very dangerous for the Egyptian court Jews until the rebellion against Ottoman rule in 1768.

Despite these hazardous and changeable conditions, the Jewish community of Egypt succeeded in maintaining a lively commercial and religious life, at least until 1735. Jews were of course deeply involved in trade, participating in the country's medial position in commerce between Africa, the Mediterranean, and Europe. As the responsa show, Jews participated in many other trades there as well. Egypt was particularly noteworthy during the Ottoman period for its great rabbinic scholars, several of whom wrote works that continue to be studied today. Among these figures were talmudists, legal scholars, mystics, and messianic activists. Another interesting and sometimes challenging aspect of Jewish life in Egypt was the presence of a large Karaite community there. The Karaites were members of a loose sect originating in the eighth century whose philosophy centered on their rejection of the Jewish oral law tradition, embodied in the Talmud. The Karaites attempted to live strictly according to the laws of the written Torah, which created clashes in both ideology and practice with the main, or "Rabbanite," Jewish community.[34]

Important Jewish communities could be found across the coast of North Africa, many of which had major Sephardi components.[35] Esther Benbassa and Aron Rodrigue have described the development of an integrated Maghrebi Jewish culture, made up of Sephardic and local elements, which they refer to as "'Sephardized' Judeo-Arabic culture."[36] The major communities in this region include Tripoli, Tunis, Algiers, Oran, and Tlemcen, among others. Tripoli fell to the Ottomans relatively late, in 1551, after a long period under the rule of Spain and the Knights of Malta. Sephardim arrived, both from the Iberian Peninsula and from Livorno, Italy (see below), in the late sixteenth and seventeenth centuries. Among the interesting personalities who resided there were Hakham Simeon Lavi, the first author of a complete commentary to the Zohar, and Dr. Abraham Miguel Cardoso, a major theologian of the Sabbatean movement.

Tunis was a somewhat less desirable port for escaping Sephardim because it was under a long-term threat of Spanish invasion in the sixteenth century. In the seventeenth century, for complex reasons, Tunis Jewry became very closely tied to the community of Livorno, which was composed largely of former *conversos*. In Tunis there was a sharp division between the Spanish/Livornese ("Grana") and native Tunisian ("Tou-

---

[34] See David, "On the End"; Nemoy, *Karaite Anthology*; Polliack, *Karaite Judaism*; Landau, *Jews in Ottoman Egypt*; Sambari, *Divrei Yosef*, 254ff.; Beinart, *Sephardi Legacy*, 2: 72–76 (Barnai); *EJ*, s.v. "Aleppo," "Damascus," "Egypt."

[35] See Hirschberg, *History*, vol. 1; Beinart, *Sephardi Legacy*, 2: 68–71 (Barnai); *EJ*, s.v. "Tunis," "Algiers," "Morocco," etc.

[36] Benbassa and Rodrigue, *Jews of the Balkans*, xvii.

ansa") Jews, which caused a complete and hostile break between the two in 1710. Tunisian Jewry suffered rough treatment at the hands of the Muslim authorities, but had commercial success with coral, woolens, and gold trade.[37]

Algiers, which had a population of French and Majorcan Jews already in the fourteenth century, began receiving fleeing Jews and *conversos* from Spain after the 1391 riots. Tension arose from the fear of competition from these Sephardim; in one case, a Muslim judge actually overturned the Jews' attempt to force a boatload of *conversos* to return to Spain. The pattern we have seen elsewhere occurred in Algiers as well: Sephardim became a majority and created a separate community from the native (*must'arib*) Jews. Several outstanding Spanish rabbis arrived, creating a major center of Torah study in Algiers in the fifteenth century. The Ottomans arrived in 1519, and they encouraged both Jews and former *conversos* to conduct commerce there. Again, many Livornese Jews came to Algiers in the seventeenth century, and they, together with the Portuguese former *conversos,* formed an elite. This group acted as agents for European governments and as diplomats on behalf of their own country.

Spanish attacks on Algiers were repulsed on several occasions, but the Algerian port of Oran was not so lucky. All the Sephardic refugees there had to flee when the Spaniards captured the town in 1509, and their property was confiscated. Strangely, however, a group of wealthy families (including Sasportas, whom we will meet in these pages) was readmitted in order to serve the Spanish as diplomatic and commercial agents. These Jews, too, were expelled in 1669; some returned when Oran came back under Muslim control in 1708, but it was reoccupied by the Spanish in 1732. Tlemcen, another Algerian city with a noteworthy Jewish community, underwent similar tribulations, falling to the Ottomans, then the Spanish, then the Ottomans again. The Jews suffered tremendously in the repeated sacks of the town. Many were enslaved and only ransomed later by their coreligionists in other countries. Perhaps the most noteworthy aspect of Algerian Jewry in this period is the way the Jews' skills in languages and diplomacy, and their international connections, gave the community a modicum of protection from wholesale exploitation.

The situation of Moroccan Jewry was altogether unique. There were a number of important Jewish communities there, including those in Tangier, Tetuán, Fez, Meknès, Casablanca, Safi, Marrakesh, and Mogador. Moroccan Jews had a long, impressive history of intellectual and com-

[37] Ibid.

mercial achievement long before the Sephardim arrived. The community was in a period of decline by the time Spanish exiles began appearing in numbers after 1391, and the poor-to-middling sorts of Sephardim who came did little to help the situation. Political and religious unrest led to serious persecutions of the Jews in the fifteenth century, including the near destruction of Fez Jewry in 1465. The sultan, however, warmly welcomed the fleeing Sephardim after 1492. Unfortunately, local bandits took much advantage of the refugees and killed many, while others could not find accommodations and were locked out of the cities. Many important Spanish rabbis did succeed in settling there, though a number of them subsequently left for Europe or Palestine. The common pattern of reception repeated itself in Morocco: the Sephardim (*megorashim*), with their strong culture and identity, threatened to overwhelm native Jewish communities (*toshavim*), creating great tension. In the south the Sephardim became more accepted and dominant, but in the north there was serious resistance to their presence. In Fez, for example, the non-Sephardic native Jews retained many of their own institutions and traditional practices throughout the early-modern period. The Sephardi hakhamim in Fez, meanwhile, introduced the "decrees of the Castilian exiles" concerning marriage and inheritance into local Jewish practice.[38]

Morocco was not part of the Ottoman Empire. Portions of the country were occupied by Portugal in the sixteenth century, but the Portuguese kept up good relations with the Jews in order to use their skills for commercial and diplomatic advantage. Most of Morocco was ruled by mulays, or local governors, who often battled for position among themselves and with the Portuguese. Among the charges of Jewish diplomats, mainly Sephardim, was keeping the fragile peace between the various Muslim principalities and the Portuguese. A paradoxical result was that Moroccan Sephardim often found themselves in Portugal (and sometimes Spain) on missions of diplomacy, despite the laws against the existence of practicing Jews there.[39] Their presence undoubtedly encouraged the stream of escaping *conversos* making their way to Morocco, where their wealth, technical skills, and commercial acumen were welcomed. While this created a wealthy Jewish elite, the majority of Moroccan Jews were in fact laborers and craftsmen whose living was regularly sucked away from them by random taxations and fines.[40] Even the Jewish advi-

---

[38] See Bentov, "'Residents'"; Corcos, *Studies*, chap. 6; Gerber, *Jewish Society in Fez;* Ben-Asher, *Spanish and Portuguese Jews in Morocco* (including the extensive introduction); Zafrani, *Two Thousand Years.*

[39] See García-Arenal and Wiegers, *Man of Three Worlds.*

[40] See Gerber, *Jewish Society in Fez;* Zafrani, *Two Thousand Years.*

sors to the different local sultans suffered as these potentates battled each other for primacy and often took their Jewish advisors down with them when they were bested.

Moroccan Jewry was generally very pious, and the communities produced many great rabbis. They were particularly dedicated to the works of Maimonides on the one hand, and the mystical book *Zohar* on the other. Shabbatai Zvi had a strong following there. Moroccan businessmen and hakhamim were often persuaded to leave the country for the opportunities afforded by the new European Jewish communities that arose in the seventeenth century. Amsterdam, for example, imported a number of its early spiritual leaders from Morocco and Algeria.[41]

While this description constitutes only the barest thumbnail sketch of the Eastern Sephardi diaspora and its communities, it should offer enough orientation to give a sense of the world in which the majority of responsa below were composed. Several major communities of Jews that are sometimes today referred to as "Sephardim" are not discussed here, including those of Persia and Yemen, because they are not made up largely of Spanish and Portuguese exiles. A number of the included responsa do concern a somewhat different group of Sephardim, those of western Europe, who had a rather different profile than the Eastern Sephardim but were part of the same world of Iberian Jewish refugees.

The Western Sephardi Diaspora

The *conversos* of Spain and Portugal were a class that should never have existed. According to Church doctrine, they should have been treated like other Catholics and not singled out in any way. However, popular prejudice and the fact that a fair number of *conversos* (especially in the first generation) secretly clung to some Jewish practices combined to bring persecution upon them. The Inquisition hunted for any signs of Judaizing, and jealous neighbors or competitors were often willing to testify against them. Even the best Catholics among the *conversos* led anxious lives.

Most of the time it was against the law for *conversos* to leave the Iberian Peninsula. They and anyone abetting their escape were subject to very severe punishment. If a person had already been tried by the Inquisition and was now caught trying to leave, it might even mean death. Nevertheless, there were windows of opportunity when flight was per-

---

[41] See Corcos, *Studies*; *EJ*, s.v. "Morocco"; Gerber, *Jewish Society in Fez*; Hirschberg, *History*, vol. 1; Landau, *Jews in Ottoman Egypt*.

mitted, and there were always *conversos* willing to take the risks of escape even when it was not. Still, many others chose voluntarily to remain in their comfortable homes, hoping they would never come to the Inquisition's attention.

The escaping *conversos* faced a number of choices, including where to go, whether to revert to Judaism when they arrived, and how to make a living once they got there. These choices were closely linked together. If *conversos* wished to escape merely to avoid the scrutiny of the Inquisition but had little interest in practicing Judaism, or were willing to keep their practice secret, they could go anywhere Catholics lived. That might include southern France, the Americas, or anywhere in western Europe. These were all fine opportunities for those who wanted to engage in trade because the Atlantic world was beginning its great boom. If the *converso* wished to revert to Judaism, on the other hand, these choices were not attractive because Jews were forbidden to live in all those places. Such a person would have to go to an existing Jewish community in the Ottoman Empire, Morocco, Italy, or elsewhere, and re-convert.

The nature of this choice changed over time as well. Spanish and Portuguese *conversos* who left within a few years of their conversions were most likely to want to return to the practice of Judaism. They had been raised as Jews and could easily reintegrate into the Jewish community, though other Jews might look down on them for having lived as Catholics for a period. After a generation or two, however, the gap between *conversos* and practicing Jews would have widened. The *conversos* had commercial, educational, and social opportunities that Jews never had, and many took full advantage. But even an educated, wealthy *converso* arriving in Saloniki or Fez would be embarrassed by a lack of any living knowledge of Jewish practice. The Jews increasingly looked askance at these *conversos* as a foreign element, and the *conversos*, for their part, felt increasingly uncomfortable with the less worldly, poorer Sephardim they encountered. In some cases, then, even those *conversos* who wished to practice Judaism were so uneasy with anyone but fellow *conversos* that they created their own communities alongside existing Jewish communities.

By the late sixteenth century the Iberian *conversos* were a century removed from Jewish practice. Even the Judaizers among them increasingly preferred to live in enclaves in western Europe. There they would not be troubled by conflict with existing Jewish communities, they could take advantage of the mercantile economy, and they could continue their crypto-Jewish practices in secret as they had in Spain or Portugal. Groups of these merchants appeared in southern France, Antwerp, Amsterdam, London, and other cities in which Jews were forbidden. This is why the Western Sephardi diaspora did not come into being until a century after the Expulsion.[42]

Such enclaves always contained *conversos* of different stripes, including some strong Judaizers and some who had little interest in Judaism. The Judaizers frequently organized worship services, and even brought teachers or rabbis in secretly to lead their communities. The Judaizers were often the leaders of the groups, and the whole enclave would take on a crypto-Jewish character. In some cases, such as in Antwerp, the *conversos* were eventually evicted. In other cases, however, their secret Judaizing became known one way or another, but they were not thrown out because their commercial value was too great. In Amsterdam and London, the Protestant religious values of the country played a part in the decision to allow the *conversos* to remain. Once the secret was out and the determination to tolerate their presence had been made, these colonies organized themselves as practicing Jewish communities, though they generally had to keep a low profile for some period. This was the genesis of the Western Sephardi diaspora.

Amsterdam was unquestionably the predominant community of Western Sephardim. While its origins are shrouded in legend, it appears that in the first years of the seventeenth century a group of escaped Portuguese *conversos* in Amsterdam was discovered practicing crypto-Jewish rituals by the Dutch authorities. While conservative church leaders wished to have them expelled, the city fathers were loath to see wealthy, well-connected merchants move their assets elsewhere. Some Christians made the argument that when these Jews were exposed to the beauty and gentleness of Dutch Protestant Christianity, rather than the cruelty of Catholicism to which they were accustomed, they would certainly convert. Foremost jurists were consulted on the case, and ultimately the authorities decided that the Jews could stay if they kept a low profile.

Over the course of the seventeenth and early eighteenth centuries, thousands of escaped *conversos* and their progeny made their homes in Amsterdam, where their presence was increasingly accepted. Two generations after their arrival, both the Spanish and Portuguese Jews, and the Ashkenazim who arrived in their wake, were able to build synagogues on a grand scale. A *mahamad,* or board of lay leaders, ruled the community.

---

[42] I have integrated two approaches to the birth of Western Sephardi communities here: an economic one and a socioreligious one. The economic approach comes from two works by Jonathan Israel, *European Jewry* and *Diasporas*. The socioreligious one comes from Rivkah Cohen, "Some Problems of Religious and Social Absorption of Ex-Marranos by Greek Jewry Under Ottoman Rule After 1536", in Ankori, *From Lisbon to Salonica*, 11–26.

The Amsterdam rabbis tended toward broad religious and secular erudition rather than talmudic prowess. They performed a double role as leaders of their newly Jewish congregants and as resident experts on Judaism for European Christian savants. Several very active Hebrew and Spanish-Jewish presses made the city a center of the Jewish book trade. Amsterdam Jewry probably enjoyed more liberty than any other community in the world at that time. It was also a hotbed of heterodox ideas, because some of the escaped *conversos* were unwilling to accept the authority of the *mahamad* and of the rabbinic tradition.

Amsterdam Jewry took much of its communal structure from the older Venice Sephardic *kahal,* and in turn, Amsterdam served as the mother community to a group of other *converso* enclaves. One of these groups was in London. The Jews had been expelled from England in 1290, though London had been home to small groups of secret *conversos* on and off through the sixteenth and early seventeenth centuries. Eventually, in the 1650s, two factors contributed to the the exposure of this colony. One was that they had to explain to the English government why they should not be seen as enemy nationals when England was at war with Spain. In reply, they said that as secret Jews, they had suffered at the hands of the Inquisition and their co-religionists had been expelled by the Spaniards, so they had a great hatred for Spain. At around the same period, an Amsterdam rabbi, Hakham Menasseh ben Israel, came to London to plead before Oliver Cromwell, the Lord Protector, for the readmission of the Jews to England. His mission inadvertently brought attention upon the group of *conversos* living in London, a result many of them did not welcome. Nevertheless, Cromwell, presented with the existence of a de facto Jewish community in the city, tried to get Parliament to agree on readmission, but the matter was too controversial and went nowhere. This may have been just as well, because soon Cromwell died, King Charles II returned from exile, and all the laws promulgated under Cromwell were nullified. The Jews were able to stay, though with no official charter, and they enjoyed comparative comfort there.

The history of Hamburg's Spanish and Portuguese congregation is generally similar to those of Amsterdam and London. When the authorities discovered a secret Jewish conventicle, popular sentiment urged the Jews' immediate expulsion, but again, the city fathers insisted that they could stay because of their economic utility. The Hamburg group boasted several important rabbis and intellectuals, as well as ambassadors acting on behalf of various European countries—including Portugal. A Hebrew press printed a number of titles there. Hamburg's Sephardim were particularly active in the Atlantic trade and related financial operations. They were among the founders of the Bank of

Hamburg. A crushing tax caused the wealthier Sephardim to depart after 1697.

Livorno (Leghorn), a Tuscan port city on Italy's northwestern coast, was still an undistinguished village well into the sixteenth century, but the Medici rulers determined to transform it into a major port. In 1593 they issued a very generous invitation to merchants from all over Europe to come trade in Livorno. The guarantees of religious freedom and amnesty were clearly intended to attract former *conversos,* who indeed came in numbers and established an important Sephardi community there. Thus, the origins of the Livorno congregation were quite different from those of the other Western Sephardi enclaves. The original promises were kept, and Jews continued to immigrate there well into the eighteenth century. The Livorno Jewish merchants specialized in multi-directional mercantile trade, sending agents to North Africa (as noted above) and other ports to create strategic networks. Livorno was the only major Italian city that did not keep its Jews in a ghetto. An important Jewish printing press existed there for centuries.

The situation in southern France was perhaps the most complex in western Europe. *Conversos* had been arriving there since the expulsion from Spain and continued to come deep into the eighteenth century. This was partly because it was relatively easy to get to southern France from northern Spain or Portugal. There were certainly large numbers of *conversos* who were not interested in returning to Judaism; they assimilated into the local population, and only the common Sephardi names among the Catholic populace there bear witness to their arrival. There were also, however, those *conversos* who wanted to practice Judaism to one degree or another. This was well known to their neighbors after a while, but the French authorities in Bayonne, Bordeaux, and their environs chose to turn a blind eye to the fact. There were thus active Jewish communities in these regions that kept up the barest veneer of Catholic life for the sake of appearance over more than a century. Like the other Western Sephardim, those of southern France were deeply involved in international trade, particularly coral and chocolate.

Members of these western European Sephardic communities, along with smaller numbers of Eastern Sephardim and Italian Jews, established their own small congregations in strategic trade centers all over. This was the origin of several American communities, such as Recife, Pernambuco, Barbados, and Curaçao; and others in India, Africa, and Russia. We hear little of these outlying communities in the responsa, probably because the types of Jews attracted to these far-flung colonies had little interest in the finer points of Jewish law.

One important thing to keep in mind about the Western Sephardic communities is that they were composed mainly of former *conversos*, most of whom had never lived in any other Jewish community before. They were third-, fourth-, or fifth-generation Catholics with only vague family traditions of their Jewish origins. The paradox of a Jewish congregation made up of people whose whole religious universe was Catholic was surprisingly invisible from the outside. Visitors to Amsterdam commented on the decorum of the synagogue, the excellent education system, and the elegance of the sermons.

Hidden under the surface, however, were characteristics that marked these communities as distinct from those of the Eastern Sephardim with whom they shared linguistic and cultural affinities. The dedication of even the lay leaders at the center of the congregation to the details of Jewish law, particularly those parts dealing with business practices, was questionable at best. The synagogue was the place for religion, and it was observed scrupulously there; the bourse and warehouse were a secular domain. While there were always Jews in every community who were less than scrupulous in their observance, this was particularly common among the Western Sephardim. The religious skepticism made famous by Amsterdam's Barukh Spinoza was widespread in a more subtle form across the group. Particularly important for our purposes was the sizeable contingent of marginal *conversos* living alongside these congregations, who shared a national and cultural background with the community members but declined to submit to the authority of the *mahamad* and rabbis. Several of these people will appear in the responsa.

Another characteristic that was particularly strong among the Western Sephardim was their self-image as members of a cultural elite that was superior not only to the Ashkenazim but to ordinary Sephardim as well. They styled themselves "members of the Portuguese nation," or *Nação*— referring specifically to those who had lived as *conversos* and thus absorbed Iberian culture as equals with the Catholics. This identity sometimes conflicted with the separate religious category of "Jews." If one felt more in common with a fellow *converso* still living as a Catholic than one did with one's Ashkenazi or poorer Sephardi Jewish neighbors, the clarity of group definitions became blurred and thus a potential threat to rabbinic tradition. The *conversos* also absorbed the very rigid class divisions of Iberian society, which operated on a matrix of family nobility and wealth. It is ironic but not strange that these Spanish and Portuguese *converso* emigrants, who were at the bottom of the status hierarchy in their native land, crafted a system in the West that put themselves at the top and their fellow Jews down below.[43]

---

[43] On the Western Sephardim see Bodian, *Hebrews;* Coppenhagen, *Menasseh; EJ;* Israel,

Using the Responsa as a Historical Source

Historians have been using the responsa as a source of information about the past for many generations. In the later twentieth century, several scholars stepped back to examine the genre, its advantages and its disadvantages as a tool for historical study. Some of their results are incorporated in what follows, while other aspects of my approach may differ from theirs.[44]

The study of Jewish history requires different tools than the study of other national histories because the Jews, through the last two millennia of their history, were a nation in exile, moving between countries. Most Jews in most of the diaspora remained outsiders no matter how long they lived in a particular country or city, though there were occasional exceptions—the few Jews who, usually by acquiring wealth or political power, became an integral part in the national history of another nation. The historical sources usually consulted for a nation living in its historical homeland include national or local archives, birth and baptismal records, court documents, journals and memoirs, letters, and newspapers. The Jews appeared occasionally in these sorts of records everywhere they lived, but they were very often faceless Others, suspected of every evil in the world. While we can learn a great deal from such documents, they leave us largely in the dark about the lived experience of Jews themselves.

Inquisitorial proceedings are among the most useful non-Jewish sources for getting at the details of Jews' lives, particularly in the early modern period. Properly speaking, these seldom focus on actual Jews because inquisitions had jurisdiction only over people who were (or

European Jewry; Israel, *Diasporas;* Kaplan, *Alternative Path;* Kaplan, *Western Sephardi Diaspora;* Pullan, *Jews of Europe;* Barnett and Schwab, *Sephardi Heritage;* Yerushalmi, *From Spanish Court.*

[44] For example, Haas, *Responsa;* Netanyahu, *Marranos of Spain;* Soloveitchik, *Use of Responsa.* Among those to make extensive use of responsa in the history of the Sephardim are Ben-Naeh, Hacker, and Rozen, in all their cited works; Goldman, *Life and Times;* Goodblatt, *Jewish Life;* Morell, *Precedent;* Passamaneck, *Insurance;* Shmuelevits, *Jews of the Ottoman Empire;* Weissberg, "Jewish Life"; Zimmels, *Magicians.* On the use of responsa in Sephardic historiography, see Marc D. Angel, "The Responsa Literature in the Ottoman Empire as a Source for the Study of Ottoman Jewry," in Levy, *Jews of the Ottoman Empire,* 669–86. For full texts of responsa from various periods, including many interesting Sephardic exemplars, see Finkel, *Responsa Anthology;* Freehof, *Treasury of Responsa.*

were assumed to be) baptized. Furthermore, the victims of inquisitions had many reasons to lie or distort the truth about their lives. Inquisitional interviews, for all their detail and personal features, were a view from the outside. Still, these proceedings contain a wealth of material about both *conversos* and the Jews with whom they sometimes came in contact.[45]

To really get at Jewish society from within, then, the historian needs to look at material written by Jews. By the nature of things, most of these works were composed by rabbis or an elite of wealthy, educated leaders. The sources include communal record books, biblical and talmudic commentaries, sermons, letters, the rare memoir, and of course responsa.

The responsa, particularly from the early modern period, contain a great deal of material for the historian. (When I speak of responsa here, my intention is in fact more the questions addressed to rabbis than their answers.) One feature of this genre is that responsa are plentiful. Another is their wealth of detail. While medieval responsa almost always compress the questions into an extremely abbreviated form, the invention of print and more conscious treatment of texts after the fifteenth century led to preservation of queries far closer to their original forms. The print shop, working from an original manuscript, would often keep sentences intact rather than truncating them as a hand-copyist might be tempted to do. While this was not always the case, it is a general tendency that can be easily spotted through comparison.[46]

This means that early modern responsa preserve information about every aspect of Jewish life, but also (at least occasionally) the original voices of actors in the events recounted. Jewish law attempts to regulate every facet of the Jew's activities—hygiene, diet, sexual relations, finances, ethics, religious activities, and a great deal more. Thus almost anything at all can be the subject of a question referred to a rabbi. In practice, a large majority of questions in the early modern collections focus on a limited group of topics: marriage, divorce, inheritance, property rights, taxes, communal authority, and ritual infractions. Nevertheless, the entire range of human experience turns up there; and, perhaps

---

[45] See Beinart, *Conversos on Trial;* Homza, *Spanish Inquisition;* Kagan and Dyer, *Inquisitorial Inquiries.*

[46] While there are important collections of responsa from the medieval period, only a handful are cited with any regularity by early modern and modern Jewish legislators. In contrast, these legislators cite numerous early modern collections, suggesting that the genre's significance in Jewish law is mainly a product of our period. This is due largely to the impact of print on the one hand and the effects of population dispersion on the other.

most important, those involved come from every class and walk of life. The poor and the wealthy, the ethical and the unscrupulous, the wise and the foolish, women and men, young and old, all find their place in the responsa.

The original purpose for these documents was not, of course, to teach history, but to establish the law. Thus, details of historical interest are often omitted in editing, while points that seem superfluous to the historian are included because they are relevant to the legal case at hand. We must be aware, then, that most of the questions were formulated or reformulated by rabbis. Sometimes it is the local rabbi before whom the question was originally raised; sometimes it is the more prominent rabbi to whom this person brought the problem; and sometimes it is an editor. Nevertheless, if we are careful to think about how this treatment is likely to affect the presentation, we can still cull a great deal of the actors' lived experience from the words.

I will briefly suggest a method for the recovery of contextual meaning in these documents. Imagine you are sitting on the jury in a modern American courtroom hearing testimony about the alleged murder of a wealthy businesswoman by a down-and-out drug dealer. Everyone in the courtroom, including the suspect, is well dressed and groomed. The lawyers for both parties and all the witnesses use their most polished, careful English. Only one thing in that courtroom will give away the different life experiences of the defendant and the victim: the meaning of the words spoken. As a jury member, you must read behind the words you are hearing to re-create the gritty, appalling world of the defendant on the one hand and the pressured, privileged life of the victim on the other. If you think about the reality that underlies the words, the subtleties of meaning, and your own experiences in different environments, you will be able to see entire universes of meaning in those dry words. This is the method to use in studying the responsa as well. Professor Haym Soloveitchik, teaching a course in medieval responsa at the Hebrew University, once told us, "If the words do not jump off the page and dance for you, you are not getting it."

One especially exciting moment in the responsa is the occasional citation of verbatim testimony given before the rabbinical court, which very self-consciously maintained its integrity. In fact, such testimony is often quoted in the language in which it was given, which in most instances was Spanish and on rarer occasions Arabic, Turkish, or Hebrew. This testimony is most common in cases of an *agunah*, a grass widow. Witnesses came to testify about what they saw or heard concerning the husband's death in order to free the widow to remarry. This subgenre within the responsa is a rich and little tapped source of material about popular culture in the original voice.

Some sense of the rabbinic context will be helpful to understand the makeup of these documents. Jewish legislation was based on the Talmud, an enormous ancient compendium of law and lore compiled over centuries and eventually edited at the dawn of the medieval period. The Talmud is composed in a style resembling stream of consciouness. As it flows from one subject to the next, it often takes up the same topic in several places, sometimes with different conclusions. On the other hand, there is sometimes no legal conclusion at all to a discussion. The derivation of a ruling from the Talmud in any particular circumstance is extremely challenging. The Jews, living scattered in a far-flung diaspora, needed talmudic experts to answer the many questions that naturally arose in their lives. In the later Middle Ages and afterward there were legal codes to help them, particularly the *Mishneh Torah* of Rabbi Moses Maimonides (Moshe ben Maimon, 1138–1204) and the *Shulhan Arukh* of Rabbi Joseph Karo (1488–1575)—both Sephardi scholars. But specific difficulties were often not clearly addressed by these codes, and sometimes the codes themselves needed interpretation. Local rabbis were the first adjudicators of a case, and it is clear that in most instances they judged on the spot and the proceeding was finished. More complex cases and those requiring technical documentation went before a *bet din,* or rabbinic court. If there was not one locally, the involved parties might have to travel to a larger town.

The recorded responsa, which essentially constitute a body of case law precedents, come into being when a complex or politically significant case arises. There are a variety of scenarios by which a question and answer might make their way into written form and be preserved in a particular rabbi's papers. The author of the collection might himself be the local hakham in a given case. He might be the person to whom the local hakham brought a case for either a more expert opinion, or, if one of the parties had impugned the local hakham's authority, for a more objective one. He might include cases brought before his court, or cases sent by other rabbis for an opinion.

The texts in our possession in the printed volumes of responsa are also of various types. There are queries that are copied almost verbatim from the documents and testimonies presented at court. There are those that have been heavily edited by the rabbinic judge, a copyist, or a printer, preserving only the factual outlines of the case; and there is everything in between. The collections published most recently are often particularly complete renditions because modern editors are usually careful to copy from the manuscript originals with great care. I should add, though, that in the many cases where texts copied directly from autograph manuscripts can be compared to printed editions from the early modern presses, the latter often prove remarkably complete and free of tendentious editing.

Sometimes the responsa genre was used in an odd way by rabbis. Rather than responding to actual questions asked by Jews, they would invent questions themselves as a way of exploring some legal topic. One such case was recently discussed in the Israeli press.[47] I came across some responsa volumes that were composed almost entirely of such pseudo-questions. These questions are, however, easy to recognize. For one thing, the rabbi often tells us he is inventing the case—he has no interest in fooling the reader, only in expounding the law. In cases where the author does not state that he is inventing a question, it is usually clear when he is doing so anyway because the question lacks all specificity or extraneous detail that does not speak directly to the legal issue. (Sometimes actual cases are stripped down in this way as well.) Since the social historian is usually interested in exactly those human details, we are not likely to use these queries unwittingly.

In this volume there are two examples of self-created questions. One is in Document #25, concerning a levirate marriage to a Karaite. The questioner asks "a related question" that is clearly hypothetical. The second example appears in Document #28, concerning certain strange natural phenomena seen by Hakham Jacob Hagiz, in which he presents some obviously hypothetical questions along with ones which were actually relevant.

My selection of responsa was not designed to present systematic information about any single community, nor about the Sephardic diaspora as a whole. I searched for documents that told a human story illustrating aspects of Sephardic life as they were experienced at the individual level. I tried to emphasize local conditions obtaining, for example, in Ragusa, Amsterdam, or Kastoria, but also the interconnectedness of Sephardi communities and their common concerns. Some of the episodes recounted are of major historical importance, while many others are useful mainly for their illustrative value.

The nature of stories in historical material like the responsa is obviously different from that of fictional stories, where everything is neatly

---

[47] The case involved events in the city of Worms, Germany, in 1636. For our purposes what is most noteworthy is that the author of the responsum on the case, Rabbi Ya'ir Hayyim Bacharach, explains from the outset that the question he is addressing is strictly hypothetical. See Reiner, "Event"; Posen, "Psychological Towers"; Reiner, "Response." I am grateful to Professor Elliott Horowitz for calling my attention to this exchange.

arranged and all the pieces contribute to an orderly tale. The queries from the responsa are snatches of stories from real life. They are jagged, odd, repetitive, incomplete, and complex. They do not have a clear beginning, middle, and end. Like genuine wood next to formica wood-grain, however, it is these very qualities that offer us a window into the lived experiences of the people involved. Real life is not neat and clear. The battles of everyday existence are not played out on the grand stage of history, but in the little skirmishes between pettiness and kindness, fear and trust, fighting and running. We must also remember that the episodes that came to court represent only the instances where something went wrong with the orderly course of things. For every cheating husband who shows up in the literature, there were undoubtedly scores of faithful marriages. For every business arrangement that goes sour there must have been hundreds that came off smoothly. For each ruffian there were numerous good and pious folk. If we keep these matters in mind, and we pay careful attention to the construction of the narratives, we can mine incredible historical riches from the responsa.

Certain technical phrases and procedures turn up regularly in the questions. The term "Sages" refers to the Hebrew *Hakhamim zikhronam le-vrakhah,* by which is meant the rabbis of the Talmud. The terms "rabbi" and "hakham," both of which were used by Sephardic Jews to refer to their religious leaders, are used interchangeably here.

Witnesses testifying before the rabbinic court are sworn in with a series of oaths and warnings that are often mentioned as having been administered with all due solemnity. Testimony from non-Jews, even when cited secondhand by a Jewish witness, are deemed reliable in many situations when the non-Jew gives critical information without any prompting or leading questions by an interested Jewish party. This is called *mesi'ah lefi tumo*—speaking in innocence.

The Hebrew term *melekh* is used in rabbinic literature to refer to the highest political authority in the region or country. I have thus generally rendered it as "king" in Christian lands, "sultan" in the Ottoman Empire, and "mulay" in Morocco.

Speakers often comment that something unfortunate happened "in our multitude of sins," a formulaic piety; and they insert phrases like "may God preserve him," or "may his repose be in Eden." I have deleted these in a few places, when they unduly interrupt the narrative flow.

Responsa collections are often divided into the four sections of the law codes *Tur* and *Shulhan Arukh: Orah Hayyim* (The path of life: laws of everyday behavior); *Yorah De'ah* (Teacher of knowledge: laws of the permitted and forbidden in foods, relationships with parents and teachers, and other fields); *Even ha-Ezer* (The rock of help: laws concerning women and marriage); and *Hoshen Mishpat* (The breastplate of judgment: laws of business and money). When a responsum appears in one of these divisions I have noted it by placing the abbreviations O.H., Y.D., E.H., or H.M. before the number. Identifying responsa by number rather than page makes it easier to find the reference among several editions of the collection.

In many instances, names of individuals and cities have been replaced in the responsa by generic terms to protect privacy. A person or place might be described as *"ploni"* (so-and-so). Places are often called by the names of famous cities in the Land of Israel: Jerusalem, Tiberias, Tzipori, Safed. (This can cause confusion because legal disputes sometimes involved these actual cities.) Women are referred to pseudonymously as Dina, Rachel, and Leah; men as Reuben, Simeon, and Levi. Sometimes we are luckier and the names have been preserved. The responsa are also full of pronoun problems, which often complicate our understanding of the story. The authors try to forestall this difficulty by constantly referring back to the parties as "the abovementioned Reuben" or "the abovementioned Sarah," which results in little clarification, but a clumsy English reading. I have dropped these small reminders in many instances.

I have translated the Hebrew term *Togar* as Turk in most cases, though it might as easily mean any Ottoman Muslim.

Another difficulty arises when cities changed names or were referred to by various names. So, for example:

Old Name	New Name
Constantinople	Istanbul
Smyrna	Izmir
Adrianople	Edirne
Ragusa	Dubrovnik
Spalato	Split
Leghorn	Livorno

When studying the episodes recounted in a responsum for the reconstruction of communal or individual history, the method is to examine all responsa and other documents related to that case. Since systematic reconstruction of this type is not the goal of the present work, I have not attempted to search out all these related documents. I cite certain background literature in some instances, and in one case (Document #31) I quote several parallel texts to show how this looks. Many of the texts I use here are already well known to the tiny cadre of academic experts for whom their details are historically significant.

I attempt to create prose that reflects the legal, technical quality of many of these texts on the one hand, while still eliciting something that is readable in English on the other. I strive to preserve the meaning with precision, but there are places (particularly with idiomatic phrases or undue repetitions) where I depart slightly from a literal translation. I insert commas and periods liberally because without them the text is almost unreadable. There are spots where I am uncertain about the meaning of the text, in which case I insert a question mark in square brackets [?]. In many places I feel the text needs a few extra words for clarification, or some words are better skipped. In other spots I add the original Hebrew term used. I place both these and a summary of the author's response in square brackets as well. While I am certain that my prose will look clumsy to many readers, and not sufficiently precise to experts in the field, I still hope I have presented something that will be useable and interesting.

SHORT BIOGRAPHIES OF THE HAKHAMIM

For convenience, names with a patronymic or hereditary title, such as ibn, ben, ha-Levi, or ha-Kohen, are listed under that patronymic or title. These biographies are mainly based on Azulai, *Shem ha-Gedolim; Encyclopedia Judaica* [*EJ*]; *Jewish Encyclopedia* [*JE*]; and Ya'ari, *Sheluhei Eretz Yisra'el,* unless otherwise noted.

Algazi, Isaac b. Abraham (fl. seventeenth century). Hakham Algazi, member of an illustrious rabbinic family, was rabbi of Chios. He studied in Istanbul under Hakham Hayyim Benveniste, who published some of his responsa. The rest of these remained in manuscript until their publication in 1982. He wrote a book of homilies, *Doresh Tov,* at the age of seventeen, and said that he was assisted in this and his other writings by some of his famous relatives.

Almosnino, Joseph b. Isaac (1642–1689). Hakham Almosnino, who came from a famous Spanish rabbinic family, followed a common pattern: he left his native Saloniki as a youth to study in the great academy of Hakham Jacob Hagiz in Jerusalem. He moved to Belgrade around 1666 and succeeded his father-in-law as chief rabbi in 1668. Belgrade suffered from a great fire in which many of his own writings were lost, and in 1688, disaster struck again when the city fell to the Ottomans. Many Jews escaped, but some were captured, and Hakham Almosnino went to Germany to raise money for their ransom. This background is reflected in his responsum translated here.

Alsheikh, Moses (fl. sixteenth century). Hakham Alsheikh was born in Adrianople (Edirne) and studied in Saloniki under the exiled hakhamim Joseph Taitatzak and Joseph Karo. He joined the latter in Safed, where he excelled as a preacher and halakhist and taught the famous kabbalist Rabbi Hayyim Vital. He traveled widely in Syria, Turkey, and probably Persia. He is most famous today for his extensive Torah commentaries. (See Shalem, "Moses Alshech.")

Amarillo, Solomon b. Joseph (1645–1721). Hakham Amarillo showed great brilliance as a young student in his native Saloniki, becoming a preacher at the age of twenty-one. He taught in major yeshivot and in 1691 became one of the three chief rabbis of Saloniki. Many of his responsa are really novellae on Hakham Karo's *Shulhan Arukh,* but there are genuine queries among them such as the one translated here.

Angel, Barukh (ca. 1595–1670). Hakham Angel spent his life in Saloniki, where he was a leading legal scholar, teacher, preacher, mystic, and yeshivah head. In addition to responsa, he published many novellae on Talmud and glosses on the *Shulhan Arukh* of Hakham Karo.

Ayyash, Judah b. Isaac (d. 1760). Hakham Ayyash was the son of the leading rabbi of Algiers, and himself became the leading rabbi of Algiers in the first half of the eighteenth century. In 1756 he moved to Jerusalem, passing through Livorno on the way. In addition to his responsa, *Bet Yehudah,* he published numerous other commentaries on Jewish law.

Ben Arhah, Eliezer b. Isaac (d. 1652). Hakham Ben Arhah was the rabbi of Hebron in Palestine from about 1615 until his death; he also lived for some period in Safed and Gaza. His responsa, containing questions from all around Palestine and beyond, demonstrate the respect in which he was held. They contain a great deal of important historical material for the study of seventeenth-century history in the Land of Israel. The responsa remained in a unique manuscript until they were edited and published in 1978. (See *She'elot u-Teshuvot Rabbenu Eliezer ben Arhah,* Introduction.)

Ben Habib, Moses b. Solomon (ca. 1654-1696). Hakham Ben Habib came from a very distinguished family of Spanish rabbis (usually Ibn Habib). He was born in Saloniki and raised mainly in Istanbul, but he left there as a young man to study in the yeshivah of Hakham Jacob Hagiz in Jerusalem, where many rising luminaries learned. At the age of fifteen he was married to the daughter of Hakham Hagiz. He later became chief rabbi of Jerusalem (*Rishon le-Zion*) and wrote several very important works, including the standard *Get Pashut* on laws of divorce. (See *She'elot u-Teshuvot Mahara"m Ben Habib,* Introduction, 1–2.)

Benveniste, Joshua b. Israel (fl. late seventeenth century). Hakham Benveniste is a classic example of a rabbi whose fame and respect were enormous during his lifetime, but whom history has largely forgotten. He was the brother of the still-famous Hakham Hayyim Benveniste (author of *Kenesset ha-Gedolah*); both studied under Hakham Joseph Trani in the yeshivah of Istanbul. He was a physician as well as a widely respected rabbi, and published sermons, a commentary on the Jerusalem Talmud, a work on the high holiday prayer service, and a study of divorce laws. Other works of his remained in manuscript. He wrote thousands of responsa, but most of the collection was destroyed in a fire. The few remaining ones were published in Hungary at the beginning of the twentieth century.

Berab, Jacob (1474–1546). Born near Toledo, Spain, Hakham Berab went to Morocco after the Expulsion and was almost immediately appointed a rabbi there at the age of eighteen. He was a merchant as well as a teacher, and his work took him to Egypt, Palestine, and Syria. He gained a group of disciples who revered his wisdom, but his bid to impose his authority in legal matters rankled some rabbis. His yeshivah operated as a center for all the community's scholars, in the tradition of the great Spanish academies. He is best known among scholars today for his attempt to renew the ancient Mosaic line of rabbinic ordination (*semikhah*) in Safed, which aroused a famous controversy. (See Dimitrovsky, "Berab's Academy.")

Castro, Jacob (d. 1610). Hakham Castro was one of the most important Egyptian rabbis of the early modern period. His legal opinions were widely cited by contemporaries, and he was treated with the greatest respect by Hakham Karo, whom he visited in Safed. He was from a family known for wealth as well as scholarship; his uncle, Abraham de Castro, was master of the mint in Egypt. He wrote glosses on Hakham Karo's *Shulhan Arukh,* sermons, and novellae on Talmud, in addition to his responsa.

De Boton, Abraham Hiyya b. Moses (ca. 1560–ca. 1603 or 1609). Hakham de Boton, an early member of this illustrious rabbinic family, was a student of the renowned Hakham Samuel de Medina (Rashda"m). He spent most of his life in Saloniki, though records show he visited Istanbul and Palestine later in his life, and he was rabbi at Polia for a period. He was considered one of the great talmudists of his generation, and he taught many outstanding pupils in his yeshivah. He is famous today for his work *Lehem Mishneh,* a standard commentary on Maimonides' legal code, *Mishneh Torah.* (See Ben-Sasson et al., *Studies in a Rabbinic Family.*)

De Boton, Jacob b. Abraham (ca. 1635–1687). The de Boton family were very prominent among Saloniki's Jewish scholars for many generations. Hakham Jacob de Boton, son of *Hakham Abraham Hiyya de Boton,* was born in Saloniki and studied with Hakham Hasdai ha-Kohen Perahyah. He was a member of the rabbinical court there for a very long period, but failed to be appointed chief rabbi. He wrote many responsa, but the majority (along with other works of his) were lost in a fire. Those that remain are noteworthy for the light they shed on economic matters and the author's extensive use of very old manuscript material in addition to standard printed sources. (See Ben-Sasson et al., *Studies in a Rabbinic Family.*)

Gavizon, Me'ir (fl. late sixteenth to early seventeenth centuries). Hakham Gavizon was born in Damascus and earned a living as a merchant before coming to Egypt and joining the academy of Hakham Hayyim Kaposi, a colleague of Hakham Jacob Castro. Later he was also appointed to the Cairo rabbinate. The family had been prominent in Spain, but most of them were murdered before the Expulsion. Those who escaped created an important rabbinic dynasty in the Ottoman Empire.

Hagiz, Jacob b. Samuel (1620–1674). Hakham Hagiz was the scion of a distinguished Spanish family that came to Fez after the Expulsion. He was educated by his father and mother, after which he came to Verona, Italy, as a teacher in the yeshivah of Hakham Samuel Aboab. In 1652 he moved briefly to Venice, then on to Livorno, publishing prodigiously in each city. He stayed for a short period in Pisa on his way to Jerusalem, where he established his residence in 1658. He directed a major yeshivah there and was head of the rabbinical court in the time of Shabbatai Zvi. Much of his life's work was focused on education, and he taught many luminaries of the next generation. (See Carlebach, *Pursuit of Heresy,* 19–36.)

Hagiz, Moses b. Jacob (1671–ca.1750). The younger Hakham Hagiz was born and raised in Jerusalem at a bleak time for that city's Jews. He was thoroughly educated in Torah study by his father, his mother, his maternal grandfather, and later other Jerusalem luminaries. He spent his adult life wandering through Egypt, Italy, and central and western Europe, writing extensively and engaging in a series of controversies against perceived heterodoxies, particularly those of the Sabbateans. His responsa reflect his extensive travels as well as his vast scholarship. (See Carlebach, *Pursuit of Heresy.*)

Ha-Levi, Eliyahu b. Benjamin (fl. early sixteenth century). Unlike most of the figures cited here, Hakham Eliyahu ha-Levi was not a Spanish Jew, but came from the native Turkish community. He studied with the great hakhamim Moses Capsali and Elijah Mizrahi, and later became chief rabbi of Istanbul. This background may bear on his attitude expressed in the responsum translated here. He wrote hundreds of responsa, some cited by the greatest legal authorities of his time, as well as works of poetry and ethics.

Ha-Levi, Mordecai b. Judah (d. 1684). Hakham ha-Levi served for over forty years as rabbi and rabbinic judge in Cairo and Rosetta in Egypt. His responsa indicate his wide correspondence and the respect in which he was held around the Mediterranean, though an unpleasant dispute broke out between him and Hakham Gabriel Esperanza of Safed in 1678. Among his several books, only his responsa were published. He died soon after his arrival in Jerusalem and was survived by his son, Hakham Abraham b. Mordecai ha-Levi.

Hayyim Jacob b. Jacob David of Safed (d. after 1751). Hakham Hayyim Jacob was born in Izmir and studied in his youth under Hakham Hayyim Alfandari in Istanbul. He followed his teacher to Safed, where he was living by 1717. He was sent as an emissary of the Safed community to collect funds in North Africa (1718–1728) and in Europe (1736–1739). He wrote numerous responsa while on these travels and was quoted with great respect by contemporaries. He also wrote notes on Maimonides and other works.

Ibn Sangi, Astruc b. David (ca. 1570–1643). Hakham Ibn Sangi came from a famous Spanish family of scholars that moved to the Ottoman Empire after the Expulsion. He was born in Nicopolis in what is now Bulgaria and studied with Rabbi Solomon ha-Kohen (Maharsha"kh) in Saloniki. He served as rabbi in Sofia from 1590 until he moved to Palestine around 1640, apparently residing in Istanbul for a time along the way. (See *Sefer She'elot u-Teshuvot Rabi Astruc,* Introduction [Amar]; and Amar, "A Description.")

Ibn Tzur, Jacob b. Reuben (1673–1753). Hakham Ibn Tzur was one of the greatest of the Moroccan sages in the most impressive period of that country's rabbinic flowering. Great political unrest plagued the country at the time, and Hakham Ibn Tzur suffered innumerable personal tragedies in his own family, but he was incredibly productive as a judge and author in many fields. He spent most of his life in Fez, except for a stay in Meknes from 1717 to 1730 and another in Tétouan from 1738 to 1740. He was famous for standing up against abuses by even the most powerful in the community, which sometimes caused serious friction. His compassion for the poor and the suffering stands out in his correspondence. He also had a reputation as a "practical" kabbalist. (See Amar, "A Biography.")

Ibn Yahya, Tam (Jacob) b. David (ca. 1470–ca. 1542). Hakham Ibn Yahya was born in Portugal to a famous rabbinic family. He accompanied his father from Lisbon to Naples around 1493 and settled in Istanbul by 1497. There he served as a hakham under the leadership of the chief rabbi, the famous Elijah Mizrahi. He probably succeeded Hakham Mizrahi in this post when the latter died. Legends say he was physician to Sultan Suleiman the Magnificent and a great authority on Muslim law.

Karo, Joseph b. Ephraim (1488–1575). Hakham Karo was the greatest halakhic authority of his age. Born in Spain, he left with the Expulsion and settled in Greece, where he studied at various yeshivot. He moved to Safed in the early 1530s and became a founding member of the famous circle of mystics there. He is best known as author of the *Bet Yosef* and

Shulhan Arukh, both classic works of Jewish law, and less known as the possessor of a mentoring angel (*magid*), some of whose revelations are recorded in his book *Magid Mesharim.* His responsa are collected in *Avkat Rokhel.* (See Werblowsky, *Joseph Karo,* and Benayahu, *Yosef Behiri.*)

Katzabi, Joseph b. Nissim (d. 1696 or 1698). Hakham Katzabi studied under Hakham Joseph Trani in Saloniki, where he remained as a rabbinic judge for some period. Later he was called to Istanbul to replace Hakham Moses Benveniste as chief rabbi. His decisions were considered liberal, but his legal expertise was undisputed. His responsa contain particularly rich historical data. His sermons as well as his responsa were published by his grandson. (See Weissberg, "Jewish Life.")

Malki, Raphael Mordecai (d. 1702). Hakham Malki had a background far different than most Sephardi rabbis of the period. He apparently came from a family of *conversos* and may himself have been born a Christian. He was raised in Italy and trained as a physician at a European university but moved to Jerusalem around 1677, bringing some personal wealth. There he wrote extensively and treated not only Jews but also Christians living in the local convents, with whom he had friendly relations (a fact bearing directly on his letter translated here). He was the father-in-law of Hakham Moses Hagiz, with whom he had severe disputes. Late in life he became a rabbinical judge in the Jerusalem court. (See Benayahu, *Medical Essays;* Carlebach, *Pursuit of Heresy,* 41–44; Rozen, *Jewish Identity.*)

Melamed, Me'ir b. Shemtob (fl. sixteenth to early seventeenth century). Hakham Melamed came from Morea in Greece, where his father was a well-known scholar. He studied under Hakham Joseph Ibn Ezra in Saloniki, but little else is known of his life.

Meldola, David b. Raphael (1714–ca. 1818). Hakham Meldola came from a long and distinguished line of Italian rabbis associated with the Western Sephardim. He was born in Livorno, moved with his father to Bayonne, and left there for Amsterdam in 1735. There he published both his father's books and his own and also taught various communal groups. In addition to responsa, his voluminous works included investigations into mathematics, astrology, calendrics, and talmudic methodology.

Mizrahi, Israel Meir b. Joseph (fl. early eighteenth century). Hakham Mizrahi was raised mainly by his brother after his father died quite young. He studied with Hakham Abraham Yitzhaki and became head of the Jerusalem yeshivah in the first half of the eighteenth century. He went to collect funds on behalf of the Jerusalem community in Turkey in 1727, passing through Corfu, Saloniki, and other cities on the way, where he established confraternities for the recitation of the kabbalistic midnight prayer vigil of Rabbi Isaac Luria.

Perahyah, Aaron b. Hayyim Abraham ha-Kohen (ca. 1627–1697). Hakham Perahyah was born and spent his life in Saloniki, where he was educated by the leading rabbis. He became chief rabbi of Saloniki in 1689. His many books include extensive commentaries on the Talmud, sermons, and reference works as well as his highly respected responsa.

Sasportas, Jacob (1610–1698). Hakham Sasportas was born in Algeria (then under Spanish rule) to a famous family of scholars and diplomats. He was a child prodigy, later appointed as a member of the Tlemcen rabbinical court at the age of eighteen and as its head at the age of twenty-four. He served as a diplomat as well but was jailed by the authorities and had to flee the country afterward. He spent most of the rest of his long career as rabbi in the Western Sephardi congregations of London, Hamburg, Livorno, and Amsterdam. He was famous as a halakhist but more so as the outspoken opponent of Shabbatai Zvi. (See Moyal, *Sasportas*.)

OUTLINE of the SEPHARDIC DIASPORA,
ca. 1700 (excluding the AMERICAS)

KINGDOM OF SWEDEN

RUSSIAN

EMPIRE

KINGDOM
OF
POLAND

PIRE

Buda (Ofen)
KINGDOM
OF
HUNGARY

Belgrade

Sarajevo

Sophia   Edirne
(Adrianople)

Black Sea

Dubrovnik
(Ragusa)

Istanbul (Constantinople)

Kastoria   O
T
Larissa   T
Corfu   O   Bursa
Lepanto   M
Saloniki(Salonica)   A
N   E
M
Zante   Patras   P
I
R
Izmir (Smyrna)   E

Rhodes

Aleppo

Crete

Mediterranean Sea

Damascus
Safed
Tiberias
Nablus(Schechem)
Jerusalem
Hebron

Alexandria

EGYPT   OTTOMAN EMPIRE

Cairo   ARABIA

PART I

LIFE AMONG MUSLIMS AND CHRISTIANS

In both Muslim and Christian societies in which Sephardim lived after the expulsion there were competing conceptions about how the Jews should be treated. Official religious doctrine, traditional national statutes and precedents, local laws, whims of individual governors or officers, and the attitudes of the masses all came into play in a constantly shifting miasma of influences. The responsa illustrate that in the day-to-day life of Jews, the last two factors—avaricious potentates and capricious neighbors—played the largest roles.[1] Still, the overall structure of their position in society was a function of ancient statutes.

Jews throughout the Middle Ages and the period covered here were largely self-governing. The degree of autonomy permitted to the rabbinical courts and lay leaders varied from place to place and period to period, but they tended to have broad powers.[2]

The status of Jews in Christian society was based partly on teachings of the Church Father Saint Augustine (354–430 C.E.). Augustine said that the Jews serve a purpose in Christendom because they are a living witness to the truth of the Christian faith. This is because Jews are independent (i.e., non-Christian) believers in the sanctity of the Hebrew Bible, which, in Christian thought, clearly prophesies the life and death of Jesus. So Jews serve to prove that the Christians did not forge the Bible. Augustine thought that Jews should serve their function by being scattered and downtrodden among the nations—but not expelled or killed. More specific precedents on the treatment of Jews came from later Roman law, particularly the codes of Constantine, Constantius, Theodosius, and Justinian. These included provisions that Jews must not marry Christians, hire Christian servants, hold public office, testify in court against Christians, and so on.[3] Clearly the overall purpose here was to allow Jews to live among Christians but never to wield any domestic or political power over them or become socially close with them. Judaism itself had laws against fraternizing too much with non-Jews.

Muslims did not begin with as great a prejudice against Jews. They

---

[1] The view that attitudes toward Jews and other minorities were mainly determined by specific local conditions and individuals has been strongly argued in Nirenberg, *Communities.*

[2] See Cohen, *Constantinople-Salonica-Patras;* Joseph Hacker, "Jewish Autonomy in the Ottoman Empire: Its Scope and Limits—Jewish Courts from the Sixteenth to the Eighteenth Centuries," in Levy, *Jews of the Ottoman Empire,* 153–202.

[3] Marcus, *Jew in the Medieval World,* 3–7.

usually treated Jews and Christians alike as "people of the book" who occupy a status below Muslims but above pagans. The formal place of Jews and Christians in Muslim society is described in various versions of a document called the Pact of 'Umar, many of whose dictates were copied wholesale from Christian law codes describing the treatment of infidels. Recent research suggests that the terms of the Pact had more to do with protecting a fragile Muslim identity and presence across a huge empire than with persecuting minorities. The Pact mainly lays out how Christians and Jews must demonstrate their inferiority before Muslims and keep their profile low in Muslim lands.[4] Muslims and Christians both upheld their official doctrines concerning the treatment of Jews unevenly, being extremely strict at some times and quite lenient at many others.

Popular opinion, on the other hand, tended to run more strongly against the Jews. While Jews were very often quite friendly with individual Christians and Muslims, it is clear from the responsa that the Jews were regularly made scapegoats for all kinds of misdeeds, and they were considered easy prey by robbers. Nevertheless, it would be wrong to see Jews as eternal victims among the Christians and Muslims. We often find Jews being treated evenhandedly at non-Jewish courts. Murderers of Jews were regularly convicted and sentenced to death. As one document below shows, Jews even found ways to stand up against non-Jewish officials on occasion.

What is perhaps more important to note is that for all their suffering at the hands of Christian and Muslim miscreants, Jews were probably only marginally worse off than any other common people. If Jews were sometimes blamed for unexplained deaths or other tribulations, so were witches, Roma (Gypsies), heretics, and others perceived as marginal in society. If the Jews were taxed more than others, they were not tied to the land as peasants, and they often had the means to pay even these exorbitant levies. They were frequently seen as useful to governors or kings and given certain special considerations. Even anti-Jewish prejudices could work in the Jews' favor. Tales that Jews controlled vast wealth or had the lock on major markets, which were often exaggerated, sometimes lent them a magnified value in the perception of governors and kings. The Ottomans had a certain respect for Jews that carried over from their predecessors, the Byzantine Christians, among whom the Jews had a distinctive intellectual and economic standing.[5] I will suggest, then, that some of what follows illustrates situations unique to the Jews, but much of it can be generalized to reflect the experiences of any people living in the lands described.

---

[4] Ibid., 13–19; Noth, "Problems of Differentiation."

[5] See Bowman, *Jews of Byzantium*.

1

CAUGHT IN THE MIDDLE OF

OTTOMAN-ITALIAN WARS (GREECE, 1716)

(Hakham Solomon Amarillo, *Kerem Shlomoh*, H.M. #29 and 31)

Introduction

Lepanto and Patras are neighboring cities in southwestern Greece. Lepanto is best known to historians as the site of a critical naval battle in 1571 in which the Ottoman fleet was beaten by Christian forces. Nevertheless, the city of Lepanto itself, which had become a Venetian port in 1407 and later fell to the Turks in 1499, remained in Ottoman hands. From 1687 to 1699 Lepanto was reoccupied by the Venetians, but at the peace of Karlowitz it reverted to Ottoman control once again. Patras had a small Jewish community since ancient times. The town was held by the Ottomans from 1460 until the Venetians took it in 1532. Throughout the seventeenth century the Ottomans and Venetians fought back and forth over Patras, and the Jewish population fled when life there became untenable. When the Turks decisively recaptured Patras in 1715, the Jews returned and lived in relative peace. It is presumably on the background of these battles that the following episodes occurred.

Bibliography: *EJ*, s.v. "Greece," "Patras."

(29) **Question:** Reuben owned a house in the city of Lepanto that was mortgaged to the *Vakıf* [Turkish religious foundation], and he could not find the means to redeem it from them. It remained in the hands of the Turks who ran the *Vakıf*, for Reuben had given them permission to sell the house in order to pay the debt he owed them. Now, no Jew would purchase the house from the Turks without the permission of Reuben, until finally Reuben came and gave permission to Simeon to buy the house from the Turks. Simeon did indeed buy the house from the Turks, and they prepared a deed for him according to their laws, statutes, and customs.

After Simeon had purchased the house, the city was given up to the

Christians, who had been fighting for it. The house was already in the buyer's hands under the Turks, as was mentioned, before the Christians captured the city. But then, the Turks came back and took the city away from the Christians! A rule was issued by the sultan that anyone owning a house in that city would continue to own the land, but the structure would now belong to the sultan. Anyone who wanted ownership of his house would have to pay the value of the structure to the sultan. Builders were brought to calculate the value of every house structure. Simeon came and paid the sultan the value of his house—the one he had previously purchased from them when they held the mortgage on it. They made him out a deed according to their law and custom.

Now, the heirs of Reuben have come forward to file suit against Simeon and remove the house from his possession without paying any money or price. They claim the house belonged to Reuben, their benefactor, and they know nothing whatsoever about what all occurred concerning the house. Simeon's version is explicit and needs no proof. Guide us, our teacher and righteous instructor, as to whether Reuben's heirs have a legitimate case against Simeon and can take the house from him without payment or price. For he has two deeds in hand, one showing he bought the house from the Turks in charge of the *Vakıf*, and the second from the government, as mentioned above. Moreover, the first purchase took place with Reuben's permission. May your reward be multiplied by heaven.

Response: [Hakham Amarillo replies that it is obvious Reuben's heirs have no case.]

(31) To Larissa (may God preserve it), at the request of the wise and great Rabbi Moses Mishan (may God watch over him!), in the month of Tevet 5476 [1716].
Question: Instruct us, our teacher, the great light of Israel, concerning that which has happened under the sun and is already known to be true. The city of Old Patras was in the hands of the Greeks for thirty years. Some of the homes belonging to Jews, members of our covenant, had been destroyed and were rebuilt under Greek rule. Others were completely destroyed, and in their place are orchards and olive groves.

After thirty years, the sultan (may God raise him up) waged war and battled his enemies until he overcame them and captured all these cities, including Old Patras. A decree was announced stating that all men, women, elders, and youths should return to their dwellings, their courtyards and fortresses, but with the following condition: any house that was built new under the Greeks must be sold, and its proceeds deposited in the coffers of the sultan (may God raise him up), whether it belonged to Turks or to Jews. However, any that was not built new, but remained as it had been under the rule of our lord the sultan (may God raise him up) in earlier years [before the Greek conquest] would be given for each person to return to his birthright, whether Muslim or Jew.

We now come to solicit the view of our master [Hakham Amarillo], so he will guide us in which path to take in dealing with houses that were built new, and sold according to the command of the sultan (may God raise him up). If a house had belonged to Reuben, and was bought [from the sultan through forfeiture] by Simeon, does the transaction stand up and remain valid according to the [Jewish] laws and statutes, or not? May your reward be multiplied by heaven.

Response: [Hakham Amarillo says that according to both Jewish law and communal agreements, Simeon may keep the house; Reuben no longer has a claim on it.]

2

THE FINANCIAL FALLOUT

OF A BLOOD LIBEL (RAGUSA, 1622)

(Hakham Astruc Ibn Sangi, *She'elot u-Teshuvot*, #28)

Introduction

In the period from the twelfth to the twentieth centuries, Jews were regularly charged with blood libel or ritual murder—false claims that Jews kidnapped and murdered Christian children as part of a Jewish religious ritual. These calumnies are usually associated with the Ashkenazi world because the most numerous and infamous of them happened in Italy, Germany, and England. We have already seen in the introduction, however, that a ritual murder accusation— the "Holy Child of La Guardia"—was directly associated with the expulsion of Spanish Jewry. A large number of such incidents occurred elsewhere in the Mediterranean as well. Several better-known episodes happened in the nineteenth century, but recent research has discussed cases in Istanbul in 1633, Zante in 1712, and many others. Here we will encounter two additional cases from the Sephardi context. The Ragusa case occurs in a Christian setting, the Algazi case (perhaps just a general murder accusation) in the Muslim world.

The Ragusa case is well known from other sources. In 1622, a Christian girl was found murdered in the home of a woman who was apparently somewhat mad. The woman admitted to committing the murder, but claimed that a Sephardic Jew of the community, Isaac Jeshurun, had enticed her to do it because he needed the girl's blood for Jewish rituals. He was given a very harsh sentence, but this was commuted after three years, which was considered a miracle by the Jews.

The Ragusa query before us really focuses on the financial stresses placed on the community by the ritual murder accusation. It is interesting that the governors squelched the accusation and accompanying potential for violence, but charged the Jews a huge amount of money for this benificence. This outcome looks very different from many German and Italian cases, where conflicts between local and national authorities often left the Jews vulnerable to the physical fury of the locals.

The incidental details of the case are extremely revealing as well. They give us an excellent sense of the kind of trade going through Ragusa, how it developed, and how Ragusa Jews saw their situation as different from those in the rest of Europe and the Ottoman Empire. The case also suggests something about the impact of individual wealth on the dynamics of the *kahal*.

Bibliography: Barnai, "Blood Libels"; Ivana Burdelez, "The Role of Ragusan Jews in the History of the Mediterranean Countries," in Ginio, *Jews, Christians and Muslims*, 190–97; Moises Orfali, "Doña Gracia Mendes and the Ragusan Republic: The Successful Use of Economic Institutions in 16th-Century Commerce," in Horowitz and Orfali, *Mediterranean and the Jews*, 2: 175–202; Yehudit Wimmer (Goldner), "Jewish Merchants in Ragusa as Intermediaries Between East and West in the Sixteenth and Seventeenth Centuries," in Rozen, *Days of the Crescent*, 73–150; Zvi Loker, "Spanish and Portuguese Jews Amongst the Southern Slavs— Their Settlement and Consolidation During the Sixteenth to Eighteenth Centuries," in Barnett and Schwab, *Sephardi Heritage*, 2: 283–313. My description of the case comes from Moshe Amar's note 2 (p. 176) in his edition of Ibn Sangi's responsa, with some additional bibliography.

Question: In a little city by the edge of the sea [Ragusa, now called Dubrovnik], in which a few Jews live, a very terrible and bitter affair occurred. A certain Jew from among them was arrested on a blood libel charge. The fury was visited upon the whole community with anger, rage, and suffering. They depleted large amounts of money, to the point that they had to pawn communal property in order to save the life of this Jew and pay other expenses. When God was kind to them and they were delivered from darkness into light, they concluded among themselves to institute a tax on merchandise passing through their hands from people of other cities, that is, from Turkey to Europe and from Europe to Turkey, through there. [The wording and conditions of the agreement follow.]

They agreed that the tax would be in force until they had collected enough to pay the debt on their pawned items along with the interest. They drew lots for each of them to collect the tax for three months; and anyone who failed to collect would have to pay from his own pocket. This tax ordinance was placed on the books and everyone signed, with the exception of Reuben. He had arrived in town only about two months previous to the establishment of the tax with his household (that is, his wife), to settle there. He had not been called by them to their council and they paid no attention to him. They began collecting the tax on merchandise passing from Turkey to Europe, but not on the merchandise passing from Europe to Turkey, for a period of two years. [The author explains later that at first there was not much trade going in this direction, but that it increased greatly afterward.] This Reuben became a trading agent and gave account of everything he handled going from Turkey to Europe; but they paid no attention, nor did they demand accounts from him, of merchandise passing from Europe to Turkey.

In the third year, when the majority of the holy community saw that the interest payments were eating away the communal possessions and had accumulated into a huge sum, and that everything they collected in taxes was going right back out in other expenses, they came and spoke to Reuben. Reuben told them, "I will pay half the debt from my own money, and all of you together will pay the other half. Thus we will redeem the pawned items so that the interest payments do not consume them. Afterward, each of us will collect money out of the taxes, every one according to the amount he paid in. The men were happy with this. Reuben paid more than half the debt from his own money and the community members paid the rest, so the items were returned to the holy congregation.

Now, some of the congregants asked if there was a way to recoup their property that they expended to redeem the items. This group consisted of a father and his two sons, another man along with his secretary, and two other individuals—a group of seven who took counsel together. They said, "Why should we be silent in the matter of this tax when it comes to goods passing from Europe to Turkey? It is written and sealed in our agreement that we should collect it both on what passes from Turkey to Europe, and on what passes [from Europe] to Turkey! Let us now go and implement this tax collection at the rate decided at the time of the agreement."

Everyone was happy with this except Reuben, who protested. He said to them, "What is this, and what is it all about? You want to renew the tax on goods passing from Europe to Turkey, after this entire time since you established that tax during which you never bothered to collect it? Do you want to tell me that it is because of the money you expended to redeem the property of the congregation? I alone paid more than everyone else! I am satisfied to recoup [my money] from the tax on merchandise passing from Turkey to Europe, and from the charity raised through donations the way they have been in this city for many years. It is enough that God favored us so that we were able to retrieve our pawned belongings from the hands of gentiles. Let us be repaid slowly rather than instituting new taxes, for God does not want that. Furthermore, from the start this tax was instituted unlawfully, for the great R. Solomon ha-Kohen, of blessed memory, and R. Aaron Sasson, of blessed memory, in their books, forbade the establishment of such taxes without the will and permission of the merchants themselves. You created this tax in a manner concealed from the merchants, and it is improper to take the property of our Jewish brethren without informing them.

"If you want to respond that in every Turkish city such a [Jewish transport] tax exists in order to ease the burden of [governmental] taxes, so we too will impose it to alleviate our situation, I would reply that the situations are not similar. In the cities of Turkey the Jewish inhabitants created it because merchants come from other lands and countries to encroach on their livelihood, and they take the best of the land. They therefore ask them to help pay their tax burden. In addition, they give half the [transport] tax to support Torah study. None of this is the case in our city, for the passage of goods through our city is to our own advantage; nor do we take any of it for the worship of God, for we do not even have a teacher for small children.

"There is more. The Turks are thieves and rough characters, and they exploit the Jews at every opportunity. When they behold the large amount of money, great volume of merchandise, and business conducted by Jewish visitors in their cities, their eyes see it and they are consumed with jealousy. They seek pretexts and subterfuges to increase taxes on the local [Jews], which is not the case in this city. For the Christians are delighted to see the arrival of merchandise passing through their city—it only increases their tax revenues. They [the Turkish Jews] thus have sufficient reasons for instituting a [transport] tax, which do not apply to us."

Reuben said all this and much more of the sort to those individuals of the congregation, but they did not heed his claims, for they were anxious to thoroughly enforce the said tax. In order to exert even more pressure, they wrote below the agreement that anyone who would not uphold an agreement made by the majority of community members should be excluded from among them in every way; nobody should speak with him or ask after his wellbeing. They all signed except for Reuben, who did not agree with them and did all he could to deter them.

The days passed, and Reuben did not wish to give them an accounting of the merchandise passing through his hands on its way from Europe to Turkey. They excluded him from among them and could not speak a peaceable word with him. Reuben then went and reported the matter to the government, along with all the arguments he had formulated against them. This tax was not proper in their view, and they erased it from the [Jews'] record books altogether. In their usual manner, they imposed a penalty that from that day forward, no new taxes could be levied without the desire and permission of the owners of the merchandise.

Instruct us now, righteous teacher, if the establishment of this tax was viable from the start, and whether the people of a city like this have the power to levy money from merchants without their agreement.

Response: [Hakham Ibn Sangi expresses empathy for the Ragusa community. He mentions that they had written to neighboring Jews for help and had received many donations. However, he does not think they had the right to create a transport tax like this. He strongly objects to the exclusion of Reuben from the community, which was clearly Reuben's reason for going to the Christian authorities. Hakham Ibn Sangi thinks this was a bad idea on Reuben's part, but says that since the transport tax was inappropriate to begin with, Reuben need not pay the expenses his action cost the community. Nevertheless, he thinks Reuben should repent to God privately for what he caused.]

3

A BLOOD LIBEL AMONG THE

SEPHARDIM (OTTOMAN EMPIRE,

MID-SEVENTEENTH CENTURY)

(Hakham Isaac Algazi, *She'elot u-Teshuvot*, #69)

Introduction

It is not clear precisely where and when this blood libel took place. It may have been an otherwise unknown local incident in the area of Izmir where Hakham Algazi was located. Here the whole community was arrested, and the Jews suffered physical harm as well as incarceration. This accusation, too, might have gone unrecorded were it not for the financial strife caused by the huge bribes needed to free the Jews, which led to the legal query.

Question: The following event occurred. One day a Turkish girl was found cast down the well of a certain Turkish man. The gentiles rose up against the Jews and slandered them with the claim that the Jews murdered this girl and threw her there. They were all arrested, and the Jews—both residents and visitors to the city—found themselves in a dangerous and distressing situation, for it was said that all those [Jews] in the city had plotted together to murder her. They were all caught in the trap and their names were recorded [as perpetrators] in the gentile court. By bribing the evil people the Jews were able to avoid being thrown in prison and were allowed to stand as guarantors for each other until their innocence could be unquestionably established. However, two days later, the loathsome chief of the army came and arrested the Jews again. They were beaten so badly that they were forced to humiliate themselves by sending for money to save themselves from this libel.

Now, instruct us, righteous teacher, concerning the Jews who were away from the city at the time when the fury of the libel was leveled against them, that "you murdered this soul and threw her body down the well." They were not present at the general arrest when everyone was detained because they were on distant journeys. Must they pay the tax with everyone else, or not? These individuals claim they have no part in the matter of these accusations; and that the calumny was not directed specifically at the city's [Jewish] *residents*. The proof is that visitors who happened to be there were also all arrested, and the governor claimed that all those [Jews] *who were in the city* attacked and killed the girl. He recorded their names and the names of their fathers in court, including both residents and visitors alike. Thus, it was this group's good luck to be away from the city and not be arrested. And even if they had returned to the city before these libelous antagonists were silenced, and the accusation had been leveled at them as well, they would still not have been arrested, for everyone knew they were not in the city. This is even more so in light of the fact that every single one of [the Jews present in the city] had his name recorded in the gentile court. Individuals who were not present in the city were not recorded in the book, because the suit was only against those present in town when the girl was found in the pit, whether they were residents or visitors; [the accusers] say *they* are the ones who killed her. So, these individuals [who were away] claim that they need not pay the tax for what [those arrested] expended to save themselves from the incarceration they suffered for this false accusation and lie. Those who had been arrested, however, demand it of them—even if they were not in the city, they should pay with the others. Now, instruct us, righteous teacher, whether or not they are obliged to pay, and may your reward be multiplied.

Response: [Hakham Algazi concludes that only those arrested can be forced to pay the assessment.]

4

PREPARATIONS FOR SIEGE (ALGIERS, 1732)

(Hakham Judah Ayyash, *Bet Yehudah*, O.H. #10)

Introduction

Algiers was attacked by Spain on several occasions in the early modern period, which obviously made the Jews very skittish. Rumors of an impending Spanish assault, which might strike fear into the hearts of Muslim residents as well, meant far more to the Jews—it meant that any Jew who survived the violence of the siege would be expelled and his or her property confiscated, just as in Spain. The text communicates something of the atmosphere permeating an Ottoman city in terror of a siege. It also illustrates the impressive piety of the Jews. Even under the worst conditions they trouble themselves to search out a great hakham so they can ask about a very fine point of Jewish law: if it is forbidden to pray in a bathhouse, is it permissible once its use had changed?

In the year 5492 [1732] from Creation there was great turmoil because of bad rumors. Many people were saying that the King of Spain planned to attack our city with a huge army and a heavy hand. No amount of readiness could suffice, for he had prepared instruments of death. Because of this, in our multitude of sins, the members of our community lost immense, terrible sums in rents from gardens, orchards, and so on, in order to escape with their property and their lives. They also lost money on horses and wagons on which to go up and return. As a result of all this, some individuals came and asked whether it was permissible to pray in bathhouses in the gardens; for, because of these misfortunes, they rented stables and bathhouses—two or three heads of household together in one room. Their query is this: Do we say that, since the bathing room has been scrubbed and plastered over, is lived in all the time, and is no longer used for washing, that it is altogether like a clean house? Or, since it was pushed off [i.e., unusable] it can never be restored?

Response: [Hakham Ayyash permits it.]

5

THE JEW WHO STOOD UP TO THE

GOVERNOR—BUT MAYBE NOT ENOUGH

(ALGIERS, MID-EIGHTEENTH CENTURY)

(Hakham Judah Ayyash, *Bet Yehudah*, H.M. #18)

Introduction

This episode, presumably occurring in the Algiers region, tells us something about both the modes of trade in that area and relations between Jews and non-Jews. What is most striking is the fact that one of the protagonists, faced with a local official who wanted to help himself to the Jew's horse, argued and fought back. In fact, the other Jew, who actually owned the horse, felt this man had not fought back hard enough! The case thus suggests that the balance of power in relations between Jews and non-Jewish officials was not always completely one-sided. It was sometimes possible to resist a random act of larceny, even if that resistance would ultimately fail. It seems likely that this type of predicament could have occurred as easily to a non-Jewish victim.

Reuben and Simeon each had a horse. They went outside the city during the wheat harvesting season in order to save what they had agreed upon from the hands of the non-Jews. For it was the way of the non-Jews in those days to make payments in kind, in wheat or barley, but those people [taking such payment] needed many horses in order to carry their loads.

The two of them then arranged in this manner: You will leave me your horse today to carry my load together with my horse, and tomorrow I will give you my horse [to use] together with your horse. That is to say, they made a deal exchanging one day for one day. They did as they had agreed, and Reuben began the first day. He carried on his horse and that of his friend a measure load of wheat in the standard amount. The next day Simeon took them and did the same thing. When they returned to the granary, Reuben sent someone to the place Simeon was staying to bring his horse back home, because their arrangement was over.

However, just as [Reuben's] representative prepared to bring the horse back home, a certain non-Jew showed up, an important man who was governor of the area where Simeon was dwelling. He grabbed the horse in order to carry his own things. Simeon tried to prevent him, but the non-Jew struck him and led it away. He loaded [the horse] with more than it was accustomed to carry and took it along a crooked path. The horse got into a hard spot, fell, and died.

Reuben has now come to file suit, claiming that Simeon was negligent for giving [the horse] to that non-Jew, and he must pay. For, even though the non-Jew grabbed it unprovoked, and Simeon did try to prevent him, he should have responded more forcefully and fought him as hard as he could until there was no more he could do. Simeon claims that, since [Reuben's] representative had come to return [the horse], his responsibility had ended, and it was now in the domain of the representative. "I have nothing to do with that non-Jew, and furthermore, the representative went with the horse while it was carrying the non-Jew's load, and he should have guarded it from dangerous paths or injurious places; so it is the representative who was irresponsible."

What is the law in this case?

Response: [Hakham Ayyash sides with Simeon, assuming Reuben's representative had indeed taken charge of the horse before the non-Jew arrived.]

PART II

TRADE AND OTHER PROFESSIONS IN THE SEPHARDI DIASPORA

It is hard to overemphasize the centrality of trade and finance in the responsa. One might think that, like so many other sources, the responsa mainly record issues concerning wealthy, large scale financiers or merchants. However, even the most ordinary Jews are discussed in this literature. The sums concerning which people appealed to the rabbinical court were sometimes quite small, indicating trade on a very minor scale, though other cases involved princely figures. In one document we find women and orphans scraping out a living by making small loans at interest. Some Jews made no investment of their own and worked as factors for others, settling in distant cities and overseeing storage or transfer technicalities. The goods Jews exchanged were also of tremendous variety. Textiles were always a staple, but they also traded in coral, hides, tobacco, coffee, gold, silver, jewelry, books, slaves, food, wine, spices, and any number of other things. In fine, large numbers of Jews from every stratum of society all across the Sephardi world were somehow involved in commerce.

Jews were clearly at home in the increasingly complex structures of mercantilist transactions. Many were multifaceted deals involving sets of partners in a number of ports, the use of bills of exchange (the precursor of the modern check), loans in various currencies, and several different sorts of goods. It is well to remember that mercantilism was not born in the Atlantic world, as one might be led to think from some of the literature, but in the Mediterranean, where Jews were in the thick of it. The hakhamim had to be experts not only in Jewish law, but also in the details of contemporary economics in order to adjudicate commerce claims.

The standard configuration of Jewish commercial enterprises involved two main arrangements: the partnership, usually between two or more Jews; and the family firm, in which formal or informal bases in a number of cities were manned by relatives of the controlling members. These structures allowed maximum flexibility on the one hand, and the trust necessary to trade bills of exchange on the other. Sephardi families after the expulsion tended in any case to be scattered over many lands; smart businessmen learned to turn this calamity into an advantage.

One particular religious issue arises regularly in the responsa about trade: the problem of borrowing money at interest. The Bible forbids Jews to lend money at interest to other Jews, though (in the rabbis' interpretation) it permits them to do so with non-Jews. The problem is that the mercantile economy is built from bottom to top on interest-bearing monetary loans. Various cases describe Jews' attempts to navigate the letter of these laws while still accomplishing the necessary economic ends. The efforts of Eastern Sephardim in this endeavor testify to their religious dedication. Their counterparts in western Europe, however—the former *conversos* of Amsterdam and London—did not seem to suffer the same compunctions. Having lived previously without clerical interference in business affairs, they apparently chose to ignore the interest statutes, and their hakhamim did little to interfere.

Many Jews were involved in trades outside commerce, of course. I adduce a small text below involving Egyptian Jews who raised civet cats for their musk, just to illustrate this range. Jews also show up as fishermen, ranchers, diplomats, metalworkers, artisans, shopkeepers, tailors, and so on. Naturally, there were also a fair number who were Jewish professionals of one sort or the other: rabbis, teachers, ritual slaughterers, cantors, text editors, and scribes.

The Jews in these documents are astoundingly footloose. Though the majority of those traveling were involved in trade, Jews in many fields found themselves on distant journeys. For example, certain Jews would make the rounds of obscure rural regions selling imported items and buying up old jewelry. Ritual slaughterers and kosher cheesemakers had to work in distant villages or farms. Jews were also expelled from various cities and countries at different times, or had to flee from invaders, such as the Spanish who (as we saw above) put them in particular danger. This also forced them to travel. Roads and waterways in the Mediterranean region were exceedingly dangerous. The responsa testify to the threats of robbers and murderers, storms, wild animals, strong currents, and bad roads among other hazards. The collections are full of heart-rending tales recounting how a Jew met his end in some lonely spot far from kith and kin. These stories often arise in the context of the *agunah*, the grass widow who is unable to remarry until reliable testimony of her husband's demise is established.

6

AN INTERNATIONAL LOAN GONE AWRY
(MEDITERRANEAN, LATE SIXTEENTH CENTURY)

(Hakham Abraham de Boton, *Lehem Rav*, #13)

Introduction

Hakham Abraham de Boton officiated in Saloniki, Greece, one of
the major Mediterranean seaports of the Ottoman Empire, in the
late sixteenth century. The case at hand demonstrates the type of
loans Jews were able to float for non-Jewish merchants because of
the extensive Jewish trade networks. The borrower is an Ottoman
subject, but he is presumably a Greek Orthodox Christian rather
than a Muslim. A Jew lends him a very considerable sum of money
for four months while both are in Venice, but the Turk is to pay
back the loan to the Jew's partners in Corfu. The case supports the
famous thesis of the historian Fernand Braudel that the Mediterranean in this period was really one integrated world, despite being divided between European Christian powers and Ottoman Muslims.
In the early modern period, Corfu was a crucial port on the route
between Venice and the Ottoman Empire, and the two powers
fought fiercely over it. Meir Benayahu (*Relations*, 77) points out that
the dual identity of the city between these powers was represented in
its Jewish community, which consisted of a Greek congregation and
a Venetian congregation. Despite the divisions, this document demonstrates Corfu's great importance as a base for merchants working
from both sides.

This case also illustrates the effects of shifting sixteenth-century
currency values. The voyages of discovery led to a wild exploitation
of silver and gold supplies in the New World by Europeans, while
the influx of precious metals, along with other destabilizing factors,
caused sudden bouts of inflation and debasement of coinage. We can
see in our case that money moved back and forth regularly between

Europe and the Ottoman Empire, so it was inevitable that these European monetary swings would influence the Ottoman economy as well. This domino effect peaked in 1585-86 with a major crisis in Ottoman finances that some historians have linked to an extensive decline in Ottoman power over the following period. While this responsum has no date on it, it appears to reflect this situation. Indeed, in his response to the question, Hakham de Boton expresses his familiarity with coinage debasement, which he says is very widespread in his time. Cases of inflation and debasement are common throughout the responsa for the reason we encounter here: they raised problems of interest-taking among Jews.

Bibliography: Arbel, *Trading Nations;* Benayahu, *Relations;*
Braudel, *Mediterranean;* Pamuk, *A Monetary History;*
Ben-Sasson et al., *Studies in a Rabbinic Family.*

Question: Reuben was in Venice, and he lent a certain Christian merchant from Turkey 1,000 Venetian florins [*perahim;* meaning ducats], consisting of six lire and ten soltani [soldi] per florin, according to the custom there. Each Venetian florin is reported among the merchants to be worth 50 Turkish shahis. He lent them to the aforementioned Christian in an exchange [*cambio*]. [The Christian] gave him a pledge of several garments. The money was to be sent to Simeon and Levi [Reuben's Jewish partners] in Corfu; and the pledge was with them until the Christian paid back the borrowed florins in Corfu four months later. Should he not pay the money in the indicated time, Simeon and Levi would have the power to sell the pledge and collect the debt. Then they would send this money back to Reuben in Venice.

Now the time for repayment arrived and the Christian did not have Venetian florins to fulfill his obligation according to their agreement. Furthermore, Simeon was not in Corfu because he had gone to Turkey to trade. Levi, then, went to sell the pledge, but found he could not even get two-thirds of the debt's value out of it, for the pledge was not worth as much as the loan. When Levi saw that the value of the pledge was not sufficient to cover that sum and that Reuben would lose money, Levi was forced to give the Christian additional time beyond the period agreed upon so that he could go home to Turkey and make arrangements for transmission of the money.

This was indeed the way it went. When this Christian went to his home, he began to send Levi some shahis from Turkey. (The Venetian florin was worth fifty shahis, which are 6 lire and two [read: ten] sultanis, as was stated. But in Corfu they were then worth 6 lire and 4 sultani per Venetian florin. Levi began exchanging some of these shahis for the equivalent lire at the rate mentioned and sending them to Reuben as they came. After a time, Simeon came back to Corfu and asked Levi if he had recovered the debt from the Christian merchant and sent it to its owner, Reuben, in good order. Levi responded by explaining to Simeon everything that has been recounted here about what occurred between him and the merchant, and that all he had done was unavoidable if he was to avoid losing Reuben's money. Simeon was immediately angry about it, both because of the time [Levi] had added to the period of the loan, and because he had not [immediately] sent Reuben everything he had received from the merchant. What did Simeon do? He took the rest of the money from the Turk that remained with Levi, exchanged it for the equivalent lire, and sent it to Reuben.

After this, the Christian merchant came and brought the remainder of his payment, satisfying the whole debt, and took his pledge back. Simeon and Levi began, partly together and partly individually, to exchange this [Turkish] money and sent it to its owner, Reuben, in Venice, day by day. In the process there occurred an error, a discrepancy, and an argument between Simeon and Levi, in the amount of 100 florins. Each claimed, "Such-and-such an amount was in my hand, and I have sent that amount already"; but there remained a discrepancy of 100 florins. The argument of Simeon and Levi continued until the value of the Venetian florin increased; they are worth 6 lire and 4 sultani—[a rise in] value of 8 shahis. [If I understand correctly, the value of the florin increased in *Venice* to this value, which it had already held in Corfu for some time.]

In any case, Reuben now came to Turkey or to Corfu, found Simeon or Levi, and demanded the 100 florins, the discrepancy that had fallen out between Simeon and Levi, that was owed him. He further demanded lire in the value of 50 shahis, to make up 6 lire and 4 sultanis, the [new] value of a Venetian florin. Therefore, instruct us, our teacher, whether Reuben can demand the 100 florins, the remainder of his money that Simeon [and Levi] lost; and whether he can demand 6 lire and 4 sultani, which are the equivalent of one florin, now that the value has inflated.

Response: [Hakham de Boton answers that Simeon and Levi must indeed pay Reuben. If they are unable to agree on who owes the money, they should go to arbitration. As for the value of the money, however, he says that if the loan was formulated in the standard manner, Simeon and Levi may pay back the same amount in the same currency that Reuben originally lent; they need not be concerned about its inflated value. He points out that there are coins of better and worse quality, and that the loan must be paid in coins of the original quality.]

7

THE WOMAN WITH A STEEL WELDING MONOPOLY
(ALEPPO, CA. 1559)

(Hakham Moshe Alsheikh, *She'elot u-Teshuvot Mahara"m Alsheikh,* #57)

Introduction

In the Eastern Sephardi Diaspora, many women worked in business and crafts at every level. In the highest realms of finance were wealthy bankers like Doña Gracia Nasi and Bienvenida Abarbanel. We also know of two Sephardic women who managed the sultan's harem around the turn of the seventeenth century (Kobler, *Letters* II, 391–92). Legal sources supply insight into the more mundane lives of women engaged in handicrafts. This document offers a fascinating window onto such a life.

Note the suspicion this woman must counteract; apparently people questioned whether she had actually done the welding herself. She is also forced to take a male partner, for which there might be two reasons. One (as Lamdan notes in *Separate People,* 121, quoting Meir Benayahu) is that the business required two people: one to oversee the oven and take out the molten steel while the other welded. Another reason for her to take a man as a partner was to have him act as the official male "front" for the business. This particular man apparently assumed he could cheat her with impunity.

One notable detail is that the woman was a widow. The economic independence of single women in their fathers' houses, and that of married women with their husbands, was severely limited. Widowhood thrust women into a frightening unsupported state on the one hand; but on the other hand, it offered enterprising women an unusual opportunity to compete in the male world of business (see Lamdan, *Separate People,* chap. 12). The two best-known Jewish women of the early modern period—Doña Gracia Nasi and Glückel of Hameln—were both widows, a fact that had direct bearing on their individualism in both business and social life. Later we encounter widows in Jerusalem who support themselves through small-scale moneylending.

Research on Jewish women in the early modern Middle East has been placed on an entirely new footing by Ruth Lamdan and her book *A Separate People,* which provides excellent background for understanding this case.

Bibliography: Brooks, *Woman Who Defied Kings;* Kobler,
Letters, 391–92; Lamdan, *Separate People,* 121 and throughout;
Joel L. Kraemer, "Spanish Ladies from the Cairo Geniza,"
in Ginio, *Jews, Christians and Muslims,* 237–67.

Instruct us, our teacher: Leah, during the lifetime of her husband, had learned the art of welding, which she would do with steel, and there was no other person in the land who knew how. She tried to obtain a license from the sultan (may he be raised up!) to practice this craft, since there were those who claimed it was really feigned. When she was widowed, she was forced to teach it to Reuben as a secret that could never be allowed to reach a third party. She feared that he might accept investments from additional persons and work at the craft for himself, thus causing harm to her, so she put him under oath that he would not be allowed to practice this trade with any other Jew or Aleppan. They made a contract saying the following:

> Before us, the undersigned witnesses, Reuben undertook never to engage in welding here in Aleppo or in any place under the rule of the governor of Aleppo, with any man, be he Jew, Turk, or Aleppan, except with Leah. Reuben accepted all this upon himself with the force of a solemn oath before God, blessed be He, and before all those who swear in truth, and before the aforementioned Leah, and before us who have signed below, to uphold and fulfill all that is written here, to the exclusion of every possible renunciation, and he hereby nullifies any testimony to such renunciations. We received an agreement from Reuben for all that is written and explicated above through a complete acceptance beginning now, by means of an instrument suitable for assuming commitment. This took place on Sunday, 21 Shevat of the year 5319 [1559] from Creation, here in Aleppo. All is reviewed, resolved, and abiding. Similarly, Leah swore not to engage in welding with any person, as mentioned, so long as Reuben would be her partner, and this was resolved.

The essential intention was that this craft should be found nowhere except with these two.

Now, however, Reuben has gone into business for himself, together with others. Tell us, teacher, how we should judge this man.

Response: [Hakham Alsheikh condemns Reuben. Others who adjudicated the case—Hakhamim Trani and Karo—allowed Reuben to practice the craft alone but not to take an active partner or teach the profession.]

8

DEATH OF A SALESMAN IN PERSIA

(BURSA AND PERSIA, LATE SIXTEENTH CENTURY)

(Hakham Moshe Alsheikh, *She'elot u-Teshuvot Mahara"m Alsheikh*, #118)

Introduction

This letter is interesting for the light it sheds on the interaction between Sephardic communities and neighboring non-Sephardic Jewish groups. While the Ashkenazim appear in Sephardic responsa with some regularity, and the local Romaniote or Musta'rib Jews are always present among the Sephardim, this case bears witness to the Ottoman Jews' penetration into markets further east, in Persia. Bursa is in western Turkey near Istanbul (Constantinople), while Hormuz is in the far south of today's Iran, near the Persian Gulf. Nothing strikes the parties writing as unusual about this great distance being traveled by Sephardic merchants in search of business, and clearly there were travelers to take the letter back to Turkey. Indeed, Joseph Pico, a merchant with a Sephardic name, resides in Shiraz. Within Persia itself, Judah Gabbai of Bursa traveled very widely.

Both the arrest of those who murdered the Jew, and the ease with which they achieved their freedom through a bribe, are typical of the dealings of Middle Eastern justice in the period. There is no particular reason to believe it would have been handled differently were the victim not a Jew.

Like many others among the most interesting cases of the responsa, this letter was prompted by the concern for an abandoned wife who needed to know the fate of her husband.

Bibliography: Gerber, *Economy and Society.*

The following letter was sent from Hormuz to Bursa:

To the holy communities of Bursa: the following lines are to inform you about a certain man from your city who came here to Hormuz. His name was Judah Gabbai, and he left here through Agam [Agha?]. After some days, Jews from Agam came and stated that he had been killed on the road to Isfahan, five or six miles from the city. Here is their testimony, word for word. They said that they were in Isfahan when the Arab caravan arrived on a Sabbath day. In Isfahan was a man named Isaac Mattuk [or Mi-Attuk] who was a close friend of the same Judah Gabbai. This Jew [Mattuk] knew that Judah Gabbai wanted to go to Isfahan because when he (Isaac Mattuk) was in the city of Shiraz, he saw him [Gabbai] and he expressed desire to go to Isfahan. He [Mattuk] said, "Come and we will go together." He replied, "I am unable to go with this caravan, for I still have some business pending; but I will come with the next caravan." He [Mattuk] went to Isfahan, leaving him in Shiraz. In Isfahan he saw the [next] caravan arrive on the Sabbath. He went and asked them if there was any Jew with them. They said that there had been a Jew, "but because of the Sabbath [when he would not travel] he stayed behind and did not continue with us." Based on this, he knew it had been Judah Gabbai.

Afterward, when he noted a day passing, then three days, and he still did not arrive, [Mattuk] went and asked the Arabs, "What is this business, when you say there was a Jew with you? Look—three days have passed and he has not arrived!" They said, "We know nothing of all this. What should we have done about him? But we do know that he had been with us, except that, because of the Sabbath, he stayed behind. See, here is his merchandise that he sent with us." When the aforementioned Isaac went to examine the merchandise, he saw the bag that had belonged to the murdered man and also recognized the clothes he used to wear. On the basis of this he knew that the murdered man was Judah Gabbai.

After this, the aforementioned Isaac went to the authorities and arrested the Arabs who had remained with [Gabbai] on that Sabbath [that Gabbai stayed behind]; for the men of the caravan pointed them out to him. They admitted that they had murdered him, but they bribed the authorities, who confiscated all the murdered man's goods and set [the murderers] free.

This was the testimony of the Jews of Agam, who were there at the time this all occurred. A few days later, a certain Arab came and said, "I was with Isaac Mattuk in Shiraz when Judah Gabbai was also in Shiraz. The aforementioned Isaac and I said to him, 'Come with us,'" and he responded that he could not go with them, for he still had a bit of business to conduct. He and the aforementioned Isaac left Isfahan, after which the events [i.e., the murder] occurred. The Arab testified to the same matters as the Jews, for this Arab was a friend of both of them—the aforementioned Isaac and the murdered man, may God avenge his blood—and called him by name.

Furthermore, a letter arrived from Joseph Pico of Shiraz, who writes simply, "Be aware that Judah Gabbai has been murdered," and nothing more, as your honors will see in the letter, which we have sent to you along with this letter. We, of the holy congregation of Hormuz, decided to send your honors this statement in order to inform you about the matter, in case he has a wife there, so that she will be unencumbered by means of this testimony, as your honors will see to it.

This was the wording of the letter. Inform us, our teacher, if the law would see fit to permit [the wife to remarry] or not.

Response: [Hakham Alsheikh permits her to remarry, based strictly on the testimony of Joseph Pico.]

9

A CASE OF MISTAKEN IDENTITY
(CONSTANTINOPLE, LATE
SEVENTEENTH CENTURY)

(Hakham Joseph Katzabi, *She'elot u-Teshuvot Mahara"m Katzabi*, #21)

Introduction

This text raises an interesting human problem, and one that still occurs with particular frequency with Middle Easterners: How do you
distinguish between people with the same name? Like the responsum below about the Indian impostor, this case illustrates difficulties
of identity and identification in early modern life. Natalie Zemon
Davis's work on Martin Guerre demonstrates how the increased
mobility of Europeans with the decline of feudalism made identification a problem in Europe. It had been an issue far longer in the Mediterranean world, and it would be surprising if cases like this did not
arise rather often.

Another interesting aspect of this episode is the use of parallel
documents from Jewish and Muslim courts, in a case where the parties were of different faiths. The responsa are full of this kind of cooperation between courts, which does appear to increase over the
period discussed in this book.

Bibliography: Davis, *Return of Martin Guerre*.

Question: Reuben planned to go to Egypt. Simeon came and said to him,
"Could you do me a great kindness when you arrive in Cairo? Find a certain Turk there who owes me a sum of money, for which there is a certificate of debt [*Temessük*] closed with his seal, and collect the money on
my behalf. Reuben agreed, and they went to the [Muslim] court to draft
the customary document of agency with the conditions to which each
agreed. He [Simeon] also drafted a power of attorney according to our

[Jewish] laws, giving Reuben the authority to act as he would see fit, just as a person would do for himself, for crediting or collecting debts. In addition, he gave him a certain length of London fabric [Londrina], adjuring him to take it there and sell it or trade it, whether for something of greater or lesser quality, as he saw fit; and if he ran up expenses in recovering the debt, he should deduct them from this venture. Whatever he said would be trusted, even if it came to the whole value of the [cloth] venture.

Reuben went on his way. When he arrived in Egypt, he went to find the Turkish debtor, but instead happened to meet another Turk by the same name in the very district that was written on the certificate of debt. He demanded the money from him, and the Turk responded that it never happened, that "I never took anything from the man!" They went to court, but before they even appeared before the ruling magistrate, they [the Turks] spoke out very strongly against the elders and officers of [Reuben's] nation. Finally Reuben pulled the certificate of debt from his pocket, and it was found that the document was dated from after the date when this Turk had left Constantinople [where, presumably, the original loan had been made]. He further showed them his seal, which did not at all resemble that on the certificate of debt. The [Turk] began to quiver exceedingly and exclaimed, "Look, will you, at this Jewish man who has come to laugh at me and mock me with a forged document!"

Reuben answered him, saying, "I am simply a representative for someone else! Here is my letter of agency!" He produced this for them and they read it. But they noted that while this letter was executed from Simeon to Reuben, the certificate of debt was written in the name of Levi [i.e., a different person]; for he [Simeon] had made it out at that time in the name of Levi [rather than himself] for some reason. At the time the letter of agency was drafted, however, Simeon made that out in his own name [i.e., the two documents did not match].

When the men at the gates [the Turks] saw this, they became furious over the matter and determined to place the whole case before the presiding judge. They took revenge on that man [Reuben] and threw him in prison. Reuben became terrified and disconcerted until he managed to strike a deal with the jailor for a certain amount of money [to free him]. This sum he took from the business [i.e., the cloth] he had with him, so as to save himself as well as to retrieve the certificate of debt and letter of agency from them.

Simeon, meanwhile, had died. His heirs now sued Reuben for the business [i.e., the cloth] their father had given him, [claiming] one may not save one's self with someone else's money, even if Reuben's claims were true. Furthermore, he should have stood up before the city magistrate and pointed out that there might have been another Turk who did owe this money, and that he [Reuben] simply did not know or recognize him, since he came as an agent, having been told nothing but a name and address. He need not have been so afraid, for why should he die? What had he done?

Reuben countered that he was the one who had gone through all this suffering himself; and whatever had been given [by Simeon] was given for his own use. He further pointed out that [Simeon's] carelessness had caused it all, since he had not been precise in writing the letter of agency, so that it disagreed with the certificate of debt, as was recounted above. This was the cause of his being taken as a forger and having to fear so much for his life.

Response: [Hakham Katzabi elaborates the merits of both parties' cases but ultimately decides in favor of Reuben.]

10

THE DEATH OF TALL ASLAN
(ALEPPO AND TURKEY, 1681)

(Hakham Moses Ben Habib, *She'elot u-Teshuvot,* vol. 1, #144)

Introduction

Despite the lack of details about the location and the depressing subject matter, I was immediately drawn to this responsum. There is the obvious curiosity of the opening of the first testimony. It beautifully demonstrates the type of thing that can happen when original voices permeate the curtain of time. It is also fascinating to listen to various people describe the same person and the same event, each in his own way. The witnesses meander a bit, as people do when they talk, and the details they drop along the way give us a sense of their lives. Among these we find information about coffee and tobacco use, and some reasonably positive relations between Jews and Muslims. Finally, the role of the cow adds an almost whimsical note.

An inquiry concerning an *agunah* [grass widow] on which six testimonies were received.

Testimony 1:

Mr. Rahamim Chriqui testified that he met a certain gentile, who, unsolicited, told him the following:

The Jews are not all the same. So-and-so, so-and-so, and so-and-so [i.e., three Jews he knows] eat from our food and the meat we slaughter. They buy from the market and bring it to us; then we cook it for them and we eat it all together. But Tall Aslan from your city, may he rest in peace—he was a Jew who held fast to his faith. He would not eat our food or taste what we cooked, and he conducted business faithfully, with truth and honesty.

He, I, and his partner were together in a certain market, and he and I wanted to cross the river to a certain other place. That day there was a big storm. I still had some business to do at the market, so they went ahead of me and boarded the boat. When I arrived at the riverside to make my crossing to the same place, I was told that Tall Aslan and his partner had boarded a small boat which had then capsized. No person had come out of that boat except for one woman who had held on to the horns of a cow [see Testimony 3]—she alone came out.

Testimony 2:
Before us, the rabbinic court, Mr. Nissim Atruti testified as follows.

We came to make the Sabbath in one of the villages—I and Samuel Jabli. We arrived at the house of a certain Jew to make the honor of the Sabbath, but we did not find the master of the house at home. I told my partner, "Since the man is not at home, I do not wish to make the Sabbath in the company of women." Just then, however, the master of the house arrived home from his journey, and we asked after his health. We sat down to gab about nothing important, and we said "Praised be [God's] blessed name! For on a day just like this one we were once with Aslan."

This Jew, the master of the house, responded, "This very week I found a certain Christian in Kahu [probably Kaunos, on Turkey's southern coast] who told us about them. He said that he had seen two Jews—one fat and one thin—who had been traveling around the towns thereabout. They boarded a boat when a storm wind came and overturned the boat. The thin one immediately drowned and was never seen, while the fat one bobbed up twice, but the third time he came up, he went down never more to be seen. Three days later he [Aslan] turned up at the side of the river wearing a money belt. They took him away, but I don't know if they buried him or not."

After the Sabbath, on Sunday, we went to the house of a certain gentile woman to drink coffee, and there were some gentiles there. They said, "Praised be [God's] blessed name! But it is too bad about Aslan, who went down into that boat along with his partner and drowned and has not been seen since."

Testimony 3:
On the day of 27 Tammuz of the year [5]441 [1681], the beloved and wise Mr. Samuel Bizini, may God protect him, came before the court of twelve [judges], and after the proper warnings and admonitions, he stated the following as formal testimony:

As you gentlemen know, I arrived at such-and-such place on Thursday twenty-eight days before Passover. There I entered the house of a gentile, such-and-such, where the Jews who travel in that region are always accustomed to stay. He brought me coffee, then said to me in all innocence [*mesi'ah lefi tumo*], "By my life I tell you, Tall Aslan and his partner, Suleiman, who used to sell coral, are dead." I asked him, "How did it happen?" He told me, "They stayed with me Monday, and they left to go to such-and-such place. On Tuesday I happened to go to that same place, and there they told me that two Jews had passed through there, one tall and the other short. Tall Aslan did not want to go on, and he argued with his partner that he did not want to go. Afterward he was forced to board a boat, on which there was one Turk, one woman, and four oxen. The boat capsized. The Turk, the Jews, and the boat's captain drowned, but the woman who was with them grasped the tail of an ox and came out on the other side of the river."

Testimony 4:
He continued to testify that he and other Jews were in such-and-such place at an inn smoking, when a certain Christian came in to smoke as well. The Christian opened a conversation, saying that before their great holiday [Easter] (which was approximately the time mentioned above), two Jews drowned—one tall and one short—on a boat that capsized. "I was standing right there. The tall one came to the surface with his purse on his shoulder, then came up again before he drowned. He returned to the surface three times before he drowned and was never again seen. The other one never came up and was never seen from the moment he went down in the river.

Testimony 5:
Two more witnesses came: Mr. Samuel Jabli and the above-mentioned Mr. Nissim [Atruti]. They reported that they had heard something from the above-mentioned Mr. Samuel Bizini, who learned more from a certain Christian. . . . This second Christian added that after a number of days had passed, he had seen the tall Hebrew Jew [!] dead on the bank of the river. He had on a money belt, but he [the Christian] saw that they had taken the money. Then they returned and threw him into the river so the current would carry him somewhere else.

[The sixth testimony adds nothing substantial. In the response we learn that Tall Aslan came from Aleppo, and that two other major rabbis had already adjudicated the case.]

Response: [Hakham ben Habib comes to the same conclusion as the others: the evidence of Aslan's death is sufficient, and his wife is completely free to remarry.]

11

EGYPTIAN JEWS WITH CIVET CATS
(EGYPT, MID-SIXTEENTH CENTURY)
(Hakham Jacob Castro, *Shu"t Oholei Ya'akov*, #22)

Introduction

This small question is interesting because it exemplifies the wide range of Jewish trades in early-modern Egypt. While the records are full of information about Jews in international trade, textiles, and other better known fields of endeavor, we learn here of Jews involved in several aspects of the perfume industry. The fact that the query concerns the lending of money at interest—a law only relevant when both lender and borrower are Jews—indicates that the perfumers who were customers of the cat owners were also Jews. The question also raises a very widespread issue in the early modern Sephardic world: Which of the new mercantile techniques transgress the injunction against taking interest? Here the idea is something so widespread today as to seem unworthy of attention, but apparently it was not very well known in the sixteenth century: pre-payment. The question is, if the seller has use of the buyer's money for a period before the goods are delivered, the seller can profit from its use, which might constitute a very low level of interest lending.

In Egypt there are some Jews who have cats from which they extract the fragrance called *al-ghāliya* [musk and ambergris perfume]. Whoever wants to purchase some of this scent first pays a sum of money to one of these cat owners, who then gives him the fragrance at a discount. Instruct us, our teacher, whether this practice raises any concern of taking interest according to the rabbis or not. May your reward be multiplied by heaven.

Response: [Hakham Castro permits the practice.]

12

JEWISH TRADE IN A WAR ZONE
(ZANTE AND VENICE, CA. 1620)

(Hakham Meir ben Shemtov Melamed, *Mishpat Tzedek,* vol. 3, #23)

Introduction

This query tells us a bit about the effects of war on Ottoman Jewish sea trade, and presumably the trade of all Ottoman merchants. When the trip from Venice to Zante (Zakynthos) in southwestern Greece became too hazardous because of the war between Venice and Spain, the Jew in question attempted a new and seemingly less hazardous route, from Venice to Spalato. Apparently, he planned to have the merchandise taken from there by land to its ultimate destination. It was his poor luck to run into Spanish marauders even on this relatively short trip.

Bibliography: Arbel, *Trading Nations.*

Question: Instruct us, righteous teacher. Reuben would send his wares to Simeon in Venice, who would sell them and send back the proceeds. Their usual practice was to send merchandise from Zante to Venice, and from Venice to Zante.

Now a rumor surfaced that Spain was going to make war with the Venetian territories by way of the sea. Simeon was the agent of Reuben, and [Reuben] wrote him a letter as follows. "I give you permission to deal with my merchandise as if it were your own. Any means by which you convey your property send mine as well. Think of it as if it were your own—whatever you do with your property do with mine too, for we are like brothers." This is what he wrote.

When Simeon saw that there was no passage at all between Venice and Zante because of the war raging between the governments of Venice and Spain, he took his own merchandise and put it on barges bound for Spalato [also called Split, a port city on the Dalmatian coast]. At the same time he loaded a container on behalf of Reuben. But when the barge passed through Spalato, an unclean [i.e., terrible] event occurred: it was captured by a detachment of the Spanish king's soldiers.

Now Reuben claims that Simeon acted improperly in sending a container to Spalato on behalf of Reuben—he thereby departed from their usual practice by not sending it through Zante. It was fine for his own [merchandise], but he had no right to do it with that of others. Simeon claims that, since he sent him the letter mentioned above, permitting Simeon to do the same with his property that Simeon would do with his own, and any route by which he forwarded his own property he should send that of Reuben as well, he did what he did and routed both his merchandise and that of Reuben through Spalato. Furthermore, since Spanish forces surrounded the sea around Venice, even if he had sent [the merchandise] by way of Zante it might have been captured; the passage through Spalato was both shorter and safer than that to Zante.

Reuben claims that when he wrote, "Any means by which Simeon conveys his property he should send that of Reuben as well," it should have been clear that he meant *any means* [he implies that his intention was *any vessel*], small or large, that would turn up going from Venice to Zante according to their usual practice—not to depart from the normal manner and send things through Spalato. For, he had sent him textiles in a small vessel to Corfu and they were not captured by the non-Jews. It would have worked the same if he would have sent these [containers in small vessels to Zante instead of to Spalato]. Simeon replied that if this were the case, why would he have needed permission? If it was just a matter of sending [merchandise] from Venice to Zante, he would have needed no special permission! As for Reuben's claim that he was giving permission simply to use smaller or larger vessels, he should have written explicitly, "and in any vessel by which you send your goods, whether it is large or small, send my goods as well." He should not have written a blanket permission in the manner that he did, that "you have permission to deal with my merchandise as if it were your own." And he further wrote, "Whatever you do with your property do with mine too." If it had been merely a matter of a smaller or larger vessel, look—he had already written, "Any means by which you convey your property send mine as well"! Why, then, did he need to go back and write afterward, "Whatever you do with your property do with mine too"? He had already given him explicit permission to do whatever seemed advisable and proper in Simeon's view!

Instruct us, righteous teacher, about all the aspects of this question, and may your reward be multiplied greatly from heaven. [Explain] about everything that Simeon has claimed: that the barges are safer than other vessels [or passages]; that the way [from Venice] to Spalato is only a third the distance of that from Venice to Zante by sea; and the matter that, from there to the place where Reuben lives is a great distance by land. Simeon claims that he made an arrangement with a certain Jewish merchant that when [the merchandise] reached land he would insure and take responsibility for it until the goods arrived at the fair where Reuben, who was going there to sell them, would take them in hand. What more could he [Simeon] do to achieve Reuben's purpose according to his best assessment?

Whom does the law favor?

Response: [Hakham Melamed, not surprisingly, takes the side of Simeon.]

13

THE TALE OF THE CLOTHIER AND THE VIZIER

(CONSTANTINOPLE, 1641)

(Hakham Joshua Benveniste, *Sha'ar Yehoshu'a*, E.H. #27)

Introduction

This is one of the most intriguing documents in the collection. The style of the tale is so leisurely and literary that it seems almost out of place in the responsa genre. In fact, its charm and meandering story-line are more reminiscent of the Arabian Nights.

Hakham Benveniste was the brother of the famous Hakham Hayyim Benveniste and served the community of Istanbul (Constantinople) throughout the middle of the seventeenth century. He wrote four volumes of responsa but they were lost in a fire; the few dozen that were preserved were published only in the beginning of the last century. The modern manuscript-based edition may be part of the reason it feels like the hand of the editor has been generous to these documents. The author takes us through the rise and fall of "Reuben." This query admirably demonstrates the potential of the responsa as a conduit for biography and storytelling. It evokes elements of the Joseph and Esther stories by using biblical language that would be immediately recognizable to the early modern Jewish reader. The tale draws out pathos through language and allusion, siding very clearly with "Reuben."

The historical points we learn along the way include the strange workings of loyalty and power within the Vizier's court; the political potential of Jews in the Empire and provinces; and the problems of competition for positions of influence among Jews. In the Ottoman context, the strong role of the sultan's mother (Valide) and wife illustrate the growing role of women at court, a matter that was criticized strongly by later chroniclers. (This is discussed by Marc Baer in a forthcoming article about the discourse on manliness in Istanbul.)

The arrival of this important Jew in the retinue of the new Egyptian governor is similar to the episode of the "Melancholy Monogamist" later in this volume.

The charity and generosity of Reuben are expressed in the language of the Torah (Deuteronomy 15) and the talmudic tale of Hillel (BT Ketubot 67v), who, though poor himself, helps a wealthy man who has fallen on hard times by supplying him with a horse and runner. The implication is clear to any educated reader of the time: Reuben has gone far beyond his duty in his devotion to his patron.

A somewhat disturbing note is struck, however, by the apparent disparity between the Vizier's warm, personal attitude of friendship toward Reuben and Reuben's seemingly utilitarian approach to his patron. Perhaps Reuben's actions belie the calculating disposition imputed to him by the narrator, for he shows warmth and personal support to the Vizier even at times when the latter is out of favor with the Sultan and a bad risk for Reuben's further investment.

Some errors occurred in the writing or transcribing of the text. I have tried to translate according to the sense of the context in places where the printed reading appears to be corrupted.

Laws of Damage to Neighbors. To the distinguished brothers, the sons of Villasid, may God protect them; 1641.
Question: In his store, Reuben carried on a trade buying and selling cloth, clothes, silk apparel, and other such things, as merchants normally do. God privileged him with a visit from a certain official of the sultan, a very great man, who came in and did business with him two or three times. From that point onward, the man was always friendly with him. He would regularly stop in when he was passing by to purchase anything he needed from [Reuben] for himself and his household. Ultimately, he became so accustomed to Reuben and to conducting business with him that the official became quite attached to him, and [Reuben] became a fixture at his home, directing the comings and goings of everything there and overseeing his affairs. Everything he needed in the way of clothes, satin [sheets], hemp, wares—anything that costs money would be bought through him. He was allowed to carry on with no outsiders involved from the time he was appointed over the household more than twenty-five years ago.

Now, during that entire time, no year passed during which the official was not indebted to Reuben around 20,000 *grush*. But he would allow him to pay it off in installments, and when the opportunity arose he would be paid back generously.

The years passed, and this official was appointed a vizier in the court. He had to purchase the entire necessary wardrobe for himself, clothes for his retinue and for his young men (and there were many), and the accompanying weapons of silver and similar materials, all according to their traditions. Reuben supplied it all on credit, from strings to shoe-buckles, until the debt reached almost 30,000 *grush*. In addition to all this, he supplied them with anything they requested; for he said [to himself], "Perhaps God will be merciful and [the vizier] will rise to a high status and become one of the great men, and *the one who tends a fig eats from its fruit*" [Proverbs 27:18].

But *there is wrath gone out from the Lord* [Numbers 17:11], and *God caused masters to become angry with their servants* [Midrash Bereshit Rabbah 25:3]. For some reason, the fury of the sultan was kindled with four of his adjutants—viziers—who serve in the sultan's gates, and suddenly the sultan's decree was announced that they should be exiled to the island of Rhodes, with no forewarning at all. [Reuben's] vizier was among those affected by this decree. He exiled them immediately, and with that took everything they had; their goods and lands went to the sultan. They did not even have a chance to take anything with them except their own bodies. They dumped them onto a boat and sent them away to Rhodes, a place where the sultan's prisoners were held.

When Reuben heard about this tragic event he was terribly saddened and upset, because the debt [owed him by the vizier] was more than 30,000 *grush*. At the same time, he himself owed money to many suppliers. What can a lamb do among wolves? They would demand their due and he had nothing with which to pay them. So, on top of everything else, he left his loss up to God, cast his load upon the Lord, and prepared to add even more to the earlier losses for which he lamented. He took 50,000 ducats in a bag for expenses of the journey, and a few of the implements for the exile—a bed, cushions, tools, sweets, and food for the road—and went off to the vizier and his retinue [before their ship sailed].

He spoke good and comforting words to the heart of [the vizier], so that the officials sitting nearby were deeply astonished by Reuben's generosity and eloquence. The vizier then began to sing Reuben's praises, declaring that he had found a faithful friend, one who had served him with love from the day he met him. And if God would ever remember him benevolently and return him to his position, raising him up to greatness again, he would repay [Reuben] according to what is proper and owed to him. They took leave of each other, the vizier going off on his voyage across the sea and Reuben back to his home to see what would happen to him.

Not much time passed before the sultan's anger subsided and he decreed that the expelled viziers, including this one, should be returned to their former places. They arrived back in the capital city broken and tossed about, dirt poor, without anything at all to support themselves, for the sultan had looted everything they had. At this juncture, Reuben again showed up to support the vizier, finding him the means to acquire the things he needed, from a horse to ride upon to a servant to run before him, so that he could return to the sultan's gates—the divan—in the accustomed manner. In time, God made this vizier pleasing in the eyes of the sultan, may God raise him up, and out of his affection for him he appointed him governor of Egypt and everything there, which is an extremely good and productive territory.

At that point, Reuben was deathly ill, his head and arms so desiccated that he could not make his way to the gates of the vizier, for his illness had overtaken him. Nevertheless, the vizier did not violate his friendship or abuse his faith in him. The very day that [the vizier] departed from the sultan in his royal finery (that is, the *khla'at*), the moment he came home with his robes of honor upon him, he stripped them off and gave the clothes to one of his servants to bring the robes to Reuben. He told him that he was granting him the role of chief financier [*şeref başilik*], so he was giving him the robes by right.

In the morning Reuben gathered his strength, and weak as he was, came and prostrated himself before the vizier. The vizier rejoiced greatly with him, then told Reuben and his brothers, "Prepare provisions for yourselves, because in three more days we are leaving. Get whatever you are taking ready in great haste!"

Meanwhile, there was another Jew [Simeon] who frequented the court of the head vizier on some matter. When he saw that this other vizier had been granted rule over the foremost territory, being placed in control of the entire land of Egypt, he plotted in his heart *to seize habitations not his own* [Habakkuk 1:6]. He requested that the head vizier command the other vizier [Reuben's sponsor] to make *him* chief financier instead of Reuben. The head vizier lost no time in doing so, writing him a directive that he should make Simeon the chief financier. This was a very bad thing in the vizier's view—so much that he got up and told the head vizier that he has a Jew who has overseen his household for many years, and to whom he has already promised the office of chief financier. Despite all this, the head vizier told his attendant, "Command him concerning the office of chief financier, for this is what I want." Since this vizier was obliged not to transgress the wishes of the head vizier, he did so, dressing [Simeon] in the robes of the chief financier.

The vizier, along with all his servants and attendants, were terribly dismayed about how this awful perfidy could have occurred. [The vizier] spoke to Reuben in secret and told him, "Do not take this to heart, stay true to me, and your reward will be very great." Now, when some of the eminent people of the land observed the exploitation and maltreatment of Reuben, they intervened between Reuben and Simeon to fashion a compromise that would help them avoid harming each other. In this they failed, because Reuben was impelled not to bring the matter to a settlement and partnership. He said, "How can I do such a terrible thing, to take bread for which I struggled and fought from the mouths of my own babies and infants, my own children, and give it to one who did nothing to earn it?" And though the mediators insisted that they would arrange a concession that would be very advantageous for him, he would not accept it and was completely unreceptive to this as well.

Simeon and his group, meanwhile, were lying in wait for this; for if Reuben would not compromise with him, he had influence with the head vizier as well as the sultan's wife and mother, and he would arrange that Reuben never go to Egypt at all. Furthermore, at that time the Flemish ambassador was here, an important man, beloved by all the officials, whose requests would not be denied. This person was helping Simeon and backing him with his support.

Reuben was in such fear of all this that when they were on their way to board the boat and he found himself alone [with Simeon] and no mediators present, the two men swore to each other to be partners in the chief financier's position, with the condition that Simeon would wear the robe of office in Cairo or Alexandria, and if not he would be exempt from this oath [i.e., he would use his influence to take the position over alone]. But even though Simeon would wear the robe, nevertheless, when it came to the sale of food, textiles, and clothing, he would have no business with them, as Reuben said, because that would all belong to Reuben.

When the ships prepared to leave the Constantinople harbor, the vizier treated Simeon like a stranger, as if nothing had ever occurred between them. He [the vizier?] spoke harshly with him once or twice, but to no effect, for he did not want him. When they reached Egypt, he immediately dressed Reuben in the robe of the chief financier rather than Simeon; and on any matter or for any need, for better or for worse, he turned to Reuben and not to Simeon. All the vizier's people, his ministers, officers, and attendants, acted as he did.

When Simeon saw that his resolution was not being followed, and ten days or so had passed without his gaining any benefit at all, he said to Reuben, "Please. I have come, but the vizier has not seen fit to attach me to any post, whether small or great. Let us make a covenant between you and me that you will compromise and give me something, and I will leave you alone so all will be well with you." With this, some reliable and understanding men were brought in to negotiate between them, and they agreed that Reuben would give Simeon 3,500 *grush*. He would also pay him on behalf of the vizier, who owed him 4,000, for a total of 7,500, and [Simeon] would go on his way. Reuben did this: he handed him the 7,500 *grush,* and they wrote up a comprehensive settlement comprising a clear and absolute acquittal of each one's claims on the other. It conformed to all the laws and statutes, with due prerogative and authority of the scribes.

Simeon left there and traveled to the Land of Israel, where he lived for a period before returning to his home here in Constantinople. Reuben remained there [in Egypt] conducting the business on behalf of the vizier as he had before. After two years had passed, the vizier was transferred from his post at the behest of the sultan and taken from his office. He set out on his journey by way of land, while Reuben, who was already weak from the difficulty of travel, went on a ship by sea and arrived home safe and sound.

Now, when Reuben arrived here in Constantinople, Simeon clapped him with a lawsuit, claiming he had been his complete partner, and wanting [Reuben] to divide all his profit with him, for he too had worn the robe of the chief financier when he was here. And, if he had agreed to a compromise in Egypt, it was only because it was forced upon him. He claimed to have a deposition to annul their settlement. Reuben claims that Simeon had threatened his life and had encroached on his rightful boundaries [*hesig et gevulo*], grabbing a position that was not his by coming into the gates [of the vizier]. For thirty years [Reuben] had earned and maintained it. How many expenses and losses had he undergone in this service; how many gratuities had he paid throughout as part of his service to the court of the vizier, as is well known to everyone! Then this Simeon shows up with high-handed methods, using force to take what was [Reuben's]. And despite all this, [Simeon] had refused to accept any compromise without the condition that *he* wear the robe of office in Egypt; yet he did not wear it. Nevertheless, in Egypt, [Reuben] gave him 3,500 *grush* before witnesses and the hakhamim of Egypt, as can be seen in the settlement document.

What does he want from him now? What will he take from him? None of this is lacking in the laws of the Torah. They will come forward together for justice, and whoever the law finds responsible must pay. Meanwhile, this Simeon has done all he can in every direction to befoul [Reuben] before the authorities, the masters of the land. God has been Reuben's support, and the truth is its own witness.

Now instruct us, our teacher, whether Simeon's case has any merit, and whom the law supports; and may your reward be sevenfold beyond the heavens.

Response: [Hakham Benveniste sides very strongly with Reuben, and bitterly chastises the rabbinical courts for allowing Simeon to impinge so inappropriately on Reuben's rights. He expresses hopes that this dismal situation of justice might at least constitute a sign that the messiah will soon arrive to return matters to a just and true path.]

PART III

LIFE WITHIN THE SEPHARDIC COMMUNITY

The community and its institutions were the essential framework of pre-modern Jewish life. While governors and sultans might decree taxes, the division of responsibilities occurred among the communal leaders. Jewish law determined appropriate behavior, but its application was ordained in the community. The following examples from the responsa show the range of topics that came up before the community's courts: debates over housing and building, strangers bringing their problems into the congregation with them, natural and man-made disaster relief, support for other communities in trouble, marginal and rebellious Jews, the welfare of widows and orphans, taxation, intervention with the national authorities, disputes between members—this is just a sampling of issues dealt with at the communal level.

Authority in the Sephardic community was generally divided between the rabbis and the board of lay leaders, called the *mahamad.* During our period, these groups, which were both dedicated to the spiritual as well as the physical well-being of the community, usually saw eye to eye. Their values and faith in traditional Judaism were of a piece, so it is rare to find them clashing. (The one topic of constant conflict was a rabbinic ruling that hakhamim should not have to pay taxes!) Moving toward the middle of the eighteenth century, this type of conflict shows up more frequently, suggesting that the unity of temporal and religious values was beginning to fracture in some places. In the Mediterranean region it appears that the rabbis adjudicated most matters and the lay leaders willingly followed their rulings. In western Europe, the rabbis' rulings in ritual matters were scrupulously upheld by the *mahamad,* but it was the latter who oversaw political and institutional affairs.

In Egypt and Morocco this formula often contained another element: a *nagid,* or temporal leader of the Jewish community. These figures were normally appointed by the government, and their main function was usually the collection of taxes and duties of various sorts on behalf of the government. Depending on who this person was, he might work in concert with the rabbis and *mahamad* or in conflict with them. His position usually depended not on communal support and respect, like that of the rabbis, but on his wealth and connections to the government.[1]

While there are only rare hints of it in the responsa, most Mediterranean communities were overseen by an elite of wealthy and learned Jews.

[1] On the office of Nagid see David, "On the End"; Gerber, *Jewish Society in Fez,* 86–94.

In other words, the rabbis and members of the *mahamad* did not agree simply out of a shared faith—they also shared socioeconomic and family background. This is not to say that the poor and disenfranchised were not treated fairly, but that the leadership cadre was often not permeable. Among the rabbis of the Western Sephardim this was not as much the case, for a couple of reasons. First, many rabbis were brought in from the Mediterranean and were not of the same *converso* background. Second, those rabbis trained in the communal schools tended to rise to success in Torah subjects based on merit, while colleagues from wealthier families might be encouraged to join the business. Figures like Hakhams Saul Levi Mortera, Isaac Aboab de Fonseca, and Menasseh ben Israel in Amsterdam were certainly not regarded with the respect of authority carried by Hakhams Elijah Mizrahi, Hayyim Benveniste, or Moses Galante in the East [see Kasher, "Menasseh," for an example of how one might know].

For anyone with a background in Talmud, watching the community leaders and courts in action is an especially rewarding opportunity. Our view of the observant segment among today's Jewry might lead us to think of Torah law as a body of complex strictures, overseen by some powerful rabbis, to which a tiny segment of society voluntarily submits itself. In the early modern Sephardic diaspora we see Jewish law operating as the living legal system of the whole community. Real communal problems are debated and adjudicated on the basis of talmudic precedent, Jewish law codes, and earlier responsa.

14

DIVORCE AND AN INDIAN IMPOSTOR

(GREECE, MID-SIXTEENTH CENTURY)

(Hakham Meir ben Shemtov Melamed, *Mishpat Tzedek,* vol. 3, #4)

Introduction

This strange case relates to the intriguing early modern problems of
identity and imposture we encountered before in "A Case of Mistaken Identity." With the waning of the Middle Ages it became increasingly easy for people to move from place to place. Adventurers
or con artists could shift identities by moving to a new location and
pretending to be something different, as long as nobody from the
person's old life recognized him or her. The case of Martin Guerre in
France is the most famous example: A man left home and returned a
few years later, except that there was a real question about whether
the one who returned was the same man who left. In the Jewish
world this problem is exemplified by the messianist David ha-
Reubeni, who turned up in Italy during the 1520s claiming to be the
representative of several of the Lost Tribes of Israel then preparing
to make war on the Muslims and win Palestine back for the Jews.
Numerous other cases, great and small, illustrate the issue of identity adaptability in this era.

The present episode involves two men from India. India was often
a medieval and early-modern euphemism for any unfamiliar land,
but here it appears to mean India proper. Small numbers of Jews had
been living in various Indian cities for a long period, and a Sephardic community had formed in the port region of Goa. It seems to me
most likely that this is the community from which the main figures
in our document came. As for the city where the events take place,
the anonymous "Tiberias" has been used, so it is impossible to
know, but it was almost certainly one of the Ottoman Jewish communities. Other communities mentioned where participants had

been known to reside were Constantinople, Saloniki, and Egypt. The participants' names have likewise been hidden by the pseudonymous "Simeon," "Levi," and "Dina."

The query begins as a solution to an *agunah,* a grass widow who is unable to remarry until her husband either formally divorces her or dies under known circumstances. It rapidly shifts gears, however, when the professed husband grants a divorce to his wife back in India, then returns and denies that he is the husband at all. The debate between the Indian agent and the purported husband reveals a great deal about how footloose early modern Jews negotiated the increasingly sticky problem of verifying identity.

Bibliography: Davis, Return of Martin Guerre;
Eliav-Feldon, "Invented Identities."

Question: In the city of Tiberias, at a time when the Jewish nation was scattered in the small towns because of [God's] attribute of strict justice [probably a plague], two Jews, Simeon and Levi, arrived there from a far corner of the earth. [They appeared] before Reuben, a local hakham, and Simeon made the following request of him. He, Simeon, was an envoy from distant lands, from the far corner of the earth. Every place he would find men from his land, which is called India, who had left their wives abandoned [without a divorce] for any reason, he was to endeavor to secure divorces from them. And so, Simeon wanted Levi, who was passing through Tiberias, to divorce the wife he had left in India. When Levi was not present, Simeon pleaded that they try hard to obtain the divorce bill from Levi, for he had apostatized in the place where his wife was located, so he could never go back there and she would remain fettered. He had already been absent for a long time.

Levi was indeed convinced at this point, and he divorced her. He declared that this woman was his wife, that his name was Levi the son of Jacob, and that his wife was Dina the daughter of Isaac. The divorce bill was drawn up and signed, and Simeon was made the agent for the divorce according to ordinance and law. The writ of agency was composed with the inclusion of the nicknames* used by himself and his father, and his name. Before the ordering, composition, and transfer of the divorce

---

* Nicknames (*kinuyim*) are included in Jewish legal documents to be sure of the identity of the persons involved, who may be known by names other than those given them by their parents. In the early modern Jewish world these could include ordinary nicknames, but also names used for business and especially non-Jewish names used by the person. This was particularly common for *conversos,* who often kept parallel Jewish and Iberian identities with names to match each.

bill, Simeon testified that this was indeed Levi the son of Jacob, the husband of Dina the daughter of Isaac, that these were in fact their names and nicknames, and that he [Levi] was a resident of that place [in India]. This was necessary because Levi had not been a resident of this city [Tiberias] for thirty days. For, about five days after he had arrived, nobody was to be found there—they had fled to a nearby village because of [God's] attribute of strict justice, where the hakham, Reuben, had taken up residence. [Levi] granted the divorce bill, vowing not to dispute the [validity of the] agent and not to annul it—all as the Sages require.

After he granted it, Levi traveled to lands across the sea, but within three months he returned to Tiberias, in whose outlying village he had granted the divorce bill, and found the agent still staying there. But now he proclaimed loudly that he was *not* Levi the son of Jacob, that his nicknames were *not* what he had claimed, and that he was *not* the husband of that woman. None of it could be possible, for he had left there [India] as a young boy, and he did not want to release a forbidden woman into the marketplace [i.e., to grant a divorce to Levi's wife, allowing her to remarry, when he was not really her husband.] It was Simeon who had beguiled him with wine and told him that he was Levi the son of Jacob, and that his nicknames were such-and-such. [Simeon's] intention was to arrange the divorce of a married woman using his name! Furthermore, he had discovered Simeon's assertion that he [Levi] had apostatized in the place where his wife lived, which he strongly protested before him [Reuben? Simeon?], shouting until he almost choked to death.

Then they asked him, if this is so, how is it that he wanted to release [i.e., divorce] her before? He answered that it was because he had been enticed; and because Simeon said he wanted to bring her the divorce bill because he would get paid for it, but that after they had given him the money he would tear up the document rather than actually delivering it to her. He swore upon a Torah scroll that he was not the woman's husband, that this was not his name, and that this was not his nickname.

The agent [Simeon], however, claimed that this was indeed Levi the son of Jacob, that his wife was Dina the daughter of Isaac, and that these were his nicknames, just as he originally said; and that he wanted to leave her anchored [*le-agnah*; i.e., unable to remarry], which is why he was recanting now. It was also precipitated by a quarrel that had arisen between them, provoked when Levi had stolen some money from a Jew in Tiberias and Simeon threatened to expose the matter. But Levi was willing to confess to the theft himself, and therefore, to spite and provoke [Simeon], he impugned the divorce bill he had granted his wife.

Levi said that he did not, God forbid, intend to do that. He only feared for his soul and the spiritual punishment [if he would release a married woman], and that he had no wife at all in the place where the divorce document was going—he had left that place at the age of fourteen. And, while he had claimed at the time he had granted the divorce that his name was Levi the son of Jacob, it was not true, for his correct name was Dan the son of Abraham, and his nickname was different as well. He produced a letter of introduction that referred to him as Dan the son of Abraham and also used a different nickname.

Simeon claimed that, notwithstanding, the man was still indeed Levi the son of Jacob, his nicknames were the same as he originally said, and the letter of introduction did not belong to him. Rather, it belonged to a certain pauper who happened to be with him in Tiberias the previous time, and he [Levi] stole it from him—this is why he now represented his name as Dan the son of Abraham, based on the name written in the letter of introduction. Furthermore, the signatures on the letter were fictional and forged, as everyone knows. This was the truth.

The divorcer [Levi] retorted that even if the signatures on the letter of introduction were forged, his name was still really Dan the son of Abraham, his nickname was different [than that on the divorce bill], and he was not the husband of that woman. Furthermore, neither his name, the name of his father, nor their nicknames were the same as those of the husband of this woman, the name of his father, or their nicknames.

Now Simeon brought a witness [who testified] that the last time he had come to Tiberias—the time all the Jews were in the outlying villages and [Levi] had concluded the divorce—he had asked [Levi] if he had a letter of introduction, and he replied that he did not. The letter he has is old. Where did he get it?

The divorcer [Levi] now added to the oath he had taken on the Torah scroll—that he was not the husband of that woman, that he did not know her, that he had not married her or any other woman in that place, and that his name was Dan the son of Abraham, known by these nicknames. Now came a witness, Judah, who testified that before the divorcer's visit to Tiberias, in Constantinople and Saloniki, people used to call him "Dan." Another witness, Naphtali, came forward and testified that for six years, when he lived in Iskederun and Egypt, he had known the divorcer as Dan the son of Abraham, and that his nicknames were different [than those on the divorce bill]. Everyone else also called him Dan the son of Abraham. He had relatives in distant parts, which is why nobody recognized the divorcer in his place [the witness's town? Tiberias?]. He also testified that they would call him by the other nickname [the one he now claimed].

The agent [Simeon] replied that this man was really the divorcer [the real husband], that he regretted giving the divorce, and that is why he

[Simeon] insists that he knows him, and that he is the husband of that woman. His name is the one written on the divorce bill. Concerning the dispute that caused them to fall out with each other because of the theft he uncovered, he said that it really happened, and that [Levi] simply regretted granting the divorce.

Instruct us about how we should treat this divorce bill and its manner of execution. For the agent insists most vehemently that [Levi] is really the husband and regretted giving the divorce, which is why he says what he does and causes the whole quarrel described.

Response: [Hakham Melamed concludes that the divorce is null and void.]

15

THE GREAT FIRE OF SALONIKI

(SALONIKI AND LEPANTO, 1620)

(Hakham Meir ben Shemtov Melamed, *Mishpat Tzedek*, vol. 3, #35)

Introduction

Before the modern period, most cities experienced major fires on a regular basis. Homes were crowded together, there were almost no building codes, most materials were flammable, and fire was used everywhere for light and heat. Saloniki suffered several cataclysmic fires in the early modern period. This one, in fact, is not even recounted in the usual lists of such conflagrations.

Like so many other responsa, the original concern of this responsum is to establish the death of a man so his widow would be able to remarry. Naturally, then, the detailed testimony is incidental to the main purpose, and thus all the more interesting and believable. The day mentioned, Tish'a be-Av, is the traditional Jewish day of mourning for the destruction of Jerusalem by the Babylonians and Romans in ancient times.

Bibliography: Mazower, *Salonica, City of Ghosts.*

Before us, the rabbinic court signed below, came the fine and wise Mr. Yohanan ben Samuel, may God preserve him, and recounted for us all the events and misfortunes that had befallen him, in our multitude of sins, in the city of Saloniki.

He reported that when he saw that the evil was inevitable, in our multitude of sins, and that the fire had taken a strong hold around the inn in which we were staying, he called out to his son, "My son, my son! We do not have the luxury to save our property. It would be good if perchance we can save even our lives! Blessed is He who decrees. Therefore, my son, look—I am going. Follow me, because from here on out I will not be able to speak to you any more because of the flames and fire that have grown up to the heavens."

Then, he told us, he wrapped himself in a cloak and told his son that he too should wrap up in his cloak so that the fire not overcome him; and that he should follow him. He called out again, "My son! Look, I am going! Follow me, because from here on out I will not be able to speak to you any more." He then went, with four other Jews following him, until he got to the entrance of the inn. There the fire closed in around them, for the flames had completely engulfed the inn. They ran right into the fire and through it, burning the cloak he was wearing, but saving himself and the Jews who passed through with him.

However, apparently his son, who had been following him, looked at the flames which had stretched up to the heavens and concluded in his mind that they must have burned up his father. He feared to pass through the flames, and it seems that he returned back into the inn because the fire had not yet inundated the inside of the inn. Evidently he heard the sounds of talking, because there were some Turks there, and he supposed that he would take refuge with those Turks. This is why his father did not see him following behind him.

In the morning of the day of Tish'a be-Av the father went all around the city seeking him—had he been seen? Had he taken refuge somewhere? Or had he been burned up? He cried out bitterly for his son, but the Turks and everyone else responded to him, "If an old man like you escaped, is there any doubt that your son, who is a youth like a cedar tree and a tough fighter, managed to flee?"

None of this calmed him down, and he entreated everyone. He went to the entrance of the inn and found a certain Turk there. He asked him, "Is there a Jew in there?" [He replied,] "There are three burned bodies. Maybe your son is one of them." So he went on top of the inn to look for his son, but because of the heat from the fire he was not able to investigate fully. Eventually his shoes were consumed right under his feet, and he came down from the inn. On the morning of the second day after Tish'a be-Av, when the fire had cooled down some, he went to investigate and saw three burned bodies, but he could recognize nothing to identify them. Then he saw another body in a corner standing on its haunches with its arms on its head. It was completely burned, and he could see no identifying feature on it, until he spotted where one of its legs had been covered by something and protected a little so that it had not burned. Even the shoe on it had not burned. The father recognized his shoe, made of black leather, which the two of them had bought together in the city of Constantinople. When he saw the shoe he recognized with certainty that this was his son; he rent his clothing and did everything necessary.

He buried him and sat in mourning for his son. The shoe was on [the son's] foot until the moment of the burial, but then [the father] took it off his foot and showed it to everyone standing there to demonstrate that the shoe was a clear sign for him that this was his son; and so that it would be a proof and a merit for his widow.

We have written and signed our names today, Monday, 25 Menahem [Av] 5380 [1620], here, Lepanto. It is all true, confirmed and established.

Response: [Hakham Melamed expresses his grief over the fire and its consequences. He permits the widow to remarry.]

16

AN APOSTATE SOLDIER OF FORTUNE

(ZANTE, CA. 1620)

(Hakham Meir ben Shemtov Melamed, *Mishpat Tzedek,* vol. 3, #27)

Introduction

This is one of those episodes that illustrates the lives of Jews living at the margins of Mediterranean Jewish society. The husband is a mercenary, an apostate, and a person of generally low character. He has undergone one conversion and is contemplating another, neither of which appears to be out of any religious conviction. He seems completely inured to the plight of his wife and child. We find, nevertheless, that he is still part of Jewish society—he is seen coming and going from the homes of Jews.

The case arises from a rumor that even after he issued a conditional divorce to his wife, they were seen consorting together, which might jeopardize the status of the divorce. As it turns out, the woman was simply trying to stay with her child whom the husband attempted to take from her by force. If the divorce he granted failed to take effect, the wife would undoubtedly be stuck in a marriage to a man who would neither divorce her nor live with her as a proper spouse. If the father succeeded in converting the baby girl, her status as a Jew would not change in the eyes of the Jewish community, but the Christians might well take her away to be raised in their faith because she had undergone baptism. (Meanwhile, it is interesting to contemplate how this case might have looked in the husband's version of events.)

The "Shkokim" here are Uskoks of Senj, in Dalmatia, who were allies of the Spaniards against Venice. The Venetians fought them between 1613 and 1618 with mercenaries. Zante belonged to Venice at this time. (I am very grateful to Mark Cohen for pointing this out to me. For Daniel Rodriga's dealings with the Uskoks, see Toaff and Schwarzfuchs, *Mediterranean and the Jews,* 1: 191.)

Bibliography: Bornstein-Makovetsky, "Jewish Converts."

Question: [The following] episode occurred in Zante. At the time that the Venetian Republic, may God protect it, was hiring people to go to war against the Shkokim [Uskoks], there was a certain man who showed up there, a debauched individual of our nation who had spent all his days following the whims of his heart. He debased himself with forbidden intercourse and prohibited foods, to which end he had earlier converted to Islam in Turkey—in order better to satisfy his lust for prostitutes and prohibited food. Even after his arrival in Zante, where he made pretense of his desire to return in penitence and revert to Judaism, he still did not curb his desires—so much so that he went and converted to the Christian religion in order to freely chase after prostitution with non-Jewish women and the like without fear.

The man hired himself out as a mercenary, changing his name to a non-Jewish one, which was how he was recorded in the register containing the names of all the mercenaries. He went and joined together with all the other soldiers in their eating, drinking, whoring, and debauchery; he even went to church like one of them. He only delayed having himself baptized because they told him that shortly, when they would arrive in Venice, they would baptize him there.

Before he left, he agreed to grant a divorce to his wife, but he would only give it for two years hence, because he joked with her that he would not accept baptism in Venice. For, in their religion, as long as one has not been baptized, even if he goes to their church and behaves like them, he can still retract any time he wants. On this basis he used to tell her that he would return to Zante a Jew. Therefore, he was granting the divorce on condition that it would be effective retroactively, in a legal and proper manner, as long as he returned to Zante a Jew within two years from that day. This was all lies, because he was a deliberate apostate.

And indeed, after he divorced her, we heard rumors that he had been alone with his wife after the divorce [!]. We wanted to investigate and know the truth, so we declared [with a threat of] excommunication before the entire holy community, may God preserve it, that anyone who had information, or had seen anything, must come report it before the three judges whom we had appointed to receive these testimonies.

Here is the wording [of the testimonies received]:

> In front of the three sitting together, we, the undersigned judges, came the honored Mr. Judah de Fano, may God preserve him. After the proper warnings he testified formally that one time he was passing by the house of Mr. Joshua Romano, may God preserve him, when he saw this apostate with his wife exiting Mr. Romano's house and walking together. This was after the granting of the divorce bill.

Mr. Raphael Kuti, may God preserve him, also came before us and testified that after the divorce bill had already been granted, he was sitting by the window of his house studying, when he saw this apostate passing by holding a baby girl in his arms with four soldiers accompanying him. His wife, Sultana, was chasing after them shouting for her baby daughter, for his intention was to take her [the baby] to be converted as well.

Mr. Isaac Israel, may God preserve him, also came before us and testified that he had seen this apostate walking with four soldiers. They had gone, entered the house of Sultana, and grabbed the baby girl. She [Sultana] came down and chased after them. Later he heard that this Sultana had stayed with them that night.

Mr. Abraham Amar, may God preserve him, also came before us and testified that one time he was in the outlying villages, when he came and found Sultana at his house. He asked her how she had committed this great transgression, that after the divorce she had gone with her apostate husband; for he had heard the rumor [*bat kol,* perhaps here meaning "women's gossip"] about it in the city. She replied that she had not gone by choice; it was because her husband had taken her daughter to convert her, and she [Sultana] chased after her with a few of his companions. She sat with him for about three hours.

Mr. David Iyad, may God preserve him, also came before us and testified that after the divorce bill had already been given he saw this apostate walking with the baby girl in his arms, and Sultana following him crying loudly. The same man also testified that one time he was in the home of Joshua Romano, may God preserve him, and the aforementioned Sultana was there. This apostate came there and slept with her under an awning, while he [Iyad] was above the awning. This was after the divorce bill had been given.

Thus far the testimonies regarding this matter.

Instruct us, righteous teacher, whether there is any suspicion about this, for from the time the apostate left, four years have passed and it does not appear that he will come back. This Sultana is sitting as a grass widow, crying copious tears. I wish to inform you concerning what is written in those testimonies from those who saw them coming from the house of Joshua Romano, that there were always people there—that is, the wife of this Joshua along with his daughter and son. They never trusted her [Sultana] enough to leave their house and possessions with her alone unless people were there guarding the house.

Response: [Hakham Melamed declares that the divorce is effective. In the next responsum in his collection he revisits the issue based on new information.]

17

THE FALLOUT FROM A TALL BUILDING (OTTOMAN

EMPIRE, EARLY SEVENTEENTH CENTURY)

(Hakham Barukh Angel, *Sefer She'elot u-Teshuvot*, #51)

Introduction

This case brings out the jealousy and calumnies with which Jews in the Mediterranean world had to deal constantly. As we saw earlier, Jews and Christians in Muslim lands were treated reasonably, but they were expected to maintain a posture of subordination to Muslims. In this instance, the construction of conspicuous homes may have contributed to the general envy felt by the Jews' neighbors, and it probably violated the conditions of the Pact of 'Umar. When an opportunity came to profit from accusing the Jews of too much success, their neighbors were happy to exploit it.

Question: Reuben built houses like everyone else in the city, but since he built them on a slope, the upper story came out a little higher than the houses of others in the city. The non-Jews grumbled about this building, saying, "Look at this building of the Jews—it is better than those of the non-Jews!" This and similar things were said against the whole collective of Jews, for this is their way; when they see any Jew who builds a new building, because of our multitude of sins, they become jealous of the Jews.

After this matter had already passed, another incident occurred. Simeon built a house with a first, second, and third story. There is no building like this in the entire city—three homes, one on top of the other. When the non-Jews saw that he had created a building unlike all the houses of the non-Jews, this new house of Simeon (because of our multitude of sins), their jealousy brought back memories of the earlier one of Reuben as well.

Now something impure [i.e., terrible] occurred. The sultan (may God preserve him) placed a tax, called *shod shati,* on the city. The non-Jews, wishing to ease the burden of this levy on themselves, sought to malign the Jews by saying that they are wealthy and had multiplied in the city. They even build new houses—newer and more beautiful than those of the Turks! This slander was a way for them to thrust on the Jews a portion of that tax greater than they should have borne.

Now the [Jewish] people of the city are agitating against Reuben, saying, "The construction of your houses caused this damage to the [Jewish] residents of the town. It was because their eyes lighted upon your house that they placed this higher tax on us and thus cause us damage. So, your houses 'stalk' [*rodfim*] us, the people of the city, and cause damage to the collective." These are matters that concerned the rabbis, and therefore, the people of the city wish to knock down the top story.

Reuben claims that the non-Jews are simply evildoers whose eyes are drawn toward the property of Jews to consume them. Therefore, even without this claim they would demand whatever they wish; for who can negotiate with someone stronger than him? And they are stronger, because of our multitude of sins. It is not because of the houses that they make this demand, for they produced quantities of libels at the time and place they gathered [to calculate the tax], like saying that the Jews had multiplied a great deal and all this type of lies, may their tongues rot.

Response: [Hakham Angel considers first whether the people of the city should not only knock down the top story, but even charge Reuben with the extra tax burden. In the end, he concludes that Reuben does not even have to destroy the upper floor.]

18

POLISH FUGITIVES IN EGYPT

(EGYPT, LATE SEVENTEENTH CENTURY)

(Hakham Mordecai ha-Levi, *Sefer Darkhe No'am*, E.H. #5)

Introduction

In 1648–49, a Ukrainian Cossack (warrior) named Bogdan Chmielnicki led a rebellion of Cossacks and Tatars against Polish landowners in the Ukraine, and then against Poland itself. Chmielnicki was extremely successful until 1651, when he was routed. But once neighboring states witnessed the weakness of Poland that Chmielnicki's war uncovered, the Russians, and then the Swedes, invaded Poland (1655). These were wars of staggering brutality, wanton murder, and destruction of property that left Poland a broken and ruined country. The Jews, perceived as lackeys of the great Polish landowners, suffered disproportionately in this terrible period, which is remembered as one of the worst episodes of anti-Jewish violence before the Holocaust.

It is on the background of these events that the present document must be understood. Refugees from the great Polish Jewish communities, which were being decimated by the Cossacks and Swedes, spread out around western Europe and into the Ottoman Empire. Here we have testimony to the widespread diaspora of these expatriates and the issues that accompanied them into their new host countries. As is so often the case, the problem of *agunot* is central here, but the circumstances are noteworthy. The women apparently fled Poland in situations where their husbands had been kidnapped or had otherwise disappeared and it was unclear whether they would ever be seen again. Now, destitute, in dangerous times, with thousands of miles between spouses, their chances for a reunion must have seemed too remote to sustain.

One of the problems involved here is the recurring theme of identifying individuals in distant lands.

The following event occurred here in Egypt. There was a group of abandoned women [*agunot*] who came from the land of Ashkenaz [Germany and Poland] at a time of disaster that transpired there: in [our multitude of] sins, men, women, and children were kidnapped and scattered among all the areas where Jews are settled.

These women who are here in Egypt hired an agent who would go to the lands of Ashkenaz and bring each of them a bill of divorce from her husband. This agent indeed went there, conducted investigations, and found the husbands of these [women]. Each of them wrote a bill of divorce for his wife before the rabbinical court in that place according to the dictates of the law. However, the agent was detained there, so he sent these bills of divorce with another agent who was coming here; for he had been authorized to commission his own agents, agents of those agents, and so on.

When the bills of divorce arrived here in Egypt, some irregularities were found in them. One issue was an investigation into whether witnesses could be found here who could recognize in each document that this was indeed the husband of the woman in question. A second was, even if someone could be located who recognizes the names, would we be concerned that there might be two [people called] Joseph son of Simeon [or whatever the name], which could well be assumed? Third, even if this cannot be assumed, perhaps, because [the documents] were carried around and traveled from place to place, even if it could not be assumed [that several men in *one* place have the same name], it is likely after [the agent has been in many towns]. For those lands are not settled as they once were. People wander around from place to place because of the chaos caused by the militaries in the area. Now, a single witness has turned up here who recognizes that the signatory in one of the divorce bills is indeed the woman's husband, but a doubt has arisen about whether a lone witness affords sufficient identification. It might require two witnesses, as the rabbinic decisors (of blessed memory) indicate; for they mention [the need for] two witnesses for identification. . . .

All of this must be settled in a proper manner, for these poor souls are grass widows: the roads are tumultuous with soldiers, caravans going [to Poland] are not available to bring new bills of divorce to them, and their husbands might never be found there because they are wandering from place to place. If the present bills of divorce are not effective, it is very likely that [the wives] will sit until their heads turn white [and never be able to remarry].

Response: [Hakham ha-Levi concludes that the bills of divorce are acceptable.]

19

THE QUARANTINE COLONY IN SPALATO

(SPALATO, SEVENTEENTH CENTURY)

(Hakham Hayyim Jacob of Safed, *Sama de-Hayye*, H.M. #6)

Introduction

Spalato (also called Spalatro, or Split) is a seaport on the Dalmatian coast that was under loose Venetian governance at the time of these events. A former *converso*, Daniel Rodriga, struggled long and hard to convince the Venetians to develop the city for trade in the sixteenth century. The Jewish community, though not large, was very active economically, politically, and religiously. As our document shows, Spalato was a major way station for goods and people traveling both directions between the Ottoman Empire and the European continent. The quarantine reflects the well-placed fear of plagues migrating with the movement of ships' cargoes and passengers, both human and animal. The question also reflects the sort of tensions between Jewish communities that were very common, especially when they concerned the payment of taxes. Sarajevo was a larger Jewish community, but it did not feel the immediate demands of a destitute itinerant population on its margins.

Bibliography: Ben-Naeh, "Poverty, Paupers, and Poor Relief"; Zvi Loker, "Spanish and Portuguese Jews Amongst the Southern Slavs—Their Settlement and Consolidation During the Sixteenth to Eighteenth Centuries," in Barnett and Schwab, *Sephardi Heritage*, 2: 283–313; Benjamin Ravid, "An Autobiographical Memorandum by Daniel Rodriga, *Inventore* of the *Scala* of Spalato," in Toaff and Schwarzfuchs, *Mediterranean and the Jews*, 1: 189–214.

Question: There is a certain small city, Spalatro, under the rule of the republic [*ha-serarah;* i.e., Venice], may God preserve it, in which few people [i.e., few Jews] live. Within it is a quarantine camp, *lazaretto* in the foreign tongue, where people and merchandise coming from the cities of Turkey generally, or from other areas in which there is fear of infection by the plague, are brought in and detained for a period of about forty days. And though it is not so pleasant, caravans and cargoes from Turkey come through because it is like a ladder—[a step] on the way to the cities of the republic or other towns, according to their needs and desires.

The [Jews] of that community realized that very destitute people would pass through in these caravans in order to get to Venice (may God preserve it) or other cities, and from Venice to the cities of Turkey, and they would be held in the inspection camp for forty days. They [the local Jews] needed to feed them with their own money, but their forbearance wore thin because the people of that city were not many and not wealthy; they could not bear the burden of this need. So, about a century ago, some individuals from Spalatro formulated a proper decree, faithfully and with intentions only for the sake of Heaven, that every Jew who came to do business there, or to transfer merchandise between countries through there, donate a set amount specified explicitly in writing in their decree. All the proceeds of this levy would be dedicated exclusively to the support of the destitute poor so that they not, God forbid, die hungry, thirsty, naked, and lacking everything; and to supply them with provisions for the journey, as the Torah of Moses and the laws of the Jewish people demand in all their dwelling places.

For many years the merchants who came through to trade or transfer goods to other cities of the republic (may God preserve it) maintained and accepted this upon themselves, for they understood that it was very worthwhile for them to maintain the *lazaretto* there rather than in the capital city [Venice].

After a time, a man arose from Spalatro named Mr. Abraham Curiel (may he rest in Eden), a representative and agent of theirs [the merchants?]; their *consulo* in the vernacular. He challenged this venerable statute. The people of the community, unwilling to be provoked into a controversy and lawsuit with one of the congregation's major figures, compromised with him: he would supply the money that had to be expended to support the itinerant poor. All their needs would be his responsibility, and none of those traveling or transferring goods through their city would be assessed. For it had never been their intention to profit by this, but only to support these wretched paupers who sojourned in their camp. Mr. Abraham Curiel (may he rest in Eden) continued this until the day he died.

After the passing of Abraham, the people of Spalatro went back to reinstate the statute as it had originally been—to return the crown to its place and the precept to its enforcement. However, the people of Sara-

jevo rose up and declared to those of Spalatro, "We are not responsible
for your decree! It is improper to do this, and nobody can just decide as
you did to enforce a decree on us. Indeed, when we wanted to instate a
similar statute on you and the people of Ragusa, a letter and legal opinion from the rabbis of Saloniki (may God preserve it) arrived here, pro-
claiming on pain of excommunication that we could not impose a
gabella [internal tax] upon Jewish merchants who come to do business in
our city. We have their decision in our files, ready to show any proper
rabbinical court. So, how would it be possible for there to be one Torah
for you and a different Torah for us? For such a decree to be permitted to
you, yet forbidden to us? The Torah is full of passages stating, *You shall
have a single Torah* [see, e.g., Numbers 15:16]. Furthermore, the decree
and establishment of the tax that you had made previously has been annulled for a number of years, and we have paid nothing. How is it that
you wish to renew it now?

The people of Spalatro answered them, "Your case and our case are
not the same; the circumstances of the one are different from those of the
other. If we come to your city to do business, it will not disturb your
livelihood because *the land is large enough* [Genesis 34:21] for both you
and us [i.e., there is plenty of business for everyone]; so why should you
wish to burden us? But we, the orphans of orphans [i.e., unfortunates]
who live in a tiny city—if you come to do business you will threaten our
livelihood. And if you transfer merchandise through our province [with-
out benefit to us], our households will go hungry. Our small income does
not suffice, which is why the law advocates that you too contribute
God's charity to support the poor who enter your borders. If you did not
have to pay for some years, it is because Mr. Abraham Curiel (may he
rest in Eden) paid on your behalf, so it was as if you yourselves did pay.
Nothing new is now being foisted on you, but rather the exact opposite:
while our ancestors made your yoke heavier, we made it lighter [by having it paid for a period by Mr. Curiel]. Thus, the law is on our side, and
you cannot abolish what our ancestors established a century ago."

This, then, is the summary of their words and claims. Now instruct us,
righteous teachers, which path we should take in the matter and what
should be done, for from Zion (your honors) comes Torah. May your reward be doubled and multiplied by Heaven, amen, so may it be His will.

Response: [Hakham Hayyim Jacob concludes that although a smaller
community like Spalatro could not normally impose an edict on larger
communities like Sarajevo, since this edict had been accepted previously
it should now remain in force.]

20

UNSCRUPULOUS PARTNERS AND THE FEAR OF FORCED CONVERSION (RHODES, EARLY SEVENTEENTH CENTURY)

(Hakham Eliezer ben Arhah, *She'elot u-Teshuvot*, #13a)

Introduction

Portugal was not the only country to forcibly convert Jews. While recent research has revealed that this was done on an occasional basis in Muslim lands as well, we find it here again in a Christian setting. Levi's experiences, and the threat to the community, come from the governor, while his wife fears groups of common thugs. The responsibility of the partners in this matter is a difficult matter to assess. On the one hand, it is likely that they turned to the government for recovery of a perceived debt because the rabbis might not have had the means of coercion needed. On the other hand, their action smacks of *halshanah*—turning an innocent fellow Jew over to non-Jewish authorities—which is a major offense in Jewish law. (Note: This responsum is not by Hakham Ben Arhah, but from Hakham Joseph ha-Levi Nazir; it is identical with the latter's *Matteh Yosef* [Constantinople, ca. 1726], Part I, Hoshen Mishpat, #3.)

Bibliography: Bornstein-Makovetsky, "Jewish Converts."

Question: Instruct us, our master, rabbi, and righteous teacher, concerning an episode that occurred in the city of Rhodes, may God preserve it. Reuben and Simeon argued with Levi, and the dispute between them became so great that they went and turned [Levi] over to the city ruler. The latter struck him injurious blows, maligned him, and insisted that he convert. All the while they were hitting him, and out of his great suffering, he made a complete confession and left the place as an apostate.

After some time, Levi betook himself to the city of Constantinople, may God protect it. There he laid out his complaints before the rabbinical court of twelve in that city. They wrote him their decision, which said that Reuben and Simeon have a legal obligation toward him to pay him a certain sum for the threat to his life, so he could move to another land and return to Judaism as before. Furthermore, they obtained for him a warrant from the sultan [governor] stating that if Reuben and Simeon do not pay heed to this legal decision [Levi] held, he would be able to serve them with this warrant. This is precisely what Levi did.

Meanwhile, when Levi's wife discovered that he had apostatized, arisen, and left her, she feared that (God forbid) tough gentile thugs would come to malign her and force her and her three sons to convert. For that reason, she too ran for her life, traveling by ship over the salt sea to the city of Alexandria, may God protect it. Now, when Levi arrived at the aforementioned city of [Rhodes], the governor of the city asked him, "Where has your wife gone?" Levi answered him, "She went to Alexandria." He further asked, "Who directed her?" Levi answered, "She went by herself." The governor took his leave of this Levi then, and prosecuted the entire [Jewish] community of Rhodes, telling them, "You directed and smuggled out the wife and children of Levi so they would not convert!" He came upon them with force and they could not extract themselves from his grasp except by paying a bribe of 470 lions thalers.

We are now asking: who is responsible for the payment of the aforementioned amount? Does it fall on the entire community? Or on Reuben and Simeon, who are the reason and cause of this incident? For, if they had not delivered him up to the governor of the city, Levi never would have come to all this, nor would he have converted, nor would we be threatened over the matter of his wife and children. Guide us, just teacher: What is the truth, the truth of the Torah? Who is obligated to pay the aforementioned sum? May your reward be multiplied by heaven, amen.

Response: [Hakham ha-Levi concludes that the damage caused by the action of Reuben and Simeon could not have been predicted, so they are not to be held accountable for the expense. They did, however, commit a grave sin in turning Levi over to the authorities in that manner, and the Rhodes community is free to fine them as a warning to others.]

21

A CHANGE OF FORTUNE, AN UNWILLING WIFE, AND A CITY IN PANIC (MOROCCO, ALGERIA, AND EGYPT, 1737)

(Hakham Judah Ayyash, *Bet Yehudah*, H.M. #4)

Introduction

Although Hakham Monson, the figure at the center of this case, was a member of the learned class, he was clearly not among the great scholars of his time. The tribulations of a mediocre figure like this give us an interesting perspective on success and failure in the Sephardic world. The man gets nowhere as either a rabbi or a businessman and is forced to move from place to place trying to make a living. His family, of course, is left behind in Tétouan. When he finally finds a sponsor, his wife invokes the standard clause from her marriage contract, forbidding him to force her to move away on the one hand and from marrying a second wife on the other hand.

The response of Hakham Ayyash is noteworthy for its compassionate tone. He places the responsibility on Hakham Monson, warning him not to use his Torah knowledge to sidestep his obligations. He emphasizes the terrible consequences of abandoning a wife and recommends a course of action for the unfortunate Monson.

In his response, Hakham Ayyash describes briefly but very poignantly the atmosphere of a North African port under threat of Spanish invasion. This was a chronic fear throughout the early modern period. In several other documents in this collection (especially #4, "Preparations for Siege," also from Hakham Ayyash, and possibly from the same occasion) we encounter similar details: the panic, the flight to rural areas to avoid the onslaught, and the lack of provisions.

The Hakham Rabbi Abraham Monson, may God protect him, was a resident of Tétouan, where he was born and raised among his siblings and relatives. When he reached the appropriate age he married a woman who was fitting for him. But it was not long before he started having a rough time, and the place became difficult for him because he could not make a living there. He had to borrow from here and there, hoping to repay—perhaps an auspicious moment would arrive to profit through some merchandise or negotiation from whose earnings he could pay his debts. Nothing helped, and he was forced to relocate. He left his land and came to our community here, where he started trying to conduct a little business with some people who did a kindness for him and sold to him on credit. He began with some success, but soon the yoke returned to his back. He lost everything he had and remained in debt to various people. From here he departed for Oran, but things went the same for him there as they had here.

He wandered various places until he arrived at the city of Cairo (may God preserve it), where he was received by a certain resident—one exceptional in his reputation and deeds. This person welcomed him into his home with great honor, supplied him with food and drink, clothed him with both weekday and Sabbath attire appropriate for that region, and arranged a special place for him to study. His friendship was so fast that he insisted on filling [Abraham's] pocket with a gift sufficient to send for his household (that is, his wife) and bring her from the western lands to the city of Cairo. All the expenses for her needs, those of her [his?] mother-in-law, those of everyone involved in their move from the moment they would leave to the moment they would reach their destination—this and all else would be covered by the aforementioned gift. The man also swore to [Abraham] that he would underwrite his salary and support his household until the day he died. The man indeed seemed prepared to do as he promised.

Now, when the aforementioned hakham saw all the honor being given him, in addition to [the opportunity] to fix times for Torah study with astute students, and even an income from it, he agreed to transfer his home there and not leave. He sent for his wife to leave the place she was, but she did not wish to do so, for two reasons. First, because of the danger from the government, which had decreed at that time that no man or woman was permitted to change residence from one place to another. In addition, she did not wish to abandon the land of her birth and the home of her father. An explicit condition between him and her was established at the time of their marriage that he would not remove her from one place to another, nor would he marry an additional wife together with her, nor would he divorce her. This was the tradition of everyone who lived in her region—they would affirm these conditions at the time they entered the wedding canopy, recording those aforementioned stipulations in the marriage contract: the husband accepts an oath upon himself to uphold every detail of these conditions.

When the said husband realized that he was bound by the conditions of his oath, he searched for a way out, researching and ransacking the books of the legal authorities of blessed memory to see if he could find license to annul his vow not to marry another woman along with her. He plunged into deep waters and came up with one precedent that would allow him permission. He also found a supporter: the rabbi of Cairo, the great and perfect hakham, the outstanding judge, Rabbi Yeshua Zin, may God protect him, who assented to release him from the aforementioned vow. This is explained at length in the holy manuscript with impressive proofs from responsa of the later authorities of blessed memory.

The hakham Rabbi Abraham sent this legal response to me to get my opinion—the opinion of an unversed man. I then sent it along to his brother-in-law in the city of Tétouan, may God preserve it—he is the great hakham and judge Rabbi Isaac ha-Levi, may God protect him. [I did so] even though when the aforementioned legal opinion arrived in my hands, there was no time for it because of the grief and dread in which we were absorbed. This was because of the fear of the angels of death, the Spanish army; we had heard rumors about them, that they planned to come and lay waste to the city with cannons. Our hearts melted and our spirits were despondent. We were all spread out across the fields, scattered in gardens and pastures, and no day passed whose curse was not greater than the last. There is no way sufficient to enumerate all the woes; they escalated week to week, from before Passover until now. On this account our reason is not sharp enough to analyze even one chapter or law with acuity. In addition, our hands are tied because all the holy writings of the early and later authorities are secured in the treasury, hidden away and sealed. We have with us only the books of Maimonides, the *Tur,* the *Bet Yosef,* and the *Shulhan Arukh.* For this reason it would be proper not to become involved in the present case at all, but since I cherish the words of friends, and it is a case now in litigation with immediate application, I did not want to withhold my evaluation, small as it is.

Response: [Despite the respect he declares for Hakham Zin, Hakham Ayyash demolishes his case in favor of Abraham Monson, and makes the following recommendation.]

If the said hakham [Monson] would listen to my advice, it is to go back and write to his wife giving every possible enticement and all the words of endearment in the world to convince her to follow him. He should also offer inducements to the family members with whom she takes counsel. If all these inducements and pleadings fail, there is nothing for him to do but return to his natural place and to his land. It is possible that when he takes it to heart to really envision her abandonment and the enormity of it, God will return and have mercy on him, and will send him respite and salvation; and he will arrive whole in body, possessions, and Torah learning. For a person must not abandon hope for mercy; and he must not let this woman's humiliation [that he is contemplating] become his impediment and stumbling block from which there is no rectification all the days of his life.

22

THE CAUSES AND CONSEQUENCES OF
A DENUNCIATION (MEKNES,
MOROCCO, 1721–1728)

(Hakham Jacob Ibn Tzur, *Mishpat u-Tzedakah be-Ya'akov,* #116)

Introduction

This complex story rapidly turns into a quagmire of interconnected circumstances and forces, to which the response only adds more confusion. It should give us pause to consider that any of the queries in the responsa literature might look much different if we possessed more particulars.

We begin with a robbery. The only really noteworthy circumstance here is the brazenness of the bandits, who come into a home, beat the residents, then beat their neighbors who come to help them. The next layer of complexity unfolds like a detective novel: the owner of the home is recently married to a divorced woman. The woman's first husband, apparently humiliated by the situation, loathes the newlyweds and is quickly suspected of setting them up to be murdered by these robbers. Now the *nagid,* the secular leader of the Jewish community, is introduced. It appears that the *nagid* and the rabbis exercised parallel (or perhaps overlapping) judicial functions. The *nagid* seems to be quite prepared to believe in the guilt of Simeon, the attacked woman's first husband.

At this point, the Muslim authorities enter the picture. Two Muslims who work with (or for) Simeon have apparently gone to the pasha, the local governor, and they now come to petition on behalf of Simeon. It is not clear at this point quite why the *nagid* flies off the handle at the men coming from the pasha, but it appears later that he feels his authority is being undermined by them. Now the *nagid* goes over the head of the pasha to the sultan (or mulay) to salvage his honor. The mulay, in classic Middle Eastern style, levies a huge fine, gets paid off (we may assume) through the Jews' bribes to his officers, and simply turns the whole matter back to the pasha.

Thus far, then, we have encountered the following conflicts: Reuben and his family vs. Simeon; the *nagid* vs. the rabbis; the *nagid* vs. the pasha; and the Jewish community vs. the sultan. For our purposes, the conflict between the *nagid* and the rabbis is particularly interesting. We learn about a division of power that goes outside the usual balance between rabbinic and lay leaders.

Then comes the response, with a whole new set of data and complications. It turns out that "Simeon" is Hakham Ibn Tzur's son-in-law; and that the hakham was directly involved in the events of the case. The conflict between the *nagid* and Simeon is clarified—the *nagid* feels Simeon is flexing his political muscles by bringing in the pasha's advocates, so he goes measure for measure by appealing to the sultan. The tension between the rabbis and the *nagid*, Sheikh Maimon, is also sharpened, as Hakham Ibn Tzur describes the insulting demeanor adopted by the *nagid* toward the rabbis. Still, we learn that the *nagid* normally showed some respect for them. Finally, Hakham Ibn Tzur exposes a further rift: that between local and outside hakhamim. After the rabbinic court of the community had already decided the case, one individual hakham, seeking (according to Hakham Ibn Tzur) a compromise not desired by either party, went to seek the views of other rabbinic courts that might overturn the local decision.

All told, this is one of the most historically revealing responsa in this volume. It contains a wealth of detail about the balance of power between Jews and Muslims, and within the Jewish community, in early-eighteenth-century Morocco.

The title given by the editor is *moser havero be-yad goy*—one who turns a fellow Jew over to non-Jewish authorities. But the *nagid* must be a Jew, indicating a complex relationship between the *nagid* and the rabbis, and unfamiliar roles for him. Criminal cases seem to go to the *nagid*.

Bibliography: David, "On the End" (on the office of *Nagid*); Gerber, *Jewish Society in Fez*, 86–94; *EJ*, s.v. "Nagid"; Amar, "A Biography" (on Hakham Ibn Tzur).

Question: Robbers and night-bandits attacked Reuben. They beat and injured him and his wife, and took everything they wanted from his house. There was a great uproar in the entire neighborhood as well, be-

cause the neighbors had come to try to rescue them but were unable—
the robbers beat them too.

As it happened, this Reuben had recently wed the divorced wife of
Simeon, and he suspected that Simeon had been behind this matter out of
loathing for him [Reuben]. Perhaps he had paid the robbers off and incited them to kill him. Reuben began crying out loudly in his house. He
sent for all his brothers and relatives, and said to them, "Look what Simeon did to me for marrying his divorced wife! He hired robbers and night-
bandits to kill my wife and me out of his hatred for us. Now, go tell all
this to the *nagid* [the leader of the Jewish community] so he will exact my
vengeance and repay the perpetrator in kind."

First thing in the morning, his brothers and relatives went and told the
nagid all about it. They said to him, "Simeon, out of his hatred for our
brother and his wife, incited robbers and night-bandits to kill them." The
nagid sent for Simeon, and immediately clapped him and his relatives in
jail. This occurred before the morning service on a Sabbath. Guards were
also placed over all the property in the homes of Simeon and his relatives
so that nothing would be taken from there.

After the morning service had ended, the rabbis of the city went to entreat [the *nagid*] to release Simeon from prison. They told him, "Since
there are no first-hand accounts or witnesses, why should he be held in
jail? Because of mere suspicion?" He then assured them that he would let
[Simeon] go free if he posted bail.

While they were still discussing this matter earnestly with him, two
gentiles from Simeon's bakery [i.e., his Muslim workers] came from the
court of the pasha to entreat [the *nagid*] as well to free Simeon from
prison. Matters escalated to the point that the *nagid* and the gentiles got
in a fight; they cursed each other until they were screaming. [The *nagid*]
became infuriated. He hurried and reported the matter to the mulay, may
he be preserved, putting Simeon in very grave danger. The mulay levied a
fine of a thousand *methqāls* on Simeon, and he had to bribe some officers
to intercede for him before the mulay [to remove the fine]. These bribes
and expenses cost him 130 *methqāls,* which he paid to the officers to intercede with the mulay for him.

The officers did intercede with the mulay, who returned him to the cus-
tody of the pasha and said, "Here, he is in your hands. Do with him as
you wish." The pasha, too, imprisoned him in his house, and he was
under arrest and imprisoned until God brought light to his case.

Now Simeon is suing Reuben for his losses in expenses and bribes to
save himself. [Simeon says] Reuben should not have sullied his name in
this way, based on nothing but suspicion, before bringing the case to rabbinic adjudication, and before bringing proof that he was the one who

incited the robbers. This kind of defamation poses a great danger to its object—the whole nation is anxious to expunge him from the world. It is all the more true when the matter reaches the captain who is responsible for the city's protection, for he will certainly harm and penalize anyone about whom this is reported. . . .

Reuben responded that this type of matter is regularly brought only before the *nagid* [rather than the rabbinic court]; and furthermore, that Simeon's loss was a result of the fight between the *nagid* and the gentiles, as explained above, so [his loss] was strictly an indirect result [of Reuben's denunciation]. He added that everyone was already buzzing with the speculation that Simeon had instigated the robbers to come out of his hatred for [Reuben], so that it would have been reported by others even without this [denunciation].

Simeon's response was that the *nagid* would not have been moved to act on the basis of mere speculative rumors bandied about by the people. Only the claims of Reuben and of his brothers, who came to redress the insult to their brother and demand vengeance on Simeon, could have moved him. And even if the *nagid* had opted to acquit him, he would only have done so with the posting of a bond, which itself would have strengthened the rumors into an indelible slander. It would have been shouted all over so it would be known among the other nations, causing a real possibility of danger, for they get heated up about this kind of thing.

Now instruct us, righteous teacher, whether Reuben must pay Simeon for what he lost or not.

Response: [The first response is a very strongly worded set of arguments in favor of charging Reuben for Simeon's expenses. There are a few subtle indications that the hakham knows more about the case than what is presented in the question, and that he is not completely dispassionate in his analysis. For example, he mentions that "Simeon is well known to all as an honest and responsible man in all his dealings with people." The reasons for this attitude become clear later. This response is couched in terms of a request for the opinion of another hakham—"We wished to learn the opinion of the master, to know what Israel [i.e., the community] ought to do."

[Apparently, the recipient of this response and request was Hakham Judah Ben Attar, for the second response comes from him and his court. (Hakham Ben Attar was a famous and respected figure in Fez, known not only for his wisdom and piety, but for performing miracles.) Hakham ben Attar points out that the query contains many irregularities, but that the case is clear enough, and should indeed be decided against Reuben. A third response comes from Hakham Jacob Malkah, who also agrees that Reuben and his brothers should pay, on condition that Simeon takes an oath that he had no part in the incident. It seems apparent from what follows that there was more discussion and argument among the rabbis about the case that is not recorded.

[Now comes a response from Hakham Ibn Tzur to one or more of the other rabbis who have adjudicated the case—probably again to Hakham Ben Attar. He begins by complaining bitterly about the abuse of the legal system by interested parties in this case: "What can I say, when the Torah is being made into a thousand Torahs, and people are using it however they wish?" Then we learn something new about the case. He writes, "Not long ago I wrote the master with a query about the matter of Mr. Joseph Ben Ullo, may God preserve him, *my son-in-law*, who was denounced by the husband of his divorced wife when night-bandits fell upon the latter" (my emphasis).

[It is now clear that Hakham Ibn Tzur was anything but a disinterested party in this episode, and one wonders how he was allowed to adjudicate it. He addresses this issue: "Indeed, I did not want to adjudicate in addressing the question, but our colleague, Hakham Abraham ben Hassin, may God preserve him, dealt with the matter, and I merely signed it." Hakham Ibn Tzur says that although his court ruled clearly against Reuben, another rabbi, identified only as the Rama"b (RM"B), "rose up and requested advice from far away places about how to exonerate that instigator and troublemaker [Reuben] who so baselessly denounces the bodies and money of Jews. For, he said, it was too burdensome to encumber one man with the debt of 130 *methqāls*. He therefore wanted to reach a compromise." As it turned out, Reuben himself was not interested in a compromise either—he wanted one party to bear the full brunt of guilt and the other to be completely exonerated. Against the continued efforts of the Rama"b to revisit the case, Hakham Ibn Tzur does something I have never seen elsewhere in the responsa literature: he retells the episode himself, from his point of view as a participant.]

I must therefore inform your honors how it actually occurred. It started out on the day of the holy Sabbath, while the congregation was saying [the prayer], "Praise the Lord, call out his name." The attendants of the *nagid* arrived and took Joseph [the "Simeon" of the original question] from the synagogue, may it be preserved, and threw him in prison. When we left the synagogue, I, the Hakham Rama"b (may God preserve him) and two or three others of the community gathered and went to the *nagid* to appease him so he would let [Joseph] out of prison. He showed us a furious countenance—he did not even want to turn and face us. Rather, he answered us with his face turned away, "I will not let him go or exonerate him!" Then the Rama"b comes along and pinches me, and whispers to me, "Why are we sitting here humiliating ourselves? It is better for us to go on our way than to be degraded any further." He started to get up, but I lingered. Then one of the congregants rose and said to [the *nagid*], "Ah, Sheikh Maimon, you are an honorable person; you do good and laudable things, and you always honor the hakhamim. Now a rabbinic court has appeared before you; it is impossible that you should turn them away empty-handed. You must perforce do something to show them respect."

He then responded and said [in Arabic], "All right then, sir, we will let him go if he will post a bond!" Even these words themselves he said angrily; and he repeated, "If he will post a bond!" four or five times with fury and rage. Those sitting before him said, "It is a good thing." I turned my face toward the ones who said "It is a good thing," and I began to say to them, "Where is the good in it for this one?" I had not yet finished speaking, explaining what I had said—that if a bond like this is given he will still not be free but will remain trapped in the net of lies. While I was still speaking, two gentile women arrived from the house of the pasha and said to him, "Good morning." Then they said to him, "Our master says to you, why are you doing this to his Jew?" They related this with soft words, but [the *nagid*] immediately became incensed and said, "Do you see that he is bringing the authorities down on me?" [I.e., the *nagid* is complaining to the rabbis that Joseph (né Simeon) is using his political clout against the *nagid*.] He leaped up and swore he would never free him, as well as speaking other hard words in his wrath. He got up from his home and went outside to walk in the market, while we remained at his house. Afterward we left with the embarrassment of humiliated people.

23

THE PERSECUTION OF A WITNESS TO
IMMORALITY (TANGIER AND FEZ, 1744)

(Hakham Jacob Ibn Tzur, *Mishpat u-Tzedakah le-Ya'akov,* #265)

Introduction

This strange case turns upon two laws. First is the biblical injunction that two or three witnesses are required in order to convict a
person of transgression. Second is the precept against slander and
defamation. The subject of the query, Rabbi Solomon ha-Kohen,
was following an order of his communal leaders to report any
amorous misdeeds in the community. It seems obvious that anyone
coming forward was understood to be acting on the very firm dictates of the leaders, not with the intent of slandering a fellow Jew.
Yet this is exactly the accusation later made against ha-Kohen.

The document is instructive in several areas. In context with other
responsa and documents from the time it might suggest that infidelity and adultery were becoming more common among the Jews
of Morocco in the middle of the eighteenth century. It gives us some
sense of relations between different Jewish communities and their
rabbinic courts. Finally, it indicates how the system of Jewish law
could break down when pressure either from within or outside the
Jewish community was exerted on the hakhamim. The absurdity of
the slander charge hints at a subtle change in both the integrity of
the rabbinate and the lay attitude toward rabbinic authority occurring in the early eighteenth century. The lay leaders were far more
concerned with the expense and embarrassment caused by the reve-
lation of impropriety than they were with justice and law. Their
ability to co-opt the hakhamim into their service demonstrates a serious lapse in both the virtue and the independence of the rabbinate.

This shift in the integrity and standing of the rabbinate is one of
the trends that led me to end this volume at roughly 1750.

It has been a long, sorrowful time that Mr. Solomon Ha-Kohen of Tangier (may God protect him) has been living here with us in Fez (may God protect it), upset, angry, and bitter. We did not know what had befallen him until the day came . . . that we investigated, inquiring into the matter, and heard from others that something improper had been done to him. The cause was certain testimony he had given in Tangier. When the matter was taken up in Tétouan, the communal heads of Tétouan (may God protect it) arose and demanded that he pay back the losses certain people sustained at the hands of the gentiles, because they claimed that his testimony had caused their losses. He is now like a refugee, for he fears that if he would return to his home in Tangier they would give him no respite until he pays. We see him walking around in a melancholy, depressed, tearful state, sighing all the time.

We therefore sent for him and asked that he present the facts of the matter to us as they had occurred. He produced for us a copy of the testimony he had given concerning a man by the name of Solomon Gerson, describing how [Gerson] had been delighted and self-satisfied to relate the affairs he had carried on with several women, some widows and some currently married—he had done with them as he pleased.

Meanwhile, rumors had been circulating there about some man and woman [having an affair], and it was confirmed, though they had tried to cover it up. When they saw this, the community, along with the hakham of the city, gathered in the synagogue (may God increase its greatness) on a Sabbath to rebuke and safeguard the [moral] fences of Israel. The hakham preached about this matter and they decreed that any Jew who knew about someone's promiscuous acts but did not come to report them is himself a concealed sinner. For this reason, the aforementioned Mr. Solomon Kohen appeared and testified what he had heard concerning the aforementioned Solomon Gerson.

After the presentation of the testimony, it stated that the said Mr. Solomon Kohen swore upon an object, a Torah scroll, confirmed on 19 Tammuz of the year 5504 [1744] in the name of God, may He be blessed, and in the name of all those who swear by His great and awesome name in truth, that everything to which he had testified was absolute fact. It is what the aforementioned Solomon Gerson had said to him from time to time, to which [Kohen] had added nothing. He also had no dislike of Solomon Gerson—quite the opposite; he had been a friend of his, etc. As long as he had seen no charge to report transgressors, he had been silent. But when he saw that the holy congregation had undertaken to regulate conduct, and had decreed that anyone who knew something must come and testify, he came and testified before the hakham. Among the things to which he swore was that all the details he had mentioned in his testimony were not divulged to him by Solomon Gerson at one time, but from time to time and on various occasions; in each instance he would recount one or two details. Furthermore, Solomon Gerson did not speak to him of all these matters in drunkenness, but in a state of full awareness.

Thus far is what we found written in that copied document that he showed us.

Another witness to this was found here [in Fez], by the name of Me'ir ben Ramokh, who had been in Tangier at the time. His testimony was received here and brought before us. It clarified that when Mr. Solomon Kohen went and testified to the aforementioned matters before the Hakham Rabbi Judah Hadidah (may God protect him), the hakham went to investigate and inquire into the matter of those women, in order to rebuke them and separate them from sin. [The next sentence appears to be an editorial insertion by the question's editor.] This is our obligation, and it is proper for us to burn the weeds out of the vineyard.

One of the women who heard the hakham speaking about this matter went and told the husband of one of the suspected women. This man (the husband of the suspected woman) now went to the governor and told him that Rabbi Isaac Kohen [another member of the rabbinic court?] and the abovementioned Rabbi Judah Hadidah had slandered his wife. The governor arrested them and was preparing to punish them, forcing Rabbi Judah Hadidah to tell the governor, "I said nothing on my own; rather, a single witness, Mr. Solomon Kohen, told me such and such." The governor then arrested Mr. Solomon Kohen to have him testify. At the beginning he denied it all, but the heads of the holy community saw that the two abovementioned hakhamim, Rabbi Isaac Kohen and Rabbi Judah Hadidah, were in distress, because the governor was preparing to punish them, and it was possible that the cup of torture would pass on to Mr. Solomon Kohen as well. So, they came to Mr. Solomon Kohen and said to him, "Why do you deny it? Tell the truth for its own sake." He replied to them, "I fear, first of all, that the suspects will forfeit money at the hands of the governor, and I will be charged for their [loss] whether or not the law demands it. I am also afraid the governor will punish me with physical torture."

The heads of the community told him, "Do not worry and do not be upset. Tell the truth and save those arrested [Hadidah and Kohen]. We will intercede to save you from physical distress as well as monetary distress. Anything you lose is entirely our responsibility, whether it is lost to the governor, the suspected women, or in any suit in rabbinic court that arises." With that, he told the governor about the matter.

Thus far is the essence of the aforesaid Mr. Me'ir ben Ramokh's testimony.

And so, the said Mr. Solomon Kohen related to us, weeping bitter tears, he summarized the whole matter for the governor. The governor then arose, arrested Solomon Gerson, and took what he wanted from him in fines. He also took a fine from the aforesaid Jacob Israel [!] based on this same testimony, and took what he wanted from the accused women, as the governors are wont to do. The matter persisted onward, and the two hakhamim mentioned, Rabbi Isaac Kohen and Rabbi Judah Hadidah, traveled to Tétouan, may God preserve it. The heads of the holy congregation of Tétouan stood against them and sullied their honor, tormenting them by asking, "Why did you do this?" They sent to Tangier to force Mr. Solomon Kohen to come before them in Tétouan, which he did. The heads of the holy community were very bad to him because of this testimony he had given. They demanded that he repay everything lost by those accused. Afterward they appeared before a rabbinic court, which assented and charged him with the repayment for the reason that since he was a sole witness, he is a slanderer! He has caused them damage and is responsible for the costs.

Thus far is what he told us.

It would have been more proper for them to hold the husband of the suspected woman who went to the governor responsible, for he should have taken matters only to the rabbis and received their judgment. The Torah says *before them*—before them and not before gentiles.* It is obvious that in going to the governor he intended nothing other than to damage, may his spirit rupture. Why was he so fearful? She [his wife] had not been forbidden to him—they were simply trying to shore up the [moral] situation from this point forward. He also claimed that he had requested the court to give him a ruling, to tell him which way they would judge him. They had said that was fine, but afterward they pushed him off from one day to the next until he could take it no longer, and he came out with empty hands.

Response: [Hakham Ibn Tzur excoriates not only the maligning husband and the adulterer, but also the community leaders in Tétouan who insulted the hakhamim and dealt unjustly with Kohen. He tries to go easier on the rabbinic court that supported them, but he sees them as at least partly responsible. Indeed, the case seems so obvious that one suspects the court had been pressured by the lay leaders to turn against Kohen.

* "These are the laws you shall put before them" (Exodus 21:1) is God's command to obey His laws. In BT Gittin 58v the rabbis expand on it to mean that Jews must go to a Jewish court of law rather than a gentile one, even if the gentiles adjudicate according to Jewish law.

Meanwhile, amazingly, a second witness to Solomon Gerson's promiscuity in Tangier was found in Fez. His testimony removes that of Kohen from the stigma of a lone witness.]

Thanks indeed go to God who has not withheld a redeemer for Rabbi Solomon Kohen. For right here was found the young Hayyim of Imran, whose testimony was properly received. He stated that when he was in Tangier in the fall of the year 5504 [1743/44], he was sitting one day in the shop of Solomon Gerson. This Solomon was proudly recounting to him that he had slept with four women—one widow and three married women—and that he mentioned them all by name. However, the scribe [taking the testimony] mentioned only three of them by name, and finished with, "and another married woman whose name is being left out for obvious reasons."

We therefore now have two witnesses to the statements of the aforementioned evildoer Gerson. Mr. Solomon Kohen is thus innocent, and is not to be called a slanderer.

[Among the many points that appear in the rest of the response is the implication that one of the lay leaders may have been a relative of one of the suspected women, and the statement that problems of adultery, promiscuity, and lesbianism are spreading. The specificity of the warning, along with the obvious proof within the case, suggests that this is not simply a standard rabbinic admonition, but a real statement of fact. A final interesting point appears near the end:]

It is also true that the first thing Mr. Solomon Kohen showed us was the receipt of testimony by four persons who stated that the governor of Tangier told them, with no instigation, that before Mr. Solomon Kohen ever declared his testimony before him, he already knew about the matter from gentiles who reported all events in their territories. However, as we have written, we have no actual need of either this testimony or the testimony of the abovementioned second witness who stated that he too had heard the same evil matters from Gerson.

PART IV

RITUAL OBSERVANCE AND JEWISH FAITH
IN SEPHARDIC COMMUNITIES

Responsa are all about the Jewish faith, insofar as Jewish faith expresses itself in observance of the law. In fact, as documents of Torah interpretation, they themselves become holy texts in the tradition of Jewish study. When a responsum concerns technical issues of law in a business or divorce proceeding, however, the reader may not feel she or he is dealing with faith issues. This facet of the rabbis' expertise comes to the fore when dealing with the matters of Jewish rituals, nationhood, and belief that arise periodically.

This is one of the areas in which English-language authors have made important contributions. Louis Jacobs's *Theology in the Responsa* is the classic treatment of this topic. It proceeds chronologically from the early Middle Ages to the late twentieth century, dealing with a very broad range of religious topics, such as prayer, dreams, mysticism, apostates, the messiah, and reincarnation. Jacobs was truly a pioneer in demonstrating how much of Jewish ritual and faith come through in this rabbinic genre. A fascinating work that has recently appeared is B. Barry Levy's *Fixing God's Torah,* a large portion of which is focused on the responsa of Hakham David Ibn Abi Zimra, a sixteenth-century Egyptian decisor. In the book, Levy asks whether Jewish authorities have always regarded the Bible now in our hands as the verbatim document given to Moses at Mount Sinai. The amount of information, and the surprising conclusions Levy is able to cull from Hakham Ibn Abi Zimra, constitutes a major contribution to the uses of responsa for understanding Judaism.

The topics in the area of Jewish ritual and faith discussed in the responsa presented here are particularly germane to the early modern Sephardi experience. The question of heresy raised in the first document was a problem for Judaism in all ages because Christians, Muslims, and Karaites all had carefully conceived theologies, whereas Judaism is based far more on practice. Whenever questions arose about the acceptable parameters of Jewish belief, the rabbi being queried had to interrogate the conflicting and idiosyncratic literature on Jewish dogma to respond. The question of relations with the Karaites raised the concern with heresy in a more oblique sense. Everyone knew that the Karaites were in direct conflict with the living tradition of talmudic Judaism, but they were unsure whether the Karaites were to be treated as heretical Jews or erring gentiles. This problem had a pressing practical aspect, since Karaites continued to live near Jews, particularly in Egypt.

If Karaites were a longstanding class at the margins of Jewish society, the *conversos* were a relatively new and equally problematic marginal group. The status of the *conversos* presented a real challenge to rabbinic Judaism for a number of reasons. First, the *conversos* were of very different types, some wishing to be part of Judaism and some wishing nothing to do with Jews. Second, much of the Sephardi world felt personally connected with the *conversos,* rendering every decision about them a potential emotional landmine. Third, the nature of the *converso* challenge changed radically over time.

While Karaites and *conversos* stood at a tricky place at the edges of the Jewish world, one would think that Christians stood outside if altogether and would thus not often be the source of ritual conflicts within Jewish law. But on those occasions when Christians related to Jews in what Martin Buber would call an I-Thou relationship, which would seem to be a positive development, it could raise disturbing issues. When a group of millenarian Protestants gave money to support Jewish communities in Palestine, and again when priests in Palestine borrowed money from Jews there, questions arose about what kinds of associations Jewish law permits with Christians.

Some religious issues dealt with by Sephardi hakhamim relate much more to their own intellectual world than to conflicts in their communities. The cases cited below from Hakham Jacob Hagiz present an amazing opportunity to see how a scholar at the axis of the Western and Eastern Sephardi communities thought about the kinds of scientific questions that occupied many natural philosophers of his age. For our purposes, it is also instructive to see that these ruminations were incorporated into his responsa.

24

THE JEW ACCUSED OF HERESY
(OTTOMAN EMPIRE, EARLY SIXTEENTH CENTURY)

(Hakham Eliyahu Ha-Levi, *Zakken Aharon*, #25)

Introduction

Christian, Jewish, and Muslim philosophers of the Middle Ages
struggled with the legacy of Aristotle. They all believed that the Holy
Scriptures contained the complete spiritual truth, but they could not
deny the utility of Aristotle in understanding the world. The problem was that Aristotle expressed certain beliefs (such as the eternality
of the world) that could not easily be reconciled with the revealed
truth of the monotheistic faiths. Great thinkers of all three religions
struggled to reconcile the Scriptural and Aristotelian systems, result-
ing in a great flowering of philosophical creativity. The conciliators
were of course not without their critics among the more theologi-
cally straight-laced elements in their respective communities.

In Judaism the Aristotelian tradition was embodied by Maimonides (1138–1204), the great Sephardic Egyptian polymath and legalist. There was an enormous debate about the propriety of Maimonides' synthesis of Jewish and Aristotelian ideas, and the opposition
party gained strength in the fourteenth and fifteenth centuries. With
the appearance of the Zohar (late thirteenth century), the mystical
kabbalistic worldview ascended, though it never fully eclipsed ratio-
nalist philosophy among the Sephardim. A new element entered the
debate during the period of conversionary pressure in Spain between
1391 and 1492. During that time, a surprising number of rabbis and
intellectuals converted to Christianity. Several important authors of
the generation of the Expulsion made the shocking claim that philosophy was the reason for this ready abdication of faith, claiming
that the rabbis had become so involved in the study of philosophy
that their faith was no longer so much Jewish as it was Aristotelian

(or Averroistic, based on the Arabic Aristotle commentaries of Averroes, or Ibn Rushd).

While Jewish philosophy after the Expulsion continued to have a vigorous independent life in Italy and Crete, fewer vestiges of its endurance are known from the Ottoman Empire. Here, however, in a responsum from the middle of the sixteenth century, we discover that the heated debate continued among Ottoman Sephardim. There clearly remained students of Aristotle in these communities, as well as vociferous detractors. Equally interesting is the position of the rabbi in this long responsum, of which I have only included about a fourth (the full text and commentary would almost call for a separate volume). Hakham Eliahu ha-Levi comes out strongly in support of scholars who study philosophy. On the other hand, he is also careful to clarify that this support is not for Aristotelian philosophy itself—on that he warns the reader to be extremely cautious. His position, typical of the Jewish philosophers of the Arab period, is that it is appropriate to study philosophy if one has already mastered the Torah and Talmud, so that one can distinguish the truths from the falsehoods.

Bibliography: Baer, *Jews in Christian Spain,* vol. 2;
Hacker, "Intellectual Activity."

You asked about Reuben, who said to Simeon before many people, "It is forbidden to pray with you, because you are a sectarian heretic. When other people pray they say, 'God of Abraham and God of Isaac'; but when you pray you say 'God of Aristotle'!" Reuben said this and similar things in front of many people, forcefully pouring out his wrath in public. He screamed like a child in the crowd, opening his mouth and cursing. He showed no concern about [the dicta] *Do not cause your friend's face to blanche* [BT Berakhot 43v; Ketubot 67v] and *Nor take up a reproach against his neighbor* [Psalms 15:3].

Response: [He begins with a strong attack against embarrassing or speaking badly of people, especially scholars.]

I must add that this mocker who came to Simeon did not denounce him alone, but holy people of the land as well. For he slandered the *ge'onim* [heads of the ancient Babylonian academies] and learned *rishonim* [medieval scholars] who studied the sciences, such as Rabbi Sa'adiah Ga'on and Rabbi Hai Ga'on, as well as other sages like Ibn Gabirol, Rabbi Judah ha-Levi, Rabbi Abraham ben Ezra, Maimonides, and sages of every generation. They established a great fortress with ramparts to fend off those who speak falsely against our holy Torah. Maimonides composed introductions to prove the truth of God's existence that were copied, commented upon, and used for betterment by the scholars of other nations. He brought proofs concerning the secrets of the Torah and its meanings, thereby banishing many doubts from the hearts of people who were confused by them in both earlier and later generations—all through learning the Torah and establishing *what to answer the heretic* [Mishnah Avot 2:14]. . . . [He continues with various proofs that great rabbis knew science, and that all Jews must do so.]

There is no doubt that anyone who ridicules wisdom in general also derides those who study it, that is, the great wise men of ages past. And although the words of the philosophers contain falsehoods in the matter of divine providence, some of which impinge on the foundations of Torah, those who study their works must not be disgraced. For their issues depend not on faith, but on physical proofs and demonstration—demonstrations visible to the eye. These are easily dismissed by anyone who has filled himself first with the bread of Torah, for he has consumed the nourishment of the mighty. Furthermore, many of them [philosophers] argue about these matters as well. Thus, anyone whom God has granted eyes to see and supplied with understanding will see with his eyes and understand with his heart that man's grasp is too limited to comprehend what is above him; it cannot be proved by demonstration. The true tradition is decisive in nullifying false conclusions that arise in the words of the philosophers. It is about such things that it is said, *Let not our pure Torah be like the idle chatter of others* [BT Bava Batra 116r]. Everyone who fears the word of God will choose their [the rabbis'] words, which are efficacious and conform to our faith, in the manner of *He ate the fruit and discarded the shell* [BT Hagigah 16v] like Rabbi Me'ir.* He will make of them *perfumers and cooks* [I Samuel 8:13]. . . . ˢ

* Rabbi Me'ir (fl. second century), a major figure of the Mishnah, was the student of Rabbi Elisha ben Abuya, who ultimately abandoned Judaism and became the archetypal Jewish heretic. Rabbi Me'ir continued to learn with Elisha even afterward, so it was said, "Rabbi Me'ir found a pomegranate. He ate the fruit and discarded the shell"; i.e., he took the proper teachings and ignored the falsehoods of his mentor. The implication here is that the Jew should learn what is useful from philosophy and discard that which is useless or false.

ˢ When the Jews demanded a king, the prophet Samuel warned them that a king would take their sons to be soldiers and servants and their daughters to be perfumers, cooks, and bakers. The verse is alluded to here to imply that the Jew should make philosophy his servant for unimportant tasks.

25

JEWS BECOMING KARAITES
AND KARAITES BECOMING JEWS
(EGYPT, LATE SEVENTEENTH CENTURY)

(Hakham Mordecai ha-Levi, *Sefer Darkhe No'am*, E.H. #59)

Introduction

The Karaites were a loosely organized group of dissidents who split from mainstream Judaism beginning in the eighth century C.E. Their main difference from traditional Jews, to whom they referred as "Rabbanites," was the Karaites' rejection of the Talmud and the authority of the rabbis. They attempted to practice the laws of the written Bible with no embellishments or changes, which proved to be far more challenging than it might seem at first blush. Some Karaites associated themselves with the Sadducees of the New Testament, who similarly rejected the Oral Law tradition. Many Rabbanite Jews, in turn, also saw Karaites as latter-day Sadducees.

The rabbis had been battling Karaite theology and agonizing over social relations with the Karaites for hundreds of years before this responsum appeared. I chose it from the numerous responsa on Karaites because it seems to raise the questions of identity nicely. Are the Karaites Jews? Can they intermarry with Jews? What is their status in legal matters concerning Jews? It also appeared relatively late, so the author cites the major early modern views on the matter.

The case turns on the biblical law of *yibum*, or levirate marriage. This law says that if a man dies childless, his wife is to marry the man's brother, though this is otherwise a forbidden union. If the brother cannot or will not marry his sister-in-law, he can choose a ceremony called *halitzah*, in which he formally declines the union. If neither *yibum* nor *halitzah* is performed, the woman is unable to marry someone else. If the brother is not Jewish, the requirement is

waived. The question here is whether *yibum* and *halitzah* are required when the brother is a Karaite. The same sort of question
arises in many cases where the brother is a *converso* still living as a
Catholic.

Such cases are complicated because the Karaites do not observe
the complex talmudic precepts about divorce. This might mean that
the offspring of Karaite women who have divorced and remarried is
that of bastards (*mamzerim*) because their mothers were technically
married to two men at once. This would create a legal assumption
that all Karaites are bastards, since some woman somewhere up the
family line must have been in this position. This, of course, is only a
problem if the Karaites are pronounced Jewish, so it would make
life much easier for the rabbis to declare all Karaites to be gentiles.
Yet we see in this case that they did not.

Bibliography: Frank and Goldish, *Rabbinic Culture*, part 1; Marcus,
Jew in the Medieval World, chap. 47; Polliack, *Karaite Judaism*;
Yerushalmi, *From Spanish Court*, chap. 1.

I was asked by the great hakham, Rabbi David Conforte (may God preserve him) about one of the Karaites who had accepted upon himself
membership [in the Jewish people], to observe all the dictates of the Sages
and be like us and all proper Jews. He married a Jewish woman, then
died childless. He has a Karaite brother who remains in his rebellion [i.e.,
he did not convert to Judaism] among the Sadducee Karaites. Does this
woman have the imperative of *yibum* from this Karaite or not? Here is a
related question: If the Karaite brother were to die childless, and his
[Karaite] wife wished to accept membership [in the Jewish people] upon
herself, would she be obliged to perform *yibum* with the Rabbanite
[brother] or not?

He [Hakham Conforte] composed a long responsum in which he
proved that they [in both instances?] do indeed have an obligation toward each other. However, before everything else [i.e., before reaching
his conclusions] he examines the words [of the rabbis] and their arguments concerning apostates and forced converts [*anûsim;* a term used
also to connote *conversos*], to see whether or not they have such an obligation. Afterward he comes to the present case of the Karaites. He leaves
no stone of the Talmud or earlier and later legal authorities (of blessed
memory) unturned. Since these studies yielded the proper ruling, I will
write only an outline based on what the deciding rabbi [Conforte], may
God protect him, has written. Afterward I will consider the matter of the
Karaites according to what I will be instructed by heaven, God willing.

Response: [Hakham ha-Levi offers a careful reading of the classical sources on this question. His conclusion is that the woman in the query has an obligation of *yibum* or *halitzah,* but that in an individual case where that is essentially impossible there might be room for leniency. In the second, theoretical case of the query, where the wife of a Karaite wants to accept Judaism, there is no obligation in place. Hakham ha-Levi then takes up the question of Portuguese *conversos,* citing Hakham Jacob Berab, who sees them as remaining Jewish even after several generations. Returning to the Karaites, he differentiates between the Egyptian Karaites, who live separately from the Jews; and those in Istanbul, who are much more closely integrated into Jewish society.]

BEQUESTS OF *CONVERSOS* AND THEIR STATUS AS JEWS (ISTANBUL, EARLY SIXTEENTH CENTURY)

(Hakham Tam Ibn Yahya, *She'elot u-Teshuvot Ohalei Tam*, #91)

Introduction

In the following responsum we see how the most mundane legal issues are the occasion for interesting historical texts. This responsum
and the next are among the many dozens of discussions preserved in
rabbinic literature between the fourteenth and eighteenth centuries
about the *converso* problem. If the Iberian society and leaders had a
problem with the religious identity of this group from their side, the
Jews had a whole parallel set of difficulties. While *conversos* are referred to in Hebrew as *anūsim* (forced ones), suggesting that they all
converted to Catholicism against their will, it was well known that
this was not necessarily the case. Furthermore, the significance of
the question of force was lost after the first generation. Children of
converts had never been given a choice, and they had never known
life as Jews. Each successive generation was even further removed.

The rabbis faced a panoply of dilemmas about the *conversos*. The
cases cited here are relatively benign, dealing with *converso* inheritance issues. But what happens, for example, when a betrothed *con-
versa* escapes from Portugal or Spain with her family, leaving behind
her groom as a Catholic? Now, living in the Ottoman Empire or
Morocco, she wants to marry another man. The first stage of Jewish
marriage, betrothal (*kiddushin*), renders her forbidden to all men
except the groom. The easy solution for the rabbis is to declare that
this woman is now Jewish, her groom—though a *converso*—is not
Jewish at all, and therefore she is free to marry another. But this
would be an extremely unpopular and problematic approach, because it would mean writing off all Iberian *conversos*, many of
whom felt themselves to be Jews in some spiritual sense if not in

practice. Jewish law declares that "a Jew, though he or she sins, remains a Jew." Escaped *conversos* now living as Jews also took this very much to heart. On the other hand, if the rabbis declared the groom in such a case to be Jewish, they would have to find a way to get a writ of divorce into the Iberian Peninsula, have him sign it, and smuggle it out. Naturally, anyone caught with such a document would fall immediately to the tender mercies of the Inquisition. Thus, such a decision was literally risking someone's life. Furthermore, if the groom was not a Judaizer, or he feared for his life if the courier was caught, he might refuse to sign. The woman would then be stuck in an unmarriable state. Various similar problems arose regularly.

This query centers on the same question: Are *conversos* living in Portugal considered Jews? Hakham Shalom is very clear that they are. There are several reasons he might be able to reach this conclusion. First, in the early sixteenth century there were already generations of precedents (since at least 1391) declaring that *conversos* should be considered Jews. Second, a large number of the *conversos* in his period were still of the first generation, and had indeed been converted by force in Portugal. Third, there would be no pressing negative consequences of such a decision. Note, however, the stark distinction between the view of Hakham Shalom in the generation of the expulsion, and that of Hakham Sasportas in the following document, writing over a century later. The ongoing condition of *converso* life forced the rabbis to reevaluate their approach over time.

Bibliography: Asaf, "Anusim"; Netanyahu, *Marranos*; Netanyahu, "On the Historical"; Yerushalmi, *From Spanish Court*, chap. 1; Zimmels, *Marranen*.

Question: There are Jewish *conversos* [*ha-yehudim ha-anūsim*] in the kingdom of Portugal, some of whom come to this kingdom in order to shelter under the wings of the Divine presence [i.e., revert to Judaism], but they leave behind their relatives. When they pass away and leave property behind, what is to be done with it? Should the rabbinic court appoint a custodian for it? Or, if they have some relative here, should it be given to that person until the heirs arrive from Portugal? Inform us, our teacher, what the law dictates, for we do not know whether they should be considered captives or fugitives. Your vision will enlighten us.

Response: [The response is not from the collection's author, but from a contemporary, Hakham Joseph Shalom. He opens with a fourteenth-century precedent about the treatment of such cases, then moves on to the present case.] This is how it is with these *conversos:* They derive from the hope of Israel [i.e., Jewish roots], despite the fact that they have been immersed among the idolaters. Their hope and righteousness endure forever—[the hope] that they will come to a city that is a haven for them in the lands of the Turk's righteous rule, may God raise him up. Furthermore, when they come to be included among the Jews, they are simply circumcised; they are not immersed [in the ritual bath] like converts who were never part of the Jewish people. They do not have the status of converts, whose goods are given to the first in line [i.e., their gentile relatives have no prior claim.] So, [the inheritance of dead *conversos*] is to be held by the rabbinic court until an heir arrives. Or, those who are living in the lands of idolatry in Portugal should be informed about it. If they either give up on [the inheritance, presumably by showing no intent of leaving] or choose to donate it to some charity, the individual or charity they designate should get it.

Out of my love of brevity I have kept it short. So speaks the one who completed it, a worm and not a man, Joseph Shalom.

27

THE *CONVERSO* AND THE CHARITABLE

FRATERNITY (AMSTERDAM, LATE

SEVENTEENTH CENTURY)

(Hakham Jacob Sasportas, *She'elot u-Teshuvot Ohel Ya'akov, #59*)

Introduction

This somewhat complex question offers a brilliant case study on the identity problems concerning *conversos* and former *conversos* in the early modern world. In addition, it contains important information about the life and attitudes of Amsterdam Sephardim.

Hakham Sasportas came to Amsterdam from North Africa. Whereas most Amsterdam Sephardim were former *conversos*, Sasportas was descended from a famous line of rabbis who had left Spain in the fourteenth century. He was known as a tough, uncompromising character. Here he is asked about a charitable fraternity among the Amsterdam Jews, the Society for Dowering Orphans, whose bylaws allowed membership to be inherited, even by heirs who were living as Christians in Spain or Portugal. Recent research has shown this type of policy to be part of a trend among the Western Sephardim to define themselves in ethnic and cultural terms—as the Nação, or Spanish and Portuguese Nation—as much as in religious terms, as Jews. This identity conception ran head-on into Hakham Sasportas's very conservative, traditional view of Jewish peoplehood.

Fraternities like this one played a great role in the lives of the western former *conversos*. Often they served as social clubs, meeting regularly for open discussion as well as charitable business, but they sometimes also brought in a rabbi to teach them classes. In this case, membership in the Society was also a sort of status symbol, because it required putting down a large sum of money at once—something the whole community would know about. But membership could be passed down in the family in perpetuity, and if a member's family fell on hard times, as happened to the man in this responsum, his daughters were given preferred eligibility for one of the Society's dowry gifts.

The fortunes of the family involved in this case are instructive. First, the whole family had put themselves at risk to escape the Inquisition and return to Judaism in Amsterdam. But the oldest son chose to return to a life of Catholicism in the Iberian Peninsula rather than remain a Jew in the Netherlands. It is hard to say whether this decision was made out of religious conviction, affection for the homeland, or economic considerations. In any case, his son reversed the process and came back to Amsterdam to live as a Jew. This gives us a sense of the complexity involved in choosing a new life as a western Jew. The family must also have suffered economic reverses, because the granddaughters of the original Society member had to take advantage of its generosity themselves. The sudden rise and fall of fortunes was very typical in the mercantile age, when a single unfortunate incident—a pirate attack, a violent storm, a battle—could destroy all of someone's investment. Wars between the Dutch, Spanish, and English could suddenly cut off trade routes on which the community depended for its livelihood. Sephardic Jews were great innovators in the area of insurance and risk distribution, but this was not sufficient to prevent economic crises at either the individual or communal level (see Passamaneck, *Insurance*).

Bibliography: Bodian, *Hebrews of the Portuguese Nation;*
Bodian, "'Portuguese' Dowry Societies"; Graizbord,
Souls in Dispute; Kaplan, *Alternative Path.*

The spirit of Reuben, one of the *conversos* of this time, was aroused by God, and he came with his three sons to the city of Amsterdam, may God preserve it, in order to return to Judaism and accept upon themselves the yoke of heavenly kingship. This is indeed what occurred with him and his two younger sons; the older one, on the other hand, went back as he had come—he hid his circumcision and returned to his error and filth.

Reuben, meanwhile, had joined the Society for Dowering Orphans, may God preserve it, by a payment of the usual and accepted sum for all who wish to gain merit through this commandment. There is an agreement between the members of this society that after a father passes away, his oldest son takes his place [as a member]. Furthermore, there is an agreement that after the death of the father, if there is still hope that the son will come out [of Spain or Portugal], then when he comes later he is given the privilege—for, since he recognizes his Creator and believes in His unity, but was simply unable to escape with his life until now, he is considered coerced [*anūs*] [to live as a Catholic].

Now, what happened is that the apostate son died as a gentile during the lifetime of his father, Reuben, leaving behind a gentile son there. The older of Reuben's Jewish sons came and petitioned the officers of the Society to grant him his father's place; for he deserved the inheritance, and there was no heir closer than him, he being the oldest of the remaining sons. They did this, and honored him with the place of his father. He married [i.e., dowered] his daughters by means of this honor, according to the tradition of that society. [Poverty-stricken members had the first claim to this charity.] He held the membership for almost fifty years.

Meanwhile, the son of the apostate [son] had come as a child to live here, and had been a Jew at this point for about forty years without saying anything concerning his father, who was the oldest brother and thus the heir. After the above-mentioned [middle] son of Reuben had held [the membership] for fifty years, he left his own oldest son, Daniel, to take his place. He [Daniel] maintained it because of the agreement [of the Society to pass membership to heirs]. Since he did not have any sons, he passed the membership rights to his married sister; although he had brothers, someone with no sons may give it as a gift to whomever he wishes.

The son of the apostate had been here during all this, but made no claim at the time. Some years after Daniel's death, however, he came and remonstrated, claiming the right of inheritance. For, according to the [Society's] agreement, it fell to his father, the oldest brother. His uncle's claim to it was based on an error, because he told the officers that he was the true heir; the officers did not know that his own father, the apostate, was the oldest, and had left behind a son who would take his place. They had therefore given the rights over to his uncle in error. He also claimed that the reason he had said nothing nor made a claim before this point was that he had not known the details of the [Society's] agreement until now. But since he had become aware that the oldest son should receive the rights according to that agreement—even if he was among the idol-worshiping gentiles, so long as his heart was with his God—he therefore came now to claim the inheritance as his father's heir.

The officers want to know whether the decision of the officers at that earlier time, giving the rights of Society membership to the oldest *Jewish* son, was the lawful thing. Also: Is there any substance to the claims of the apostate's son that it was erroneously acquired [by Daniel], so that the claim of [Daniel's] son who came after him was also worthless—nor may he transmit it to his sister, since it is not his to give? Instruct us, teacher, what the law is, and may your reward be multiplied by heaven.

Response: Everything done by those earlier officers was carried out properly and legally; it is obvious that they consulted the hakhamim of that time, who agreed with them. . . . And although she [the sister] is a woman, she still inherits. . . . Even if the principle is invoked that the rabbis could levy a fine [or loss] in order to bring someone to Judaism, this principle is not applicable here. Hope for him is lost, since he came here, then returned to his error. What help can it be to him to say that he "recognizes his Creator" and "his heart was with his God"? This virtue gains nothing, even for the one who is [himself] still in his land worshiping false gods for the enjoyment of his physical being. This is what Rabbi David Kohen wrote, and it is the more so for one who came here, then filled his soul with evil and returned to ruination to destroy his soul. His words are meaningless, for words are less to be believed than actions.

In addition, he [the oldest son of Reuben] already died during the lifetime of his father, and with the death of an evildoer all hope is lost. For the entire intention of the framers of that agreement [of the Society] was to entice him to come to the [proper; i.e., Jewish] religion in order to gain and enjoy the money. Since he died as a gentile, his rights ceased, as did the inheritance claim of the son he left behind. It was left to the older of the two Jewish sons.

28

MONSTROUS BIRTHS AND MARVELOUS CREATURES

(VENICE, MID-SEVENTEENTH CENTURY)

(Hakham Jacob Hagiz, *She'elot u-Teshuvot Halakhot Ketanot,*
part 1, #245, 249, 255)

Introduction

Several aspects of the early modern world came together in the contemporary fascination with monsters and marvels of nature. The voyages of discovery and generally increased sea traffic brought extensive
new knowledge of natural phenomena in distant lands to the attention of Europeans and Ottomans. Unknown types of humans, animals, and plants from distant shores sparked the interest of "natural
philosophers," those progenitors of the modern scientist who sought
to understand and categorize all knowledge. They began to look more
closely not only at the natural wonders of foreign lands, but at the
strange creatures God created in their own environs. They wondered
how these related to the various fauna described in the Bible, medieval travel literature, and Greek myths. Those engaged in magical
speculation concerned themselves with the possible spells or curses
that might cause monstrous births, while theologians sought to find
moral lessons and providential messages in the strange and weird.
Italy appears to have been a center for such curiosity. In the late sixteenth century, certain Jewish figures involved themselves in the study
and speculation about the monstrous and marvelous in nature.

In the responsa of Hakham Jacob Hagiz, the head of a talmudic
academy in Jerusalem during the middle of the seventeenth century,
a series of legal queries about such unusual creatures appears in a
cluster, interspersed with a few unrelated issues. It is hard to tell
whether they were originally part of a group of questions, whether
the grouping is coincidental, or whether the editor placed them together. Hakham Hagiz generally does not give the full text of the

questions originally sent him, or even the name and place of the questioner; but in this instance we know at least some of the matters arose in Italy. Query #240, which is not included below, asks whether a blessing on the marvelous is to be recited upon seeing an Ethiopian, that is, a black person. In his reply, Hakham Hagiz discusses the occurrences of white people born of black parents and black people born of white parents. In query #245 he speaks of his own experience in Italy seeing Siamese twins, one of whom is alive but inert and remains attached to his healthy brother. Query #249, again from Italy, concerns the case of Siamese twin chicks. He says they were made during the six days of creation, meaning they are a unique creature fashioned by God from the beginning of time. Query #255, apparently asked in Palestine, deals with a strange fish that in fact appears to be a salamander, a mudskipper, or some similar creature. One gains the impression that the legal questions asked in these cases are a mere pretext for discussing strange creatures; they hardly seem pressing problems of Jewish law.

The last query, concerning the strange fish, offers a special insight into the rabbinic mind grappling with a novel problem. Hakham Hagiz seems genuinely nonplussed by the bizarre creature, and he represents his incertitude in the classic rabbinic convention of biblical allusion. He imagines a connection between this animal that God has placed before him and the fish that God prepared for Jonah—both are sea creatures sent by heaven as a test of faith. He pictures Jonah, praying to God from inside his fish that he, Hakham Hagiz, will not err concerning the later fish God has put before him. The hakham's wonder at the great variety of God's creations is a common response to such discoveries.

Among the interesting aspects of these documents for Sephardic history is the evidence they offer of close relations between the communities of Palestine and Italy, and the travels of scholars.

Bibliography: Platt, *Wonders, Marvels, and Monsters*; Ruderman, *Kabbalah, Magic, and Science*, chaps. 4–5; Ruderman, *Valley of Vision*, 40–45, 135–56.

(245) *Question:* I recall that in Italy I saw a certain gentile, about twenty-five years old, who was born attached to his twin up to the navel, chest to chest, where he remained connected. He was mobile and healthy as other people, but the head of the little [twin] stuck out one side and his legs hung down to the knees of the larger one, who felt nothing but an inert limb. He existed in this state for many years with his twin. They

were unsure what the law would be if someone killed [the small twin]; and whether he would have to be circumcised [were he Jewish]; and how he existed, to the degree that he remained viable.

Response: One would have to say that his navel [i.e., the small twin] is attached to that of his twin, and the liver of his brother sends blood through the shell [!] to his liver, whence he is nourished, just as in his mother's womb. It may be possible to place him in the category of dying person [*goses*].

(249) *Question:* In Verona [Italy] they were showing a pair of chicks that were attached at the side (apparently there had been two yolks). They had two heads, two necks, and four legs, and the two heads both ate. What [is the law concerning its slaughtering]?

Response: It is a creature made during the six days of creation. And according to the opinion that humans were made thus [man and woman attached; see BT Erubin 18r], perhaps all creatures were created that way as well. . . .

(255) *Question:* I sent to have brought before me a certain fish that is called Sakankor [discussed in query #243]. I declared, "How great are your deeds, O Lord!" This is what it is like: it is long as a lizard with its tail, and its head is like a fish called a Gifalo. It has a spine and scales, but hands and feet like a man, with three joints, and five fingers with their own joints and a sort of nails at the ends. [These were used for medicine. Is it permissible to consume?] I said "The mysteries of God belong to those who fear Him," for they received [the commandment; BT Avodah Zarah 39r], "All that is permissible [to eat] in the sea is prohibited [in a creature living] on land. . . ." Who can fathom Your secrets, Creator of all existing beings?

I suffered tremendous uncertainty concerning this fish. After I permitted it, I said, "Lord, what have I done that God has appointed a fish to lead me astray? Why would You do such a thing to your servant Jacob?" Now, God commanded the fish to swallow Jonah, and he prayed from the belly of the fish: "Heaven forbid that the descendant of the holy Aaron [Hagiz was a priest, of Aaron's progeny] should permit this creature."

Response: [He ultimately reverses his earlier decision and forbids the creature.]

29

PROTESTANTS WHO SEND MONEY
TO POOR JEWS IN THE LAND OF ISRAEL
(PALESTINE, MID-SEVENTEENTH CENTURY)

(Hakham Jacob Hagiz, *She'elot u-Teshuvot Halakhot Ketanot*, part 2, #92)

Introduction

The circumstances surrounding this responsum are remarkable, and some aspects of the query itself are even more singular. The episode in question went as follows. The Ashkenazi Jewish community of Jerusalem was in dire straits in the 1650s, and sent an emissary, the famous Rabbi Nathan Shapira, back to his native Poland to collect money for their support. It was 1657 when Rabbi Shapira arrived in Europe. He found himself unable to collect in Poland because of the Swedish invasions that followed the Thirty Years' War, so he made his way to Germany and the Netherlands. His pleas for support from the Spanish and Portuguese community of Amsterdam met with paltry results—he was told they would only support other Sephardim. Searching desperately for succor for his endangered brethren in the Holy Land, he somehow came in contact with a group of Millenarian Christians based in Amsterdam and London. These figures—especially Petrus Serrarius and John Dury—believed the Second Coming of Jesus was imminent, and that Jews and Christians should come together in expectation of this great event. Like many other Christians, they believed that the Jews must return to the Land of Israel to fight the apocalyptic wars, and ultimately convert to Christianity, as part of this process. These people were willing to help Rabbi Shapira with very considerable sums of money after his own people failed him.

Some especially puzzling and bizarre facets of this event come out of a pamphlet that Dury published about Rabbi Shapira's visit. The rabbi, Dury states, had hinted at the Jerusalem Jews' openness to many Christian beliefs concerning Jesus, including acceptance of the Jews' guilt for his crucifixion, and the belief that Jesus was one of many instantiations of the messiah. This led the Millenarians to believe that they had finally found a group of Jews—in the Land of Israel, no less—who were ready to participate in the apocalyptic scenario they envisioned. This is presumably why they were so generous. It would be hard to believe that any rabbi, let alone one of Rabbi Shapira's stature, would ever say such things, yet it is hard to understand the situation in any other way. It is even more difficult because many of Rabbi Shapira's own writings are virulently anti-Christian.

In any case, Rabbi Shapira apparently accepted the money. The later responsum of Hakham Hagiz is the only known vestige left of the episode in Jewish writings. Nothing appears to be known to either the questioner or the hakham about Rabbi Shapira's possible hints suggesting Christian leanings among the Jerusalem Jews. The questioner expresses the very strange (and completely mistaken) view that the donors might be secret *conversos,* of whom there were many still living as Christians in England and the Netherlands. Both the questioner and Hakham Hagiz seem to be aware that there were Iberian *conversos* living as Catholics in England at the time of Rabbi Shapira's visit, but they are unclear about the differences between *conversos* still living in Spain and Portugal and those in western Europe.

Bibliography: Katz, "English Charity"; Popkin, "Rabbi Nathan";
Popkin, "Christian Jews and Jewish Christians."

Question: There are certain gentiles in England who do not worship images, but still join the Name of Heaven with something else [i.e., they are Trinitarian Protestants]. Among them are those whose hearts are stirred to send charity to the destitute of the Land of Israel. The question is whether it is permissible to accept it from them in order to pay debts owed to those gentiles who torment the Jews, placing them in danger. And if you will declare that it is forbidden to accept it from gentiles, nevertheless, since in our sins persecution has been decreed [on us] in that certain country [Spain and Portugal], and many there have assimilated so that they are like "children abducted among the gentiles" [i.e., Jews who were never taught about Judaism], it might be possible to say that those who donate are probably from the seed of Israel.

Response: This question was asked several years after the [Jerusalemite] emissary did what he did, and it was not asked properly. For if it was represented that there was danger involved, how can it say afterward, "And if you will declare that it is forbidden, nevertheless. . ."? If there was danger, since no usage of idolatry is involved, why should it be forbidden to accept in the first place? . . . Now, concerning the claim that there was a persecution there, and it is therefore possible to say that these are really Jews giving [the money]—the matter depends on the great oak trees [rabbis], whether these *conversos* are there because of [danger to] their lives, or whether they do not leave because of financial reasons. This would, to the contrary, be a negative factor, for there are things one may receive from a gentile but may not receive from an apostate . . . and this is not the place for that [discussion]. In the end, if he already transgressed and received [the money], it should be given to the gentiles who are owed the debts and there is no necessity for concern.

30

WHAT MAY A JEW DO WITH A NATIVITY MEDALLION? (GREECE, EARLY SIXTEENTH CENTURY)

(Hakham Joseph Karo, *Avqat Rokhel*, #68)

Introduction

In the previous text we found a discussion about whether money donated to Jews by Christians can be used, or whether it has some sort of taint. In Document 31, the hakhamim struggle with the legality of lending money to priests, especially when their pledges include pages with embossed figures. Here, Hakham Karo addresses the problem of a man who, apparently unaware of its significance, buys a medallion containing an embossed nativity (or pre-nativity) scene. The query is whether or not the man can derive benefit from the medallion, by selling it or otherwise profiting. The Torah teaches that one may not derive benefit from idolatry and its implements. The hakham who sent him the question seems certain that this is not a problem.

The Jewish purchaser's naiveté about the Christian symbolism might be explained in a few ways. It is possible that the man was from Spain and knew about Catholic symbols, but was not accustomed to those of the Greek Orthodox Church such as the ones on this medallion. It is also possible that, as a Jew from either Iberian or Greek background, he was isolated enough from his neighbors to simply be unaware of Christian ideas and emblems. A third, and possibly more likely explanation, is that he had a fair idea of what the images meant when he bought the medallion and originally planned to turn a blind eye. Then, he either suffered from pangs of conscience or was spotted by another Jew who inquired whether it was problematic.

The text states that the medallion was purchased "at *Tsaga*." It is not entirely clear if that is the name of the place (perhaps Tsakarisiánon, on the Greek island of Cephalonia) or the name of the precious metals market.

The author of the response, Hakham Karo, was the leading Jewish legalist of the generation following the Expulsion, as well as an important mystic. He expresses his irritation that the author of the question attempts to incorporate his own answer within the query itself.

A certain Muslim came to Tsaga, which is the market where silver, gold, coins, and metals are sold. He sold some antique florins, *yoshpis* [perhaps a type of coin]. And to a certain Jew he sold a round gold object weighing the equivalent of seven *methqāls* [a small coin]. It was decorated round about with strands of fringe-work, in the middle of which was drawn an embossed figure of a woman sitting on a chair. Her arms are thrown upward in the manner of a pregnant woman preparing to give birth, shouting in her pain. In her belly was drawn an infant with its right hand on its heart and to its left the image of a cross. Surrounding this image was writing in embossed Greek script; on one side, *giri valiti*, and on the other, *tiporisi*. Those who speak the Greek language explained it to mean, "Lord help he who raises me up" or "who clothes me."

After this Jew had paid his money and taken possession, and the Muslim had left, he desired to know what the meaning of this infant was. He said, "Perhaps this image is idolatrous."

Instruct us, our teacher, whether it is permissible to derive benefit from this circular item. For some Jews have claimed that it is the practice of the Christians to put these medallions in their hats for decoration.

It would appear that one can be lenient in this matter for several reasons. . . . [He enumerates them.] Furthermore, it is almost certainly correct to say that this image was not worshiped, for it is an image of a *nursing mother* with her son on her lap of which they spoke, as Rabbenu Nissim has written . . . and not the image of a *pregnant mother* with her son still inside her. What is more, even if you would say that this is an image of Mary the mother of Jesus, it is known that the Christians do not worship Mary, nor attribute divinity to her. And concerning the figure in her womb, even if you would say that it is Jesus, he has not yet come out into the air of the world. Even if it were an image of a nursing mother, in fact, Rabbenu Nissim writes there that it is possible that today such images are no longer worshiped.

Response: I see that this writer makes himself out to be asking a question, but he is actually teaching, and wishes to permit it with claims that have no substance. [Hakham Karo goes through the questioner's references and demolishes them one by one. He concludes that no advantage at all may be had from the medallion.]

31

ON LOANING MONEY TO PRIESTS

(JERUSALEM, CA. 1624)

Text 1: Hakham Eliezer Ben Arhah, *She'elot u-Teshuvot*, #13:2.
Text 2: Hakham Me'ir Gavizon, *Responsa* vol. 2, #43 [=44], 185-86.
Text 3: Hakham Raphael Mordecai Malki, in *Zera' Anashim* (Husiatin,
1902), 20; quoted in Benayahu, "A Bundle of Letters," 86.)

Introduction

Unlike Europe, the Ottoman Empire, including Palestine, was a
place where Jews and Christians lived on equal footing. Jerusalem
had gone back and forth between Christians and Muslims during
the extended period of the Crusades, but there was always a presence of Christians, Jews, and Muslims there. In this case we discover
an aspect of symbiosis: priests and monks, whose stipends from
their home communities were often delayed, borrowed money at interest from Jews and Muslims to tide them over. This was very small-
scale moneylending, carried out on an individual basis, largely by
widows and orphans.

The case can enlighten us about several matters. One is the nature
of life and intercommunal relations in seventeenth-century Jerusalem. Second is the sort of tension that increasingly flared up between
more zealous scholars and those who stuck to tradition. Although
there is no evidence of it in this case, I suspect that the spread of
mystical teachings from sixteenth-century Safed, including kabbalistic works on morals and ethics, tended to foster an almost competitive religiosity in some people. A third issue is the standing of contemporary Christians and their symbols, whose status as potential
idolatry could be argued with precedents from either side. Fourth is
the importance attached by the rabbis to a continued Jewish presence in the holy city of Jerusalem. The willingness of the hakhamim
to be lenient on the severe laws concerning possible idolatry speaks
volumes about this commitment.

I mentioned in the introduction that I was not searching out parallel and related texts, but in this case I have made an exception so that the reader may see how such texts can shed light on an incident. The three versions presented here contain different perspectives and details.

The account from Hakham Ben Arhah is missing many words where the manuscript from which the editor copied it was damaged. I have done my best to clarify or avoid the missing passages. It does contain the questioner's amazing contention that because the Apostles were Jewish rabbis, their images are not forbidden.

Bibliography: Bashan, "A Document Dated 5384";
David, *To Come to the Land.*

1. Instruct us, our teacher: Here in Jerusalem, may it be rebuilt speedily in our days, there have been [Catholic] priests since ancient times. Every thirty years others come from Rome and the previous ones return to their homes. They borrow money at interest from Jews and Muslims to tide them over until the money collected for them in Christian lands arrives to pay them. Whenever they are in need they come and take [loans], for all their business is conducted in good faith. It is particularly relevant for widows and orphans, because any one or the other who has a hundred *grush* [small coins] can bring [lend] it to them. Similarly, merchants lend to them for a profit, because all [Jews] who come to reside here do so knowing that they depend on this [profit from the priests]. For in this city, there is absolutely no other livelihood or profit to be made in any other way.

Since ancient days this city had great rabbis who did not deter this practice by forbidding it at all, for they relied on the law. . . . [Here the questioner cites legal precedents by a number of great rabbis for permitting loans to Christians. The main concern is the possibility of abetting idolatry, but the authorities since at least the time of Rashi (d. 1105) and the Tosaphists of the twelfth and thirteenth centuries said Christians in their day are not idolators because they only follow the traditions of their ancestors without real knowledge of idol worship.] Their normal practice is [to give] a certificate [saying], "We took this money in order to buy flour, wine, and goods for the home."

Now some recently arrived scholars have invented something new: they want to forbid loaning [priests] money at interest as a transgression. They would nullify all that was written by the important teachers cited above, who declared [following the Tosaphists] that in our days it is permitted, as was explained, because [today's idolaters] know nothing of the significance of their worship, but simply follow in the footsteps of their ancestors, as was explained. They further claim that on the certificates given [by the priests] are [images of] the twelve apostles, which are embossed so that they protrude [from the paper]. They [these new rabbis] do not realize that these twelve were Jewish sages from among the scholars of Israel. . . . They declared that anyone who touches them is as if he touches his own eyeball. . . . [Perhaps] these certificates could be kept in the home of a non-Jewish Muslim. . . . They also claim that [this lending] poses a threat and great damage to the city, for they will say that the Jews have so much money. . . .

Concerning their claim that it would help the city [to discontinue these loans], I see it rather as a destruction of the city. . . . [Without it there could be no] Torah study at all, and any [Jew] who arrives will simply leave again; someone who has 1,000 *grush* will do [the loans instead of the poor who profit from it now]. They support their households with the 160 [*grush*] they can make in a year, widows and orphans, each according to his or her means. If they do not have this source of income, where will they get food? From the sticks and stones on the Mount of Olives? . . . If the householders [who profit from the loans] decide to leave, what will the scholars and paupers do who are left behind? Torah study is as important as all [the other commandments combined (BT Shabbat 127r); and it would be lost from Jerusalem if there were no moneylending business to support it]. . . .

[He goes on to explain that there are many Muslims with great wealth who would be happy to step in and make the loans. Hakham Ben Arhah agrees with the author of the question that the loans are permissible, especially because they serve the critical purpose of keeping Jews and Torah study alive in Jerusalem.]

2. *Question:* The soul of the holy flock, sanctified and honest, the first of [God's] harvest who are scattered in the lands of the gentiles, longs and pines away for the courts of the Lord's house and to come to His sanctuary at His holy mountain, Jerusalem. However, the yoke of the gentiles [i.e., taxes] lies on the neck of those who, with patience and fortitude, choose to reside there. They must constantly appease the officials with money, in addition to what they need to support their households; and the judges and ministers regularly want more gratuities and gifts, both official and unofficial, as is clear and well known.

A loophole was found: Since the Christians and priests live there in order that they too may preserve a presence, they take out loans at interest from the city officials and merchants until their subsidies arrive from their lands. A few special individuals [*yihide segulah*] who had recently arrived to live there gathered together and decided to fulfill the injunction, *but to a stranger you shall lend* [Deuteronomy 23:21]—that is, to lend money to them at interest. This would yield a tenth [10 percent interest] on which they could live, as well as abiding by the words of the Sages [who say] *Living in the Land of Israel is as consequential as all the commandments of the Torah [combined]; and anyone who is buried there is like one buried beneath the altar* [BT Ketubot 111a]. It would also allow them to maintain an academy and students there, to fulfill [the verse], *For from Zion the Torah goes forth* [Isaiah 2:3] with God's help; and they would have the forbearance for all the taxes and assessments that are extorted from them anew every day. For, concerning everything that comes to them [as charity] from outside the land, *a handful cannot satisfy [the lion], nor can a pit be filled [by the dirt dug from it;* BT Berakhot 3b; meaning Jews need income from outside their own community.]

Now, recently, a group of hakhamim from the leaders of the city have been inspired to arise and declare that this practice is forbidden, each presenting his own views. They concluded an agreement to annul [it] with the threat of excommunication: No Jew, whether residing there presently or arriving later to live would be permitted to participate any more in this business at all.

But the entire nation [says] it is their livelihood and maintains the city [i.e., the Jewish population]. Their whole lives and their homes are there, and there is no other way for them to exist, for there is nothing else with which they can do business. It is almost certain that [without this business the city] will become bereft of its [Jewish] inhabitants, who will return to their errors and go practice idolatry outside the land; as the Sages say, [*Anyone who lives in the Land of Israel is like a person who has a God; and anyone who lives outside of it is like a person who has no God; as the passage states, "(I am the Lord your God, who brought you forth out of the land of Egypt)] to give you the land of Canaan, to be your God"* (Leviticus 25:38). [*Does it mean anyone living outside the land has no God? Rather it is to tell you that it is as if anyone living outside the land worships idolatry.* (BT Ketubot 110b; modified to reflect the standard wording.)]

Instruct us, teacher of righteousness, whether there is any support for the opinion of those who forbid it, and [if so] whether this would constitute a Torah prohibition or merely an extra stricture. And, concerning those who permit it (of whom there are a great many more in both number and quality), must they give heed to the decree and agreement [of those who forbid it]? What of the fact that most of the community is unable to abide by it? And even if some or most of them were to accept it at the beginning, would it be erroneous, because they would think it is forbidden according to the law? Does [the decree] require annulment by the rabbis, or is it annulled by itself?

May a response come about all of it, and may your reward be multiplied by Heaven.

[Two responses are preserved here. Hakham Gavizon permits the loans and says the decree is null and void with no further action. He suggests that the priests are not exactly idolaters in the talmudic sense, because if they were it would be forbidden to do any business whatsoever with them. The second response, from Hakham Josiah Pinto of Damascus, also permits the loans, though for slightly different reasons.]

3. There are three monasteries of priests. If they need to borrow money at interest, they come to the Jews, and they give them ten percent [interest]. They find it dependable, because if they investigate, the Muslims will tell them that the Jews control a great deal of money. They do not lend large amounts; rather, the widows and orphans give 300 [lions thalers] at a time, or 500 at most. The total amount they have borrowed from the Jews stands today at about 15,000 lions thalers or more between the three monasteries.

Now, even though it appears that there is a transgression involved, since they are giving it for the expenses of idolatry and it thus appears that [the Jewish lenders] favor the continuation of idolatry, nevertheless, since the gentiles demand much [tax money] of them, and people have no livelihood from any other source, the earlier authorities permitted it.

32

THE PENITENCE OF THE KASTORIA COMMUNITY

(GREECE, LATE SEVENTEENTH CENTURY)

(Hakham Aaron ha-Kohen Perahyah, *Perah Matteh Aharon*
[Amsterdam, 1703], #5)

Introduction

Kastoria was a small, ancient Jewish community in Macedonia not far from Saloniki. The Jewish community in the early modern period was known for its trade in furs.

This document beautifully illustrates a widely held tenet of Judaism: all evil, whether it comes through natural or human agents, is in fact a result of the sins of the Jews. This attitude reflects the fact that Jews, like members of other faiths, have a highly self-centered view of the universe. Their actions and thoughts are so important in the eyes of God that He alters the course of world events to reward or punish them. While this doctrine can promote a discourse of power, as it does for the kabbalists, it can also produce strong feelings of guilt.

In this case, the occasion for a great communal penitence is the relaxation of a set of regulations that stood on the frontier between tradition and law. Married couples were of course expected to touch, but only when the wife was not menstruating (which is a law), and not in public at any time (which is a tradition). The technical side of the question hardly matters, though. For the rabbis, there was a certain norm of modesty that was transgressed and had to be set right again. This is not an indication of assimilation or rebellion, but the sort of popular ebullience that can be found throughout Jewish history. Obviously it had happened in Kastoria in past generations, which is why there had been rules about it before. In this connection, it is instructive to compare these strictures to the communal statutes of Venice from the early sixteenth century, in which the court of the great Rabbi Judah Mintz explicitly permits mixed dancing on certain occasions. Still, this episode may be a sign that the piety and educational level of the community itself was declining.

Bibliography: *EJ*, s.v. "Kastoria"; Dan, "No Evil" (on kabbalistic ideas of evil); Bonfil, "Aspects of the Social and Spiritual Life."

Question: This is a copy of the agreement made in the holy congregation of Kastoria, may God preserve it: Whereas it is true that *the earth is rent asunder and . . . is violently shaken* [Isaiah 24:19], and *the ruined part is greater than that which stands firm* [BT Erubin 10r etc.], *for death has come up into our windows, it has entered our palaces* [Jeremiah 9:20], *for we are left but a few of many* [Jeremiah 42:2]; we are almost all black-headed, wearing black, and wrapped in black [i.e., in mourning]. No day passes whose curse does not exceed that of the previous day, with fevers, starvation, pestilence, and evil diseases, year after year for a long time.

Therefore, we, the undersigned, gathered all together as one man, friends of one mind and willing souls, to beseech the Lord our God, blessed be His name, with all our souls and all our might; and to investigate, seek out, and rectify all the needs of the city through the implementation of the decrees, fences, and hedges established by our forebears. Perhaps God will spare us and we will not be destroyed—may he return to forgive us and say we have suffered enough, amen.

The first concern is this. We have seen the bad and bitter effects of levity and frolicking. It occurred on the day ending all happiness and all joy, all grooms and all brides [a play on words on Jeremiah 7:34, etc.], that *all joy reached its eventides* [Isaiah 24:11]. A very serious intermingling occurred: the women were all made up, and were dancing in front of the Christian musicians; they performed songs for men but the women responded. Furthermore, *the men came upon the women* [literal reading of Exodus 35:22]—the relatives of the groom and bride. All the female relatives came over to their husbands, they joined hands, and they danced together, with their two faces together [BT Berakhot 61r], male and female. All the people saw it and murmured. This eruption has spread almost to the point one might have thought it had been permissible, but in fact they simply took the liberty on themselves [by becoming habituated]. We, however, remember the old days and the righteous men of the past who stopped up this breach several times until it was secured. But over time, it has been broken through again and again.

We now return to the original state of things; we accept it upon ourselves and those who come after us happily, lovingly, and willingly, of our own free choice and desire. We take a solemn oath in the name of the

blessed God and of the departed sages and the righteous and holy rabbis
of Saloniki (may God preserve it!), to shore up this breach. We will not
rejoice with the nations [see Hosea 9:1], not allow any stranger to participate in our celebrations, and not allow any song or any music made by
a gentile into our midst. Furthermore, each gender will only mix with its
own: men with men, women with women. Let them be happy to fulfill
the desire of their Creator and not change their purpose.

Response: [Hakham Perahya praises their resolve and addresses the
problems of transgression mentioned further in the query.]

PART V

MARRIAGE, FAMILY, AND PRIVATE LIFE

The private lives of individual Jews, especially women, that are divulged through the responsa are among the most important revelations this literature gives us. Apart from private letters and diaries, of which there are precious few from early modern Sephardim, no other genre brings everyday experience as sharply into focus.

Much of what comes to light in this area is, by the nature of things, rather ugly. People whose lives are orderly and proper do not usually come to the attention of the authorities. Thus we have concubines, slaves, bigamists, adulterers, secret marriages, wife abusers, and other sordid embarrassments making their appearance here. As long as we keep in mind that these cases provide a point of view from the bottom upward, and that most people did not experience these problems, we can make good use of the material to recreate the cadence of day-to-day life within the family.

The nature of marriage and divorce in this setting must be understood in order to make sense of the documents. People in the pre-modern world did not get married because they fell in love after a chance meeting at a social occasion. Social occasions were normally designed to avoid precisely such an eventuality. Unions were planned by families to create economically and socially advantageous alliances. Parents of boys sought to marry off their young men to girls from families that could help him succeed in business with either material support or connections. Parents of girls sought to marry off their young women to boys who showed promise of being good providers. Social class was also a major factor, and each side might try to "marry up" if it could. Marriages between Sephardim and Ashkenazim were very rare, usually because the former felt themselves much superior. Western Sephardim usually did not even want to marry spouses from an Eastern Sephardi background.

While it was unusual in most of the Sephardi world for men to marry before their late teens, it seems relatively common to find girls married at a young age. Girls married off before the age of twelve, however, could appear before the court when they reached the age of majority and decline to remain in the union. The man of a new family was expected to provide food and a home; the woman would prepare the food, keep the home, and raise the children. In many ways the married state was necessary for survival.

Several laws in Judaism set off the conditions of Jewish private life from those of other faiths. Rabbinic literature is rife with warnings against masturbation, which made it imperative for men to marry without undue delay. Homosexual relations are likewise forbidden. Marriage was accomplished in two stages: *Kiddushin* (betrothal that binds the couple in wedlock) and *nisu'in* (wedding), which were usually performed at different times. Once married, the couple is not allowed to cohabit while the wife is menstruating or for a week afterward. Procreation, however, is considered an extremely important biblical commandment. Without the advantages of modern medicine, couples would bear many children but see most of them lost to illness after a short time. It was not uncommon for mothers to die in childbirth, just as fathers frequently died on their travels. Jewish law allows for divorce and does not permit the husband to leave the wife at will, but some divorce situations were quite unpleasant.

A couple of our documents provide insight into the interactions between private life, communal life, relations with gentiles, and science. I have placed these in the category of marriage and family life because their central components engage these areas.

33

A *CONVERSO* AND HIS FLEMISH CONCUBINE
(TURKEY, EARLY SIXTEENTH CENTURY)

(Hakham Jacob Berab, *She'elot u-Teshuvot*, #39)

Introduction

The Low Countries, especially Flanders, with its connection to Spain, was a common place for *conversos* to flee in the sixteenth century. Trade was growing there, and enclaves of fellow fugitives from the Inquisition gathered to take advantage of their new anonymity and relative freedom. Doña Gracia Nasi, along with many other *converso* luminaries on the frontier between Christianity and Judaism, spent time in Flanders. Soon afterward, their crypto-Jewish proclivities would be discovered and they would be expelled, but at the time of this question Flanders was still a desirable destination for *conversos*.

Reuben was afflicted with one of the most common vices of well-off Iberians of all religious backgrounds: a combination of caste pride and lust. The Flemish woman is fine for a short-term relationship, and she might aspire to be wife material if she would convert to Judaism with Reuben; but with her refusal, Reuben leaves her and takes their child with him to Turkey. This document reflects the painful human consequences that could occur when Jewish law and *converso* life choices collided.

Bibliography: Ben-Naeh, "Blond, Tall"; Ben-Naeh, "Honor and Its Meaning"; Bashan, *Captivity and Ransom*.

Question: Reuben was in Portugal at the time of the persecution and was forcibly converted among the other *conversos*. At that time he went to Flanders and took a certain woman from among the Christians of that land as a concubine. She bore him a son. After that he left the non-Jewish woman, who retained her status as a Christian gentile of that place, for she had no wish to convert, only to remain among her nation in her birthplace.

After a time, Reuben fled from under that government and settled in Turkey. He brought the son who had been born to her [the concubine] in order to convert him.

Reuben now married a proper Jewish woman according to the rules for Jewish men, with a canopy and wedding ceremony. She bore him sons and daughters.

After a time, the son of that gentile concubine died, leaving behind daughters born of a Jewish woman to whom he had been married with a canopy and wedding ceremony. Then, Reuben died.

Now, the daughters of the son of that gentile concubine have come, wanting to take part together with the children of [Reuben's] Jewish wife in the inheritance of their [grand]father. The Jewish [!] children say that they [the concubine's granddaughters] have no part in their inheritance, for their father had been born of a different woman, one who came from a completely gentile family, who had been taken with the understanding that she was not at all Jewish. Thus [they said] it is obvious that the son born of that gentile woman is not [Reuben's] son and has no [legal] family relationship with him or with his children. He is like a complete gentile born of a gentile man and woman.

Instruct us now, righteous teacher, whom the law favors, and may your reward be multiplied by heaven.

Response: [Hakham Berab agrees that only the family of the Jewish mother inherits.]

34

A CONVERT REPUDIATES HER MARRIAGE
(OTTOMAN EMPIRE, EARLY SIXTEENTH CENTURY)

(Hakham Jacob Berab, *She'elot u-Teshuvot*, #44)

Introduction

Here is another case in which an unscrupulous Jewish man takes advantage of a young woman in a servile state. The conditions of her betrothal are not entirely clear. The bad character of the husband, however, is demonstrated not only in his behavior toward the girl, but in his theft of silver from the townspeople and his transgression of the Jewish dietary laws. He also spends his time with non-Jewish friends. He uses the fear of non-Jewish authority to scare the Jews, because there were strict laws against Jews converting others throughout the Sephardic diaspora. The girl is able to extricate herself from the situation by the law of *mi'un*, the annulment of marriage involving a woman wedded under the age of twelve years.

Hakham Berab's response to this question is among the shortest I have seen. I include all of it except his signature.

Bibliography: Ben-Naeh, "Blond, Tall."

Question: To our rabbi and teacher; teach us, our rabbi. A certain gentile woman came to find protection under the wings of the divine presence and became a convert. She also brought with her and converted a baby girl whom she had found abandoned in front of their houses of idolatry [a church] and raised in her home. When this girl reached the age of about eight and a half years, a certain converted man accepted money from another converted man earmarked for [the latter's] engagement to this converted girl. She herself received nothing. She was immediately brought to the wedding canopy with that convert who had sent the engagement money to the other convert—[now] the husband of this converted girl.

After the marriage, she had not lived with her husband more than about eight days, when he left. They immediately took the girl to the court of Rabbi Zakhariah, of blessed memory, and before him she formally repudiated the marriage. The rabbi investigated and examined, and concluded that this girl was a minor. The rabbi gave her a certificate of marriage repudiation [*shtar mi'un*].

Two and a half years later, her husband returned. They hid the converted girl and told him that she was not in town. Seeing this, her husband said explicitly that he would go and inform on them to the gentiles that there were people who had originally been gentiles and had been converted by the Jews. Out of fear and terror, they brought out the converted girl, and she was alone with her husband with no wedding ceremony or anything else. Afterward he stayed with her about fifteen days. During that time he took money and coins from people because he was a silversmith; then he vanished.

Immediately they sent the girl and her nurse out of the region so that, should her husband return, he would not find her there. They say that all this time he [the husband] was running about among the gentiles and eating forbidden foods with them. Meanwhile, the converted girl had reached the age of eleven years and eight months.

Now, for everything that is written here, the only testimony is that concerning the marriage repudiation, given by Rabbi David, the son of the rabbi mentioned [R. Zekhariah], before whose father the matter was carried out; and that of the converted girl and her nurse, on whose testimony everything is based.

Response: This woman is permitted to marry. It is a clear matter and there is no need to expand upon it because it is so simple.

THE MELANCHOLIC MONOGAMIST
(EGYPT, LATE SEVENTEENTH CENTURY)

(Hakham Mordecai ha-Levi, *Sefer Darkhe No'am*, Y.D. #26)

Introduction

The details of this unusual case offer some larger insights into the nature of Jewish life in seventeenth-century Egypt. To begin with, the person facing the problem that is the subject of the question is a devout Jew of Istanbul, who is an officer of the (apparently newly appointed) Ottoman governor of Egypt. He leaves his family behind, and it is unclear whether he intends to bring them down later or return to Istanbul himself at some point. He must have an important position in the governor's retinue or he would be allowed to return home without a fuss. It is likely that, like the man in our document about the clothier and the vizier, this person was a *Ṣaraf Bashi*, or chief financier for the governor.

The problem he faces is one that may seem bizarre to the modern reader for several reasons, but it is perfectly reasonable in its own context. The man is sick. He must ejaculate or expect death from melancholy. Melancholy was conceived as a broad category of diseases affecting not only the mind, but also the body. While the concept of melancholy had a very long history, its medical formulation had been articulated at great length in 1621 by the Englishman Robert Burton in his *Anatomy of Melancholy*. (The messianic figure Shabbatai Zvi may have been understood by contemporaries as a melancholic, though of a different sort. See Idel, "Saturn.") The solutions presented by contemporaries—to bring the man to his wife, to bring his wife to him, or to marry a second wife— were all impossible. While Sephardim were not bound by the ancient decree of the Ashkenazim to marry only one wife, this was nevertheless a standard condition in marriage contracts dating back at least to the eleventh century. The solutions that would seem obvious to modern readers—masturbation, relations with a prostitute or other willing woman—were forbidden by Jewish law, and this man was deeply committed to upholding the law. The only viable solution for the rabbis was to annul the oath and let the man marry a second wife, but they were reluctant to do this without absolute certainly that the prognosis and remedy were correct.

And how does a hakham know the prognosis and remedy for diseases in seventeenth-century Egypt? He first consults Jewish physicians, but it turns out they are not the most knowledgeable in this disease. The next choice is a Christian expert—but his conclusions are clearly suspect. The Jewish doctors are reinterviewed for their opinion, and then, astonishingly, the rabbis go to the medical textbooks themselves to learn of the disease. They find it in the works of the medieval Arab commentator Avicenna, who describes it to their satisfaction. They can then annul the man's vow and allow him a second marriage to save his life.

Bibliography: Burton, *Anatomy of Melancholy*, III, ii:5; Kottek and Garcia-Ballester, *Medicine and Medical Ethics;* Zimmels, *Magicians.*

It occurred that a certain gentleman from among the important figures of Constantinople (may God preserve it) arrived here in Egypt in the retinue of the governor of the city (may God raise him up), as is the well-known habit of the governors. This man [the gentleman; a Jew] was a God-fearing person who stayed away from evil and avoided sin.

From the day he arrived here we observed that he was afflicted with various terrible illnesses so that he was falling apart. The physicians tried all sorts of intense medications—from herbs to ox milk—with no success. His pain became increasingly overwhelming, his sickness worse and worse, until the [Jewish] physicians gave up. Then a certain very expert Christian physician was brought in, who saw that the illness had turned into *melancholia*. It was getting worse each day rather than better. [The doctor] told him the reason for the sickness was the impediment of excretions; for his semen had built up and created an abcess in his body, and the vapors were rising to his head and reaching the heart. If he kept up in this way without discharging, the illness would overcome him, no more cure would be possible, and a disaster would almost certainly befall him, God forbid. He should therefore hurry to marry a woman.

When he heard that his cure depended on this, the man was seized by trembling, for he had sworn a standing divine oath to his wife never to marry another woman besides her; nor could he return to his home to live with his wife because the spirit of the governor [would not allow it], and *the law of the land [is binding]*. He was completely disconcerted and sent for an opinion from the rabbinical court (may God preserve it), those standard-bearers of the Torah, to know whether his oath might be annulled in order to cure his illness.

Now we, the rabbinical court of Egypt (may God preserve it!), acceded to his request. We researched and interviewed expert physicians to know whether the diagnosis of the Christian was correct, and if a sickness like this truly exists. They declared that it was indeed correct, that such a thing does happen at times, and that if one suffers from this disease there is no cure but to purge the semen. The fact that they themselves had given up was simply because they failed to reach a diagnosis. We then sent for the Christian physician and asked him in person. We received his testimony as reported above: that no other medicine would help at all except this, and without it he could never be cured.

Even with all this, we refused to rely on [his testimony], and we conducted our own very thorough search in the books of the physicians to see whether an illness like this really exists in the world. We found in the book of Ibn Sina [Avicenna], Part X, discussing matters concerning the male reproductive organs, Section I, Chapter 11, the following. . . . [There follow two paragraphs quoted from the medieval Muslim philosopher Avicenna's commentary on Aristotle describing this disease.]

Response: [The rabbi ultimately allows the man to nullify his vow and marry a second wife on condition he swear never to marry a third. He points out that by the time they could have sent for the man's original wife and waited for her arrival, he might well be dead.]

36

THE AFFLICTED BIGAMIST

(MOROCCO, EARLY EIGHTEENTH CENTURY)

(Hakham Jacob Ibn Tzur, *Mishpat u-Tzedakah be-Ya'akov,* #143)

Introduction

This case offers an interesting comparison with the previous one. It also occurs in the North African context and many of the elements are quite similar—a religiously scrupulous man, a disease that requires copulation to cure, and a wife who cannot help. The legal problem, exacerbated by the views of the kabbalists, is that wet dreams are considered a sin almost on par with masturbation, despite the fact that the man has no control over them. The conclusion of the hakham is very different from that in the Egyptian case.

[To] our master and teacher, the great light, Hakham Jacob ben Tzur, may God preserve him. After wishes of peace to the honor of your Torah: I was asked to discharge the request of a questioner whose face overflowed with bitter tears because he did not wish to reveal before our judges the shame of his sin. He wanted first to know what the decision would be. He wanted to ask his query discreetly, which is why I have written to our master and teacher. Here is the query of the questioner.

He has (in our multitude of sins) an affliction of the soul that causes him constantly and consistently to fall to the iniquity of nocturnal emissions. He has tried various remedies and techniques for this but nothing helps. Every day he goes and comes from the ritual bath and the river because he fears sin and wishes to be purified from his contamination. His constant exposure to the frigidity of the water has caused his body to become afflicted with severe illnesses—a pain in the kidneys and other excruciating sicknesses. He searched all over until some scholars of nature [*hakhmei ha-teva,* i.e., scientists] told him that the remedy he needs is to marry a second wife in addition to the one he has, so that he will have two wives, and then he will suffer no more of the aforementioned blight.

The man's luck became worse yet, for his wife miscarried and has been discharging ever since, according to an unceasing rumor. This was about three months ago, and she remains in her state of ritual impurity, so that he has been separated from her altogether. His pain has grown excruciating. He responded with a bitter cry and distressed heart, "Look and see if there is any pain like my pain! For even if she were ritually pure and her menstruation were regular like other women, I would still be sinking in a quagmire; how much the deeper today, when her functions have been disabled—my suffering and my sins are vastly multiplied over what they were before!"

We have found nobody who is lenient about this sin [wet dreams]. The earlier and later authorities all recount heavy punishments for it in this world and the next. For this reason he claims that "it would be better for me to marry a second wife in addition to the one I have, and I would have no transgression of the oath I swore" [not to marry an additional wife, because of this one's illness]. He has already attempted various treatments for her which have not helped. He therefore [claims] he cannot be held legally accountable when he maintains and complains about his evil nature even when she is ritually pure, and all the more so today; for *it is not good for man to be alone* [Genesis 2:18]. [He claims] further that those knowledgeable about the nature of the world revealed that their diagnosis is that he must marry an additional wife along with her, as mentioned above, so he can be saved from this sin. He also insists he does not know what else to do now that he has these terrible illnesses in his body that endanger him.

His wife responds and says, "What am I supposed to do for him? What he says about his evil nature is of no interest to me. If the issue is that my menstrual cycle is damaged, *his field is flooded* [BT Ketubot 2r-v; i.e., it is his bad luck]. He has already fulfilled the commandment to bear children—why should he now ask for rulership [!]? I will never absolve him of the oath he swore not to marry [another wife], that I should have a competitor with me."

These are their claims. And so, we beg your forgiveness, but we need to learn. Instruct us, our teacher, with whom the truth lies, and let two [additional members of the] rabbinical court sign with your honor on the back of the question. At this time there is no call to say more except to wish peace to your honor.

—Me'ir d'Avila

Response: [Hakham Ibn Tzur excoriates the man, insists that there is indeed no leniency in the matter, and gives a contemporary version of the "cold shower" advice. The man must simply suffer through the situation as best he can.]

37

A SUSPICIOUS PREGNANCY

(SHEKHEM [NABLUS], PALESTINE, 1721)

(Hakham Israel Me'ir Mizrahi, *She'elot u-Teshuvot,* O.H. #1)

Introduction

In this query and the next we return to the rogue's gallery of suspicious and marginal Jews. Women getting pregnant from men other than their husbands has been a fairly common problem in all societies. In fact, perhaps 10 percent of children in western societies today are believed not to belong to their assumed fathers (*Globe and Mail,* December 14, 2002, F1). This case contains some interesting details, however, that can teach us about the Sephardic context in the early eighteenth century.

The rumors suggest that the child's real father is either a gentile neighbor or the mother's own brother. While I have seen a number of cases involving adultery with non-Jews, I have not seen fathers or brothers named in extramarital paternity cases elsewhere. It is probably a spurious rumor, but the very fact that such an idea occurred to these Jews suggests an atmosphere of less than sterling piety. The apparent familiarity between the gentile neighbor and these Jews is instructive as well. A couple of hints suggest that these may have been very poor people—the need of the husband to leave in search of sustenance less than a week after his marriage, and the arrangement of an entire family sleeping in one bed.

I originally had doubts whether these events really occurred in Nablus, or whether it is just a Palestinian city name being used in place of the actual town. I am fairly certain it is really Nablus, however, because there was indeed a Jewish community there at this time and it was not the usual choice of a Palestinian town name for purposes of anonymity. This, too, is interesting, because there is limited evidence about the history of the Jewish community there. The other residents were Muslims, Samaritans, and probably some Christians.

Question: An episode occurred in the following manner. Reuben was married to Leah . . . on 25 Tishri of the year 5481 [1720]. He had relations with her in the normal manner. He remained in the city with his wife on the twenty-fifth and twenty-sixth. On the twenty-seventh of Tishri he was forced to leave and travel about to find sustenance for them. He did not have relations with her any more.

The news was soon circulating that she was pregnant from her husband; God had remembered her. In the month of Kislev [about two months after the wedding] all the women gathered for a party and saw that Leah's clothes had blood on them. Amazed by this, they asked her what was going on. She replied that she was having her period. Despite this, she still claimed to be pregnant, [and said] that she had seen blood another time as well, but she did not concern herself because, she said, there are also women who see blood during pregnancy, so consider me one of those. Thus, all continued to consider her pregnant.

When the time came for her to give birth according to the calculation, her husband, Reuben, was called home to celebrate the child who was about to be born. Reuben did so, arriving home on the fifteenth of Nissan of that year [six months after the wedding]. He remained in the city until her nine months had passed, but God prevented Leah from giving birth—she did not give birth until the sixth day of the month of Mar Heshvan of the year 5482 [just over a year after the wedding]! She bore a living, healthy son; but according to the calculation, from 27 Tishri when her husband left, until 6 Heshvan when she gave birth, twelve months and nine days had passed, including the day of the birth. From the day Leah entered her tenth month, the whole city was in an uproar. The nation is bad—they mock her saying, Why does she hold on to this fiction? Her husband did not remain in the city after her required immersion [in the ritual bath (*miqvah*); required when a woman marries] except for those days mentioned!

There are those who say some women saw Sarah, Leah's mother, plotting to feed her sesame oil which is used to abort the fetus. Others suspected a certain gentile who lives in her neighborhood, and there was a reason for it. For one day, they were speaking with this gentile, and asking him, "Why are you so excited by lust, especially by that woman, so-and-so (an extremely ugly gentile woman)?" The gentile replied to these Jews, "I would never get close to her! If I wanted, I would slake my desires with my neighbor, Leah, the wife of Reuben, for she is as beautiful as the moon!" This led them to suspect Leah [of sleeping] with this gentile.

There are others who spread it about that maybe Hanokh, the brother of Leah, is the one who got her pregnant, because he is a single young man, and he and his mother would sleep with his sister all the time her husband, Reuben, was abroad. Perhaps his evil inclination got the better of him, for her brother, Hanokh was a *big man* [I Samuel 17:4, concerning Goliath] who followed wherever his eyes led him, into the homes of women.

Because of all this, Reuben's soul led him to come and ask what the status of the child would be, and what he should do about his wife. He cried like a child that if he was a bastard, he would divorce himself from both his wife and her child. But if it was his son, she would be his wife as before, and he would ignore the rumors. Also, when he circumcises him and redeems him [from divine service with a payment to the priests], since he is a firstborn, should he pronounce the blessing on the circumcision and redemption like any father for his son? Teach us about all of it, righteous teacher, and my your reward be redoubled by heaven.

Response: [Hakham Mizrahi declares that the boy is his son in every way in the eyes of Jewish law.]

38

THE UNREPENTANT ADULTERER
(WESTERN EUROPE, 1730)

(Hakham Moses Hagiz, *Shete ha-Lehem*, #31)

Introduction

With this case we return to the Western Sephardim and their particular foibles. The man at the center of this case is accused of almost
every major transgression in Judaism. Note, however, that despite
biblical sins of the worst sort—adultery, theft, shaving the beard
with a blade, profaning the Sabbath, and so on—the man attends
synagogue at times and feels it is important to be part of the community. He is a textbook case of the sort of marginal former *converso* inhabiting the fringes of the Western Sephardic world and ex-
asperating the rabbis no end.

Another noteworthy facet of the episode is the pattern we have
seen in other cases, where *conversos* travel with apparent ease between western Europe and the Iberian Peninsula. Naturally, the
couple would have had to live as Catholics for as long as they were
in Spain, which may be the occasion for the author of this query to
refer to the man as an idolater.

While we do not know where the fugitive couple began or con-
cluded their journey, we do know that they spent time in Spain and
London, and that the congregation in which the man ends up is called
Beth Jacob. The authority to whom the query was sent, Hakham
Moses Hagiz, spent a large part of his life in western European Se-
phardic communities as well, suggesting to me that the affair began
and perhaps ended in Hamburg, Livorno, Amsterdam, or southern
France.

The responsum was probably sent to Hakham Hagiz for his opinion, but the response is signed by two other rabbis, David ben Uzziel
Finzi and Aviad Sar Shalom Basilia of Mantua.

Bibliography: Carlebach, *Pursuit of Heresy;* Goldish, "Jews,
Christians, and *Conversos*"; Kaplan, *Alternative Path*.

There was an episode concerning the arrival of an evil man known by his name, so-and-so (though if it is necessary his name and memory will be mentioned for a curse and damnation). He transgressed the most severe commandments of the Torah: idolatry, forbidden relationships, murder, kidnapping, thievery, profanation of the Sabbath, and violating the words of the Sages. That is, he stole the wife of the cantor away from him in the city in which he lived, along with everything [the cantor] had in his house, and went off to the cities of Spain—the lands of persecution. The result was damage to the husband caused by the worry in his soul.

After several years passed during which the adulterer and adulteress remained in Spain, their money ran out; from fear of the Inquisition they fled and came to the holy congregation of London. The husband came there and divorced her, then proceeded to his brothers, where he survived on charity. Because of the suffering he endured from the loss of his wife and his money, he finally died of terrible illnesses. In his confession at the moment of death he declared that he forgives everyone who angered or offended him with the exception of the adulterer and his wife, the adulteress.

When some time had passed this adulterer came to live where he now is. One of the zealous [persons close to the cantor] ran into him, and said to him in the middle of the city street, "Who brought an evil adulterer like this to this country? He must be expelled!" But the work of Satan succeeded for [the adulterer]. He found another evil man of his own sort to support him. That man advised [the adulterer] in his own manner, and with the efforts of one of his wife's relatives managed to get an affidavit from one of the hakhams reading as follows:

> I, the undersigned, attest that I am urged in the name of [the adulterer] to resolve the penitence he must perform and uphold concerning the persistence of grave sins he has transgressed. For he has found himself contrite and remorseful, agreeing with complete acquiescence never again to perform sins like these. Among the other things I told him to do was to go to his regular synagogue, ascend the pulpit, and publicly beg forgiveness of God with a broken heart as he implores remission of his sins; and [he must ask forgiveness] of the whole congregation for the desecration he caused with them. He must let his beard grow out for a set period; and in his regular synagogue he must always sit in a spot lower than the rest, etc. In order that the matter be known in every place it should, I have signed this with my own hand in the holy congregation of so-and-so, on the fifteenth day of Tammuz, 5485 [1725].

Everything mentioned here was written in foreign [la'az; i.e., Spanish] script and language. The name of the hakham, signed in Hebrew, is Simeon ben Jacob [again, a pseudonym].

Now, here is the text of the request for forgiveness he pronounced, according to a witness. He ascended the pulpit and declared:

> I come as a penitent to beg forgiveness of all Israel and from this holy congregation, for the sin I committed against the blessed God. I therefore ask absolution with a contrite and pleading heart. From this day forth I will act as a proper Jew, upholding the commandments of the holy Torah and of the hakhamim. And, I will pay the cost for penitence assigned me [presumably, restoration of the money he stole]. Peace be to Israel.

Below this is written: "I, the undersigned, along with the cantor of the holy congregation of Beth Jacob, confirm that this man fulfilled all that is stated above, in order that the world may know the truth. I sign in the holy congregation of so-and-so this day, the second of Av 5428 [1728]."

Based on these statements, a certain hakham, a rabbi near that city, was asked whether this man could be called up to ascend to the Torah, inasmuch as the man had done all these evil things mentioned. [The hakham] responded, "You may call him to the Torah, for he has already been confirmed by a hakham to be a penitent." On his authority they would call the man up to the Torah on any Sabbath he might put in an appearance at synagogue; for he was never habitual about his synagogue attendance as the rabbi who oversaw his penitence had stipulated for him in the abovementioned conditions. In the place he lived he would shave his beard with a blade, even on the intermediate festival days, contrary to his obligation in his request for forgiveness. In addition, he would sell in his shop on the holy Sabbath.

One day—and the reason can only be from God—a brother of the wronged man, now deceased, came to the place where the adulterer lived. He was an old man of eighty-two years, from an excellent family. When this elderly blood-redeemer saw the adulterer holding his head high, *performing the actions of Zimri and demanding the reward of Pinhas* [Numbers 25 and BT Sotah 22b]—being called to the Torah in synagogue like any proper Jew, holding the Torah for Kol Nidre, and other such matters that showed him honor, *like a gentile that had done righteously* [Isaiah 58:2]—his heart pounded within him. He cried,

> Where is God? Is there no Lord over Israel? Where are the Heavens? Who has seen such a thing? Who has heard such a thing?
>
> For, the man continues his defiance. He is not adhering to all he had promised in the terms of his pardon reproduced above. When he committed to paying the cost of the penitence prepared for him, it is obvious that this payment was necessary in order to be [reconciled] with God and man against whom he sinned. Concerning his repentance before God, whatever he did is done, since he did it according to the instructions of a hakham.

But we do not see that his penitence for sins committed toward his fellow man has been fulfilled.

For he has sinned against my brother and me by tainting us. The bad name he has given us, and the money he stole from us (for *blood touches money*) caused my brother to die from distress. At the moment of his death, he said that he forgives everyone except this adulterer, so-and-so, etc. Everyone knows that these transgressions between man and his fellow man are not atoned for by Yom Kippur, but only when the wronged person has been appeased. Now, my brother is dead, but I am alive, and none of my other brothers has seen any appeasement offered to us. What do we care for the notarized writ of his repentance that he brought from the rabbi who arranged it for him, or his request for forgiveness from the pulpit? None of it has any relevance to private sins he has committed toward his fellow man, whether they are known or hidden. I therefore demand that he not be called up to the Torah or be given any other religious honors until he returns that which he stole and embezzled from my dead brother; and he goes with a group of people to ask forgiveness at his grave three separate times as the Torah requires; and he upholds that to which he swore and committed in the penance he requested—that is, to keep the commandments of the Torah and those of the sages, which he transgresses (as was mentioned above). Only then can he be treated like other Jews and called a penitent. . . .

[The people turn to the hakham who arranged the penitence. He explains and upholds his actions with various citations from rabbinic law. Another hakham steps forward, however, and repudiates all the arguments made by the other one. He adds:]

What will the gentiles say? That the slightest penitence will excuse transgressions of this severity! Therefore, the opinion of he who is jealous for his God prevails in all aspects in favor of the old man's demands, while that evil man is responsible on all counts. . . .

[Confronted with these conflicting opinions, the community determines to ask various hakhamim in the region and follow the majority opinion. Their letter is signed, "This day, Friday, of the portion *Speak to the congregation of Israel and tell them, you will be holy* [Leviticus 19:2] . . . in the year . . . 5492 (1732).]

Response: [The Mantua rabbinical court whose response is recorded in the text sides strongly with the dead cantor's aged brother and excoriates the alleged penitent.]

39

A SLAVE AMONG THE WARS IN BELGRADE
(BELGRADE, LATE SEVENTEENTH CENTURY)

(Hakham Joseph Almosnino, *Edut be-Yehosef,* vol. 2, #20)

Introduction

The background to this case is the series of wars between the European Habsburg Empire and the Muslim Ottoman Empire that raged throughout the early modern period. The wars were particularly fierce in the Balkans at the time of this responsum, presumably written between 1686 and Hakham Almosnino's death in 1689. The Ottomans besieged Vienna in 1683, and, while failing to capture the seat of the Habsburgs, threw a dire fear into the hearts of European Christians. The Europeans redoubled their efforts against the Turks, pushing them back from Vienna. In 1684 they laid siege to the Turks at Budapest, which had been held by the Ottomans since 1541, and captured it in 1686 (the Jews sided with the Turks).

The balance of power was slowly shifting away from the Ottomans toward the Habsburgs at this time. In 1687, after the Ottomans lost Budapest, an enormous battle occurred at Mohács, a city located between Budapest and Belgrade. The Ottoman army was partially disbanded and the angry soldiers headed south toward Belgrade, which was the largest fortress in the region. There was soon a full-fledged rebellion against the sultan. The Habsburgs tried to pursue their advantage and laid siege to Belgrade in 1688. They captured the city, but in 1690 it fell again to the Ottomans. This is the tumultuous setting behind the question at hand.

This question tells us some things about social conditions in Belgrade. Jews, it seems, managed to negotiate a tightrope between the forces, though they clearly saw themselves as subjects of the sultan. To maintain their safety, they had agreed not to buy captured slaves so as to avoid the religious conflicts caused by the Torah law that slaves must convert to Judaism—partially while in servitude, and fully when they are freed. Reuben apparently breached the agreement.

Jews are seen in this document to be slave owners like everyone else, but the attitudes toward slavery exhibited by both Jews and non-Jews are instructive. The girl is removed from her abusive environment, and, as one kidnapped in childhood, is able to petition for her freedom from the gentile courts (though it is not clear if these are Muslim or Christian). It is also interesting that she has her own money with which to buy her freedom.

The conditions under which Simeon ultimately marries the converted woman attest to the lowly state of a converted slave in Jewish society—she is clearly classified at the very bottom of the social hierarchy. In a bizarre way, the match between the captured woman and Simeon becomes mutually desirable. Though he had sexually abused her when she was a child, she needs him to achieve some kind of status and security in the Jewish community. He needs her to oversee his household because circumstances have (justly, we might feel) thrown him, too, to the bottom of Jewish society. As a Jewish male, he always has enough standing that someone will be willing to marry him. The only thing standing in the way of this woeful couple is the fact that Simeon's earlier liberties with the captured woman are well known and might cause the rabbinate to forbid their marriage now.

The document is difficult to interpret in some places because of a combination of foreign terms, apparent printing errors, and pronoun confusion.

Bibliography: Bashan, *Captivity and Ransom*; Davis, *Christian Slaves*; Parvev, *Habsburgs and Ottomans*.

The following event occurred. For many years, while our sultan (may God raise him up) was at peace and had good relations with the Caesar [the Holy Roman Emperor], it was normal that Muslims called *Jitta*, from the town of Bodon [Buda or Ofen; now Budapest] and its environs, would kidnap subjects of the Caesar from his cities to hold them for ransom. [If they were not redeemed] they would sell them as male and female slaves. Similarly, the Caeasar's men, called *katonas* [soldiers] would do the same thing to the Muslims, while the two kings turned a blind eye. Sometimes, too, the Muslims would illegally kidnap each other, ransoming people like bandits from the towns and cities that pay tax to the sultan, called *Re'aya*, and selling them in secret for their own enrichment. For this reason, the sultan (may God raise him up) decreed that anyone

buying a male or female slave from the lands of the Caesar and their environs must obtain a written affidavit, called *fingia*. It was also a law of
the country that nobody should buy slaves, be they male, female, or children, who are of a different religion, for fear that Muslim captives might
be converted to their [Christian] faith [?].

Now, at the time mentioned, the Muslims captured a young gentile
girl, about seven or eight years of age, and sold her to Reuben. While she
was still growing up in his home, a rumor spread in town that she was
sleeping with Simeon—and she was really just a girl! Eventually, he
[Reuben] brought her here and sold her to Levi, in whose house she remained for many years. This Levi died, leaving behind a minor daughter
as his heiress. After a time, this woman slave petitioned her mistress to
manumit her in the gentiles' court, called *Azhatalhama*. For, if she requests before the *Azhatalhama* to return to her nation and her God, nobody may prevent her, for such is the ordinance of the government. Her
mistress was satisfied to do her bidding, but with the condition that she
redeem herself with money that she had [i.e., buy her freedom].

At that time they came to ask my opinion. . . . [Hakham Almosnino
mediates the manumission arrangement in order to sidestep some technicalities of Jewish law, and it is all settled.] After this they went to the gentile court. Her mistress made the following declaration before them: "I
hereby release her . . ."; and it was written in a court protocol. A day or
two later, the two of them called upon me to convert her and immerse
her [in a ritual bath] for the purpose of making her a free woman. Before
two other rabbinic judges, her mistress, and ourselves, she was immersed
for the purpose of making her a free woman; thus she declared three
times explicitly, accepting upon herself the Jewish faith as the Sages say.

Something over two years later, the accused Simeon came here from
Bodon as a widower. Here he married a proper woman, for he would
never have considered marrying this converted woman. After about three
years, his second wife also died, and he was reduced to the most abject
poverty, unclothed and lacking absolutely everything. He could not even
find a lame or blind woman who would marry him. He remained a widower for two years, until this converted woman came, and, through
monetary appeasement, she arrived at an agreement with him that he
would marry her. Since he could not find anyone else to marry him, as
was mentioned, he was satisfied to take her.

One of the matchmakers, pretending he was not a matchmaker, asked
me whether this woman was allowed to marry without a certificate of
manumission. I answered that, in consulting my notes, I remembered
that she did not need one, as I explained above [because of the way her
freedom had been arranged through the hakham himself]. This match-

maker asked further, "I have heard that this Simeon wants to marry her."
And I, ignorant of his purpose, responded to him, "Let it be so, and if he
marries her [the court] would not separate them. Nevertheless, as a
proposition it does not look heaven-sent, since he was accused of taking
advantage of her in Bodon." It appears to me that the matchmaker went
through this [ruse] in order that I would not conceal the facts of the law
from him.

A month later, the matter was brought before me as a *fait accompli*—
this suspected individual [Simeon] had married her before witnesses.
Now I have been asked by the leaders of the minions of Israel, the es-
teemed notables representing the congregation (may God preserve it),
what to do. Does she need a certificate of manumission? And do we force
this suspect man to divorce her?

Response: [Hakham Almosnino says it is an ugly case, but that the
woman does not need a certificate, and the couple are permitted to remain married.]

40

A SEXUALLY ABUSED WIFE (OTTOMAN EMPIRE, LATE SEVENTEENTH CENTURY)

(Hakham Jacob de Boton, *Edut be-Ya'akov,* #31)

Introduction

Early modern Sephardic responsa are replete with cases of sexual misdeeds—homosexuality, bigamy, infidelity, and others. This fact should be understood to reflect that the vast majority of Jews married, had children, and led devoted family lives. Only abberant cases were cause for comment and concern. Here the woman is extremely naive and has apparently never been informed by her mother or other female relatives what to expect in bed. It only occurs to her to report the matter to her father when the husband stops sleeping with her altogether, which she recognizes as abnormal behavior.

This is the type of question that reveals aspects of Sephardic Jewish life that could not be known from other sources. Only the rabbis would be privy to private secrets of this magnitude. The question also offers us some insight into the role of an Ottoman Jewish father in the life of his married daughter. He still sees himself as the protector of his grown child, though he seems to blame her for not being more assertive. Jewish law, for its part, has stipulations for the case of a rebellious wife who will not sleep with her husband, but is less prepared for abuses by the male, which must have been far more prevalent but less often prosecuted. Note that this case would not have been put before the rabbis without the intercession of a male, usually as in this case the woman's father.

This document, full of elaborate usages and containing numerous grammatical errors, was unusually difficult to translate.

Bibliography: Ben-Sasson et al., *Studies in a Rabbinic Family;* Ben-Naeh, "Moshko the Jew."

I was asked for a righteous judgment concerning a woman of embittered spirit who claims that her husband, *a chief man among his people,** abused her, because every time he was intimate with her his manner was to *bend his bow like an enemy* [Lamentations 2:4]—to lie with her in the manner of homosexual relations [i.e., anally] rather than in the normal manner. She suffered and was deeply troubled, increasingly silent and depressed by it. Now, her father would come occasionally to check on how his daughter was doing, and he saw that her demeanor had changed. He asked her the reason she seemed the saddest *of all the daughters of my city* [Lamentations 3:51], and she answered modestly, saying nothing. But when her days of suffering had gone on a long time, he [the husband] stopped sleeping with her altogether. Finally, she called her father in tears and begged him to *bring her soul out of prison* [Psalms 42:8], for she could suffer it no longer. Her mouth was agape with anguish, and she said to him, "He has been doing it to me this way and thus, from the very day I knew him."

Upon hearing this, her father *spit before her* [Numbers 12:14] and demanded to know why she had not told him of all this before. She answered that she had held back until now because she had known nothing of homosexual relations, and assumed that *this is the way of they that are foolish* [Psalms 49:14]—that all people suffer thus. "For that reason I did not know to ask. I was too humiliated and sunk within myself to let my *voice be heard abroad* [acc. to Isaiah 42:2]. *My eye affected my soul because of all the daughters of my city* [Lamentations 3:51], the daughters of Israel who live with their husbands and speak nothing about it. When he stopped sleeping with me completely, I told you about it, and here is the kindness you must do for me: *Bring my soul out of prison* [Psalms 142:8], out of this house." She points the finger at [the husband] and says she will die if she is forced to remain in the house with him, while her father is burning up with irritation.

When he [the father] heard all this, he immediately removed her from [the husband's] house and settled her in his own home, where she eats his bread, drinks his wine, and has been supported entirely by him until this day, when they came themselves before this rabbinic court. Her father *goes on his way weeping* [Psalms 126:6] about the whole matter.

Any wise person must ask himself whether a woman in these circum-

* The passage, Leviticus 21:4, is speaking about the *kohanim* (priests), the descendants of Aaron, the high priest and brother of Moses. It reads, *He shall not defile himself, being a chief man among his people, to profane himself.* The author may be suggesting that the man in question is a *kohen*, that he is an important person, that he has defiled himself with his behavior, or any combination of these; or possibly none of them.

stances can be judged a rebellious wife who refuses to have intercourse according to the law (since she has come with this claim) or not. It must also be determined what the law says about her marriage contract [*ketubah*], dowry, and additional gifts [promised her at the wedding]. Then, too, what does the law mandate concerning the feeding and support of the woman during this entire period?

About all these matters, may the words of the righteous teacher come forth, and may he in turn be righteously treated by [God], blessed and exalted be He, amen.

Response: [In a response that strikes the modern reader as rather unsatisfying, Hakham de Boton says that no answer can be adduced until a number of factors are investigated further, including the precise manner of the events, the woman's trustworthiness as a witness, and so on. He does consider the husband an evil man and seems to take the wife's side.]

41

ON THE MANIPULATION OF WOMEN'S RIGHT TO DIVORCE (EGYPT, MID-SEVENTEENTH CENTURY)

(Hakham Moses Ben Habib, *She'elot u-Teshuvot,* vol. 1, #193)

Introduction

It goes without saying that the rights and roles of women in pre-modern cultures were radically different than they are today. Women were expected to oversee the home, raise children, and perhaps help add to the family income. Divorce was rare and usually implied extenuating circumstances. In Jewish law, the husband could not simply decide to divorce his wife for no reason, but on the other hand, the wife's ability to initiate divorce proceedings was much more limited.

Families and rabbinic courts would sometimes intervene on behalf of a suffering wife to facilitate a separation. In this fascinating case, we discover that certain Egyptian Jews found a way to make the discrepancies between Jewish and Muslim law work for them as a tool to threaten recalcitrant husbands. It was, however, a risky business. Terrible repercussions could result if the Muslims knew their courts were being manipulated in this manner.

Like the case of moneylending in Jerusalem (and in the same period), this incident features a stringent ruling that goes against earlier practices. Hakham Jacob Castro sided with the husbands in circumstances like these and forbade the method described in the document, but the rabbis who dealt with such cases could not abandon it so easily. Both the cooperative atmosphere between Jewish and Muslim courts and the strategic manipulation of that relationship by the Jews are worthy of note.

I have rephrased the question where necessary in order to render it into readable English.

Question: Some of the poor members of the nation in Egypt [do as follows]. When a man fights with his wife and their marriage is not working out, and the wife wants to divorce but the husband does not, they are not able to force him to do it through the rabbinical court. The father and other relatives of the woman will go to the gentile courts and make a claim against the husband there. They bring false witnesses who report that he has declared before them that he divorces her, saying *Tekhuni talqa batalta*—that is, according to the laws of gentile courts, any man who says those words (which mean, "Behold you are divorced from me") three times is thereafter forbidden to his wife until she marries another. After that, if she divorces the second husband, she can return to the first. This is the policy of the gentile courts.

The purpose of the woman's father and relatives in carrying out such divorces through the gentile courts is to separate them [the couple]. They formalize a document in the gentile court with the signature of the responsible [judge] that she is divorced from her husband three times [i.e., he has declared it three times] and she is therefore forbidden to be with him. The husband is thus forced to separate from his wife. When this has gone on a month or two, some Jewish conciliators come to the husband and say, "What good does it do you to leave a woman stranded? We will counsel her that you will give her a certain sum of money [presumably less than the marriage contract dictates] and free her with a writ of divorce according to the laws of Moses and Israel."

An event like this occurred many years ago, in the year [5]366 [1605/6] in Egypt, and the rabbinic court arranged a writ of divorce for her according to the laws of Moses and Israel. After she was divorced by the rabbinical court, the husband came to protest that the writ of divorce he had provided was forced upon him by the document from the gentile court, which was issued based on a falsehood: that he had divorced her thrice with [the declaration] *Tlaq al t'laata.* Therefore, the writ of divorce is void. The rabbinic court that arranged the writ of divorce freed her without heeding the husband's protests because his divorce from her was not forced on him by a *Jewish* court.

The Rika"sh [Rabbi Jacob Castro], however, in his manuscript responsum #132, disputes with that rabbinic court and says the law favors the husband, who is considered coerced, since it was testified in a gentile court that he had divorced her thrice, and he is forbidden to her by the laws of the gentile courts. This is the substance of that earlier controversy.

The later judges in Egypt, when it was clear to them that this method was being used . . . would trouble their courts to investigate the man's original intentions. . . . And thus the tradition spread in the land of Egypt to heed the words of the Rika"sh [and not allow divorces through this subterfuge].

Now something terrible has occurred. Against the husband's will it was written [in a gentile court] that he had divorced [his wife] with *Tlaq al t'laata*. He was forbidden to his wife and other demands were made of him. In his anguish the husband became an apostate. The apostate and his Jewish wife remained separated from each other. Then conciliators approached him and promised him money if he would divorce her by the laws of Israel, and he was persuaded. The rabbinic court told them that they should try to obtain an affidavit from [the court of?] ten saying she is permitted to him, in order that it not appear that he was coerced to give the divorce, and thus to uphold their tradition of adhering to the views of the Rika"sh [that the husband can not be forced]. This delayed matters.

Meanwhile, the divorced woman and her father heard that someone planned to reveal their secret—that the whole thing was deception and fabrication—to the gentile court; and the father and the entire household of the divorced woman were constrained to apostatize out of fear and danger. All these burdens of the period made [the rabbis] look for a way to modify the decision of the Rika"sh. [To conform to Rika"sh they had to obtain the extra affidavit that they were permitted to each other, a document which could endanger them if the gentile courts saw it]. For this reason the great rabbinic court of Egypt, may it be established in righteousness, wished to investigate whether the view of Rika"sh must be heeded when an event like this occurs.

[The response is missing.]

42

A MOTHER'S QUEST FOR JUSTICE

(BELGRADE, 1698)

(Hakham Solomon Amarillo, *Kerem Shlomoh*, H.M. #10)

Introduction

This case contains some familiar themes. The backstory is clear: a woman's son was murdered, the murderer was known, but without paying bribes he would not be brought to justice. So, as we have observed repeatedly, justice in the early modern world cost money. Another familiar theme is the man who must be hired to help, and his attempt to take advantage of the woman who hired him.

Other aspects of the case are compelling. The woman is clearly somewhat wealthy or she would not be able to expend money so aggressively for her cause. She is also independent minded and very dedicated to her pursuit of justice for her lost son.

Question: Rachel, widow of Jacob, appointed Mr. Jacob Alexandri (may God protect him), with absolute responsibility and complete representative powers, to go distribute money and bribes among the officials in order to avenge the blood of her son that had been spilled on the ground. [He was to do it] whether the cost was great or small, and he could not say, "You sent me to repair, etc."* It was all agreed with guarantees for all expenses, as is laid out explicitly in writing in the document of authorization that was brought before us. All this was carried out by the said Jacob, who went with alacrity to fulfill her orders. He distributed as much money and bribes among the authorities as was necessary to

---

* BT Ketubot 85r and elsewhere: "You sent me to repair, not to damage." This is a claim that an agent might make to explain why he did not carry through his mission, in a case where his judgment suggested that the mission would cause damage rather than good. Rachel's point is that Jacob Alexandri must not find any excuse not to carry out his charge.

achieve vengeance for the blood of that wretched man that had been spilled on the ground.

Now, the said Jacob has come with the document of authorization in his hand to file suit against the said Rachel for 300 *grush* which she still owes him for his expenditures. She claims she already paid him all the money for his expenses when he returned from his journey, according to his own statement.

Is Jacob creditable if he swears an oath [that Rachel owes him the money], or not? May your reward be doubled and redoubled by Heaven.

[The question is followed by a précis of the document of authorization, written partly in Hebrew and partly in Spanish. Rachel commits everything she has to this mission, "down to the last dime." She even pledges her marriage contract and the very clothes off her back to pay whatever is necessary for justice, calling it a "sanctification of the Divine Name."]

Response: [Hakham Amarillo declares that Jacob has no grounds for swearing an oath and collecting more money, since the account had already been settled according to the terms of the contract.]

43

THE RUNAWAY GROOM (BAYONNE, 1742)

(Hakham David Meldola, *Divrei David*, #73-76)

Introduction

Clandestine marriages were apparently a problem in both Jewish and European society throughout the early modern period. This was undoubtedly another function of the growing freedom to create and manipulate identities. As we learn at the end of this responsum, the French government had ordinances forbidding unsanctioned unions. Rules about clandestine marriage can be found in the 1507 Venetian *kahal* statutes and in numerous communal rule books from that time onward. The main reason that the establishment objected to such alliances was that they almost always involved two partners who were "in love" but not socially or economically well matched. This can enlighten us a great deal about how the nature of marriage was perceived.

In the present case, a young man from a well-off family became infatuated with a woman from a poorer and perhaps more promiscuous background. The woman's family actively aided and abetted the clandestine relationship. They were anxious to see the union take place because it was highly advantageous to them. In order to facilitate this end, they brought in the usual suspects of the Western Sephardic milieu: young men of bad reputation who lived on the margins of the community. In southern France, which was itself somewhat on the margins of the Jewish world, individuals of this stripe were undoubtedly not hard to turn up.

Bibliography: Bonfil, "Aspects of the Social and Spiritual Life"; Goldish, "Passion at the Periphery"; Kaplan, *Alternative Path*, chap. 12; Malino, *Sephardic Jews*.

I have come before your exalted honor to present you with the facts about what happened so that it will all be revealed and visible to you, and in light of it you can offer us a complete response, telling us your learned opinion. Teach us lessons, for you are our lifeline.

Before all else, you should know that here in the holy congregation of Nephutzot Yehudah in the city of Bayonne, which is in the kingdom of France (may God preserve it) there has been an agreement in place since long ago, backed by pain of a stringent excommunication, that no man may become engaged to a woman in secret, without the permission of their fathers. This can be seen in another agreement preserved in writing in the community's record books from the nineteenth of February in the year 5460 from creation [1700]. Here is its wording, for we were unable to find its predecessor. [Here he quotes this document and a related one from 1703, in Spanish. The latter is countersigned by the rabbis of the Amsterdam community.]

Now, the following event has occurred. The heart of a young man of the better sort strayed after his eyes, and he was seduced by some empty and worthless people to chase after an alien woman [ishah zarah] who was not fit for him or his family. They beguiled him so relentlessly with lures and inducements that one day he suddenly called together three men from the marketplace, without telling them for what purpose he needed them, and had the girl brought before them. The girl's mother took a ring from a box and gave it to the young man, who then used it to become engaged to her, without ever receiving permission from his father or relatives. This is all detailed below, in the testimonies received from these witnesses.

With this engagement, but without waiting the seven days of [menstrual] cleanness, and without the girl immersing herself for the commanded immersion [in the ritual bath] as the law requires, they seduced the young man to sleep with her while she was still in her menstrual state. They hid him in the home of his fiancée for about twenty days, at which point the young man ran away from her house and returned to his father's home, begging forgiveness for all these things he had done without his permission or desire. He claimed that everything he had done was because of the seductions with which they had beguiled him; that they had forced him and misled him, and he regretted the whole matter. He now wished to move someplace far away so as not to be led astray by her again, etc. But after only a few days had passed, his impulses coerced him back to his earlier error in the home of this prostitute. They held him in her house and hid him about another two months, at which point a rumor began circulating around the city that the girl had become pregnant by her illicit relations with the fiancé.

Now the brothers and mother of the girl went and gathered in their house seven empty and unscrupulous men from among the Jewish sinners of the city. One of them had been caught eating and drinking on Yom Kippur; two more were apprehended stealing money from the permanent charity box for the Land of Israel at the synagogue; and two others were apprehended robbing the homes of community members in the mists and darkness of night. With everyone together [including the brothers] they came out to a total of ten, and with them they completed the wedding by reciting the seven blessings. Some days later, one of them composed a marriage contract [*shtar ketubah*] in which he wrote that the dowry the bride would be bringing to the groom from the house of her father was such-and-such a sum, calculated as the equivalent of 10,000 liters in the French currency. Three other discontented types were induced by the money offered them to sign the marriage contract before witnesses. One of them did not even know how to write at all; the others held his hand and guided him, holding the pen in his hand in such a way that he "signed" his name.

When this news reached the ears of the community leaders, they announced in all the synagogues of the city that these people [the couple? the witnesses?] were transgressors who were excommunicated and removed from the congregation of the people of Israel. It was forbidden for any Jew to sit within four cubits [about six feet] of them lest he or she trespass the excommunication and decree of the holy congregation, as mentioned above; and because they were bodily sinners of Israel in whom there is no faith or Jewishness, etc.

[There follow the three testimonies of witnesses to the secret wedding.]

I thus wish to ask you if this engagement has any validity, and whether the young man must release her with a proper writ of divorce before she can marry someone else. May your good word come concerning all of it. . . . Written and signed here in the holy congregation Nephutzot Yehudah in the city of Bayonne which is in the kingdom of France (may God preserve it), the second of February in the year 5502 [1742] from creation, the humble Moses de Robles.

Response: [The first response, listed as #74, comes not from Hakham Meldola but from Hakham Moses Sinai, who gives various reasons that the engagement is null and void: the ring, which constitutes the legal gift for sealing the engagement, was not properly acquired first by the groom; the witnesses were not valid; the community statute that forbids secret marriages; and so on. Hakham Sinai mentions that there had never before been such problems in Bayonne, where everyone kept the laws strictly, so the current hakhamim should take strong measures against these transgressors. He also chastises them for not being able to answer such a simple question themselves. Afterward, in #75, Hakham de Robles responds to this letter and adds other reasons of his own to nullify the engagement, including this one.]

(#75) . . . Another reason to nullify engagements of this type is because [of the talmudic principle that] "The laws of the state are law." For it is also a statute of the kingdom in all these lands that no man under the age of twenty-five, no matter who he is, may marry a woman without the permission of their [respective] fathers. The punishment for anyone who transgresses this law is just short of death.

[In #76 Hakham Meldola gives his response to all this, in which he agrees with the general conclusion to nullify the engagement. In typical rabbinic style, however, after apologizing for not being focused because his father is very ill, he writes a forty-two-page treatise dealing in depth with every aspect of the question and answers.]

BIBLIOGRAPHY

Journals

Jerusalem (Quarterly) (On the city of Jerusalem)
Mi-Mizrah u-Mi-Ma'arav ("East and Maghreb")
Pe'amim (Hebrew with English summaries)
Sepharad (Spanish and other European languages)
Sefunot (Hebrew with English summaries)
Shalem (Hebrew with English summaries; on history of the Land of Israel)

Works in English and European Languages

Angel, Marc D. *The Jews of Rhodes: The History of a Sephardic Community.* New York: Sepher-Hermon Press, 1978.

Arbel, Benjamin. *Trading Nations: Jews and Venetians in the Early Modern Eastern Mediterranean.* Leiden: Brill, 1995.

Assis, Yom-Tov, and Yosef Kaplan, eds. *Jews and Conversos at the Time of the Expulsion.* Jerusalem: Zalman Shazar Center for Jewish History, 1999 [English and Hebrew].

Ayaso Martínez, José Ramón. "Tarsis, 'Aspamia', Sefarad: mitos antiguos y modernos acerca de la antigüedad de la diáspora judía en la península ibérica." *Miscelánea de Estudios Árabes y Hebraicos* 40:2 (1991): 143–80.

Baer, Yitzhak. *A History of the Jews in Christian Spain.* 2 volumes. Philadelphia: Jewish Publication Society, 1962.

Barnai, Jacob. "'Blood Libels' in the Ottoman Empire of the Fifteenth to Nineteenth Centuries." In *Antisemitism Through the Ages,* ed. Shmuel Almog, 189–94. Oxford: Pergamon Press, 1988.

Barnett, Richard, and Walter Schwab, eds. *The Sephardi Heritage, Volume II: The Western Sephardim.* Grendon, Northants: Gibralter Books, 1989.

Beinart, Haim. *Conversos on Trial.* Hispania Judaica no. 3. Jerusalem: Magnes Press, 1981.

———. "The Records of the Inquisition: A Source of Jewish and Converso History." *Proceedings of the Israel Academy of Sciences and Humanities* 2 (1968): 211–27.

———, ed. *The Sephardi Legacy.* 2 vols. Jerusalem: Magnes Press, 1992.

Benbassa, Esther, and Aron Rodrigue. *The Jews of the Balkans: The Judeo-Spanish Community, 15th to 20th Centuries.* Oxford: Blackwell, 1995.

Ben-Naeh, Yaron. "Blond, Tall, With Honey-Colored Eyes: Jewish Ownership of Slaves in the Ottoman Empire." *Jewish History* (forthcoming)

———. "Honor and Its Meaning Among Ottoman Jews." *Jewish Social Studies* 11:2 (2005): 19–50.

———. "Moshko the Jew and His Gay Friends: Same-Sex Sexual Relations in Ottoman Jewish Society." *Journal of Early Modern History* 9:1–2 (2005): 79–105.

———. "Poverty, Paupers and Poor Relief in Ottoman Jewish Society." *Revue des études juives* 163: 1–2 (2004): 151–92.

Ben-Sasson, M., W. Z. Harvey, Y. Ben-Na'eh, and Z. Zohar, eds. *Studies in a Rabbinic Family: The de Botons.* Jerusalem: Misgav Yerushalayim, 1998 [English and Hebrew].

Bernardini, Paolo, and Norman Fiering, eds. *The Jews and the Expansion of Europe to the West, 1450–1800.* New York: Berghahn Books/John Carter Brown Library, 2001.

Bodian, Miriam. *Hebrews of the Portuguese Nation: Conversos and Community in Early Modern Amsterdam.* Bloomington: Indiana University Press, 1997.

———. "The 'Portuguese' Dowry Societies in Venice and Amsterdam: A Case Study in Communal Differentiation within the Marrano Diaspora." *Italia* 6 (1987): 30–61.

Bowman, Steven B. *The Jews of Byzantium, 1204–1453.* Tuscaloosa: University of Alabama Press, 1985.

Braude, Benjamin. "The Rise and Fall of Salonika Woollens, 1500–1650: Technology Transfer and Western Competition." *Mediterranean Historical Review* 6:2 (1991): 216–36. Reprinted in Ginio, *Jews, Christians, and Muslims,* 216–36.

Braudel, Fernand. *The Mediterranean and the Mediterranean World in the Age of Philip II.* 2 vols. New York: Harper and Row, 1972.

Brooks, Andrée Aelion. *The Woman Who Defied Kings: The Life and Times of Doña Gracia Nasi, A Jewish Leader During the Renaissance.* St. Paul, Minn.: Paragon House, 2002.

Burton, Robert. *Anatomy of Melancholy.* London, 1621.

Carlebach, Elisheva. *The Pursuit of Heresy: Rabbi Moses Hagiz and the Sabbatian Controversies.* New York: Columbia University Press, 1990.

Cohen, Mark R. *Under Crescent and Cross: The Jews in the Middle Ages.* Princeton: Princeton University Press, 1994.

Corcos, David. *Studies in the History of the Jews of Morocco.* Jerusalem: Reuben Mass, 1976 [English, French, and Hebrew].

Cowan, Alexander, ed. *Mediterranean Urban Culture, 1400–1700.* Exeter: University of Exeter Press, 2000.

Dan, Joseph. "'No Evil Descends from Heaven': Sixteenth-Century Jewish Concepts of Evil." In *Jewish Thought in the Sixteenth Century,* ed. B. D. Cooperman, 89–105. Cambridge, Mass.: Harvard University Press, 1983.

David, Avraham. *To Come to the Land: Immigration and Settlement in Sixteenth-Century Eretz Yisrael.* Tuscaloosa: University of Alabama Press, 1999.

Davis, Natalie Zemon. *Fiction in the Archives: Pardon Tales and Their Tellers in Sixteenth Century France.* Stanford: Stanford University Press, 1987.

————. *The Return of Martin Guerre.* Cambridge, Mass.: Harvard University Press, 1983.

Davis, Robert C. *Christian Slaves, Muslim Masters: White Slavery in the Mediterranean, the Barbary Coast, and Italy, 1500–1800.* New York: Palgrave Macmillan, 2003.

Davis, Robert C., and Benjamin Ravid, eds. *The Jews of Early Modern Venice.* Baltimore: Johns Hopkins University Press, 2001.

Eliav-Feldon, Miriam. "Invented Identities: Credulity in the Age of Prophecy and Exploration." *Journal of Early Modern History* 1:3 (1999): 203–32.

Fellous, Sonia, ed. *Juifs et musulmans en Tunisie: Fraternité et déchirements.* Paris: Somogy éditions d'art, 2003.

Finkel, Avraham Yaakov. *The Responsa Anthology.* Northvale, N.J.: Jason Aronson, 1990.

Frank, Daniel, and Matt Goldish, eds. *Rabbinic Culture and Its Critics: Jewish Authority, Dissent, and Heresy in Medieval and Early Modern Times.* Detroit: Wayne State University Press, 2008.

Freehof, Solomon B. *A Treasury of Responsa: A Selection of Important Rabbinic Correspondence During the Last Thousand Years.* Philadelphia: Jewish Publication Society, 1963.

Galante, Abraham. *Histoire des Juifs de Turquie.* 9 vols. Istanbul: Isis, 1988.

Gampel, Benjamin R., ed. *Crisis and Creativity in the Sephardic World, 1391–1648.* New York: Columbia University Press, 1997.

García-Arenal, Mercedes, and Gerard Wiegers. *A Man of Three Worlds: Samuel Pallache, A Moroccan Jew in Catholic and Protestant Europe.* Baltimore: Johns Hopkins University Press, 1999.

Gerber, Haim. *Economy and Society in an Ottoman City: Bursa, 1600–1700.* Jerusalem: Hebrew University Press, 1988.

Gerber, Jane S. *Jewish Society in Fez, 1450–1700: Studies in Communal and Economic Life.* Leiden: Brill, 1980.

————. *The Jews of Spain: A History of the Sephardic Experience.* New York: Free Press, 1992.

Ginio, Alisa Meyuhas, ed. *Jews, Christians, and Muslims in the Mediterranean World After 1492.* London: Frank Cass, 1992.

Goffman, Daniel. *Izmir and the Levantine World, 1550–1650.* Seattle: University of Washington Press, 1990.

Goitein, Shelomo Dov. *A Mediterranean Society: The Jewish Communities of the Arab World as Portrayed in the Documents of the Cairo Geniza.* 6 vols. Berkeley: University of California Press, 1967.

Goldish, Matt. "Jews, Christians and *Conversos*: Rabbi Solomon Aailion's Struggles in the Portuguese Community of London." *Journal of Jewish Studies* 45:2 (1994): 227–57.

————. "Passion at the Periphery: The Contexts of a Clandestine Converso Conjunction." *Zutot* 1 (2001): 124–32.

————. *The Sabbatean Prophets.* Cambridge, Mass.: Harvard University Press, 2004.

Goldman, Israel M. *The Life and Times of Rabbi David Ibn Abi Zimra.* New York: Jewish Theological Seminary, 1970.

Goodblatt, Morris S. *Jewish Life in Turkey in the XVIth Century, as Reflected in the Legal Writings of Samuel de Medina.* New York: Jewish Theological Seminary, 1952.

Graizbord, David L. *Souls in Dispute: Converso Identities in Iberia and the Jewish Diaspora, 1580–1700.* Philadelphia: University of Pennsylvania Press, 2004.

Gross, Abraham. *Iberian Jewry From Twilight to Dawn: The World of Rabbi Abraham Saba.* Leiden: Brill, 1995.

Haas, Peter. *Responsa: Literary History of a Rabbinic Genre.* Atlanta: Scholars Press, 1996.

Hacker, Joseph. "The Intellectual Activity of the Jews of the Ottoman Empire During the Sixteenth and Seventeenth Centuries." In *Jewish Thought in the Seventeenth Century,* ed. Isadore Twersky and Bernard Septimus, 95–136. Cambridge, Mass.: Harvard University Press, 1987.

Haliczer, Stephen, ed and trans. *Inquisition and Society in Early Modern Europe.* Totowa, N.J.: Barnes and Noble, 1987.

Hirschberg, H. Z. *History of the Jews in North Africa.* 2 vols. Leiden: Brill, 1974.

Histoire communautaire, histoire plurielle: la communauté juive de Tunisie. Manouba: Centre de Pulbications Universitaire, 1999.

Homza, Lu Ann. *The Spanish Inquisition, 1478–1614: An Anthology of Sources.* Indianapolis: Hackett Publishing Company, 2006.

Horowitz, Elliott, and Moises Orfali, eds. *The Mediterranean and the Jews,* vol. 2. Ramat Gan: Bar-Ilan University Press, 2002.

Idel, Moshe. "Saturn and Sabbatai Tzevi: A New Approach to Sabbateanism." In *Toward the Millennium: Messianic Expectations from the Bible to Waco,* ed. Peter Schäfer and Mark Cohen, 173–202. Leiden: Brill, 1998.

Israel, Jonathan. *Diasporas within a Diaspora: Jews, Crypto-Jews and the World Maritime Empires (1540–1740).* Leiden: Brill, 2002.

———. *European Jewry in the Age of Mercantilism, 1550–1750,* 3rd ed. Oxford: Littman Library, 1998.

Jacobs, Louis. *Theology in the Responsa.* London: Routledge and Kegan Paul, 1975.

Kagan, Richard L., and Abigail Dyer. *Inquisitorial Inquiries: Brief Lives of Secret Jews and Other Heretics.* Baltimore: Johns Hopkins University Press, 2004.

Kamen, Henry. *Inquisition and Society in Spain in the Sixteenth and Seventeenth Centuries.* Bloomington: Indiana University Press, 1985.

———. *The Spanish Inquisition: A Historical Revision.* New Haven: Yale University Press, 1997.

Kaplan, Yosef. *An Alternative Path to Modernity: The Sephardi Diaspora in Western Europe.* Leiden: Brill, 2000.

Kasher, Asa. "How Important Was Menasseh ben Israel?" In *Menasseh ben Israel and His World,* ed. Y. Kaplan et al., 220–27. Leiden: Brill, 1989.

Katz, David S. "English Charity and Jewish Qualms: The Rescue of the Ashkenazi Community of Seventeenth-Century Jerusalem." In *Jewish History: Es-*

says in Honour of Chimen Abramsky, ed. A. Rapoport-Albert and S. J. Zipperstein, 245–66. London: P. Halban, 1988.

———. *The Jews in the History of England, 1485–1850.* Oxford: Clarendon Press, 1994.

Kedourie, Elie. *Spain and the Jews: The Sephardi Experience 1492 and After.* London: Thames and Hudson, 1992.

Kinross, Lord. *The Ottoman Centuries: The Rise and Fall of the Turkish Empire.* New York: HarperCollins, 1977.

Kobler, Franz. *Letters of Jews Through the Ages.* 2 vols. New York: Horovitz, 1952.

Kottek, S. S., and L. Garcia-Ballester, eds. *Medicine and Medical Ethics in Medieval and Early Modern Spain: An Intercultural Approach.* Jerusalem: Magnes Press, 1996.

Lamdan, Ruth. *A Separate People: Jewish Women in Palestine, Syria, and Egypt in the Sixteenth Century.* Leiden: Brill, 2000.

Lawee, Eric. *Isaac Abarbanel's Stance Toward Tradition: Defense, Dissent, and Dialogue.* Albany: State University of New York Press, 2001.

Lazar, Moshe, and Stephen Haliczer, eds. *The Jews of Spain and the Expulsion of 1492.* Lancaster, Calif.: Labyrinthos, 1997.

Lehmann, Matthias B. *Ladino Rabbinic Literature and Ottoman Sephardic Culture.* Bloomington: Indiana University Press, 2005.

Levy, Avigdor, ed. *The Jews of the Ottoman Empire.* Princeton: Darwin Press; Washington, D.C.: Institute of Turkish Studies, 1994.

———. *Jews, Turks, Ottomans: A Shared History, Fifteenth through the Twentieth Century.* Syracuse: Syracuse University Press, 2002.

Levy, B. Barry. *Fixing God's Torah: The Accuracy of the Hebrew Bible Text in Jewish Law.* New York: Oxford University Press, 2001.

Malino, Frances. *The Sephardic Jews of Bordeaux: Assimilation and Emancipation in Revolutionary and Napoleonic France.* Tuscaloosa: University of Alabama Press, 1978.

Marcus, Jacob R. *The Jew in the Medieval World: A Source Book, 315–1791.* Reprint, New York: Atheneum, 1983.

Mazower, Mark. *Salonica, City of Ghosts: Christians, Muslims and Jews, 1430–1950.* New York: Knopf, 2005.

Meyerson, Mark D. *A Jewish Renaissance in Fifteenth Century Spain.* Princeton: Princeton University Press, 2004.

Morell, Samuel. *Precedent and Judicial Discretion: The Case of Joseph ibn Lev.* Atlanta: Scholars Press, 1991.

Nemoy, Leon. *Karaite Anthology.* New Haven: Yale University Press, 1952.

Netanyahu, B. *Don Isaac Abravanel: Statesman and Philosopher.* Philadelphia: Jewish Publication Society, 1982.

———. *The Marranos of Spain, from the Late 14th to the Early 16th Century, According to Contemporary Hebrew Sources,* 3rd ed. Ithaca, N.Y.: Cornell University Press, 1999.

———. "On the Historical Meaning of the Hebrew Sources Related to the Marranos: A Reply to Critics." In *Estudios Hispania-Judaica*, vol. 1, ed. Joseph M.

Sola-Salé, Samuel G. Armistead, and Joseph H. Silverman, 79–101. Barcelona: Purvill-Editor, 1980.

———. *The Origins of the Inquisition in Fifteenth Century Spain.* New York: Random House, 1995.

———. *Toward the Inquisition: Essays on Jewish and Converso History in Late Medieval Spain.* Ithaca, N.Y.: Cornell University Press, 1997.

Nirenberg, David. *Communities of Violence: Persecution of Minorities in the Middle Ages.* Princeton: Princeton University Press, 1996.

Noth, Albrecht. "Problems of Differentiation between Muslims and Non-Muslims: Re-reading the 'Ordinances of 'Umar' (al-Shurut al-'umariyya)." In *Muslims and Others in Early Islamic Society,* ed. Robert Hoyland. Aldershot: Ashgate, 2004.

Pamuk, Şevket. *A Monetary History of the Ottoman Empire.* Cambridge: Cambridge University Press, 2000.

Parvev, Ivan. *Habsburgs and Ottomans Between Vienna and Belgrade (1683–1739).* Boulder, Colo.: East European Monographs, 1995.

Passamaneck, Stephen M. *Insurance in Rabbinic Law.* Edinburgh: Edinburgh University Press, 1974.

Platt, P. G., ed. *Wonders, Marvels, and Monsters in Early Modern Culture.* Newark: University of Delaware Press, 1999.

Polliack, Meira, ed. *Karaite Judaism: A Guide to its History and Literary Sources.* Leiden: Brill, 2003.

Popkin, Richard H. "Christian Jews and Jewish Christians in the 17th Century." In *Jewish Christians and Christian Jews,* ed. R. H. Popkin and G. M. Weiner, 57–72. Dordrecht: Kluwer, 1994.

———. "Rabbi Nathan Shapira's Visit to Amsterdam in 1657." *Dutch Jewish History* 1 (1984): 185–205.

Pullan, Brian. *The Jews of Europe and the Inquisition of Venice, 1550–1670.* New York: Barnes and Noble, 1983.

Raphael, David, ed. *The Expulsion 1492 Chronicles: An Anthology of Medieval Chronicles Relating to the Expulsion of the Jews from Spain and Portugal.* North Hollywood: Carmi House, 1992.

Rivkin, Ellis. "The Utilization of Non-Jewish Sources for the Reconstruction of Jewish History." *Jewish Quarterly Review* N.S. 48 (1957/58): 183–203.

Roth, Cecil. *A History of the Jews in Venice.* New York: Schocken, 1975. Reprinted from *Venice.* Philadelphia: Jewish Publication Society, 1930.

———. *A History of the Marranos.* New York: Schocken, 1979.

———. "Romance at Urbino." In Roth, *Personalities and Events in Jewish History,* 275–82. Philadelphia: Jewish Publication Society, 1953.

Rozen, Minna. *A History of the Jewish Community in Istanbul: The Formative Years, 1453–1566.* Leiden: Brill, 2002.

———. *Jewish Identity and Society in the Seventeenth Century: Reflections on the Life and Work of Refael Mordekhai Malki.* Trans. G. Wachsman. Tübingen: J.C.B. Mohr (Paul Siebeck), 1992.

Ruderman, David B. *Kabbalah, Magic, and Science: The Cultural Universe of a Sixteenth-Century Jewish Physician.* Cambridge, Mass.: Harvard University Press, 1988.

———. *A Valley of Vision: The Heavenly Journey of Abraham ben Hananiah Yagel*. Philadelphia: University of Pennsylvania Press, 1990.

Sachar, Howard M. *Farewell España: The World of the Sephardim Remembered*. New York: Random House, 1995.

Scholem, Gershom. *Sabbatai Sevi: The Mystical Messiah*. Princeton: Princeton University Press, 1973.

Shmuelevits, Aryeh. *The Jews of the Ottoman Empire in the Late Fifteenth and the Sixteenth Centuries: Administrative, Economic, Legal and Social Relations as Reflected in the Responsa*. Leiden: Brill, 1984.

Stillman, Norman A. *The Jews of Arab Lands: A History and Source Book*. Philadelphia: Jewish Publication Society, 1979.

Suarez Fernandez, Luis. *Documentos acerca de la expulsion de los Judios*. Valladolid: Ediciones Aldecoa, 1964.

Toaff, Ariel, and Simon Schwarzfuchs, eds. *The Mediterranean and the Jews*, vol. 1. Ramat Gan: Bar-Ilan University Press, 1989.

Usque, Samuel. *Samuel Usque's 'Consolation for the Tribulations of Israel'*. Ed. and trans. Martin A. Cohen. Philadelphia: Jewish Publication Society, 1987.

Waddington, Raymond B., and Arthur H. Williamson, eds. *The Expulsion of the Jews: 1492 and After*. New York: Garland, 1994.

Weissberg, Victor H. "Jewish Life in Seventeenth Century Turkey as Reflected in the Responsa of Rabbi Jacob Alfandari and Rabbi Joseph Katzavi." Ph.D. dissertation, Hebrew Union College/Jewish Institute of Religion, 1970.

Werblowsky, R.J.Z. *Joseph Karo: Lawyer and Mystic*. Oxford: Oxford University Press, 1962. Reprint, Philadelphia: Jewish Publication Society, 1977.

Yerushalmi, Yosef Hayim. *From Spanish Court to Italian Ghetto: Isaac Cardoso, A Study in Seventeenth Century Marranism*. New York: Columbia University Press, 1971; Seattle: University of Washington Press, 1981.

———. *The Lisbon Massacre of 1506 and the Royal Image in the Shebet Yehudah*. Cincinnati: Hebrew Union College Press, 1976.

Yogev, Gedalia. *Diamonds and Coral: Anglo-Dutch Jews and Eighteenth-Century Trade*. Bristol: Leicester University Press, 1978.

Zafrani, Haïm. *Two Thousand Years of Jewish Life in Morocco*. Jersey City, N.J.: Ktav, 2005.

Zimmels, H. J. *Magicians, Theologians, and Doctors: Studies in Folk Medicine and Folklore as Reflected in the Rabbinical Responsa*. London: Edward Goldston, 1952.

———. *Die Marranen in der rabbinischen Literatur*. Berlin: R. Mass, 1932.

Works in Hebrew

Amar, Moshe. "A Biography of R. Jacob ben Tzur (Yaavets)." *East and Maghreb* 3 (1981): 89–124.

———. "A Description of the Collection of the Responsa of Rabbi Estruc ibn Sandji and the Sages of His Generation." *East and Maghreb* 4 (1983): 37–60.

Ankori, Zvi, ed. *From Lisbon to Salonica and Constantinople*. Tel Aviv: Tel Aviv University School of Jewish Studies, 1988.

Asaf, Simhah. "The Anusim of Spain and Portugal in the Responsa Literature." *Zion* 5 (1932/33): 19–60. Reprinted in Asaf, *Be-oholei Ya'akov*, 145–80. Jerusalem: Mossad Harav Kook, 1943.

Avitsur, Shemuel. "Safed: Center of the Manufacture of Woven Woolens in the Fifteenth Century." *Sefunot* 6 (1962): 41–70.

———. "The Woolen Textile Industry in Saloniki." *Sefunot* 12 (1971–78): 145–68.

Avrahami, I., ed. *Le memorial de la communaute Israelite Portugaise de Tunis: Les Grana, 1710–1944.* Lod: Orot Yahdout Hamagreb, 1997.

Azulai, Hayyim Joseph David. *Shem ha-Gedolim.* Jerusalem, 1970. Originally published in Livorno, 1774.

Bar-Asher, Shalom, ed. *Spanish and Portuguese Jews in Morocco (1492–1753): Sefer Hataqanot—The Book of Communal Ordinances.* Jerusalem: Academon, 1990.

Bashan, Eliezer. *Captivity and Ransom in Mediterranean Jewish Society (1391–1830).* Ramat Gan: Bar-Ilan University Press, 1980.

———. "*Conversos* Returning to Judaism in Turkey According to Reports of a British Diplomat in Istanbul, 1784." In *Hispano-Jewish Civilization after 1492,* ed. M. Abitbol, Y-T. Assis, and G. Hasan-Rokem, 47–58. Jerusalem: Misgav Yerushalayim, 1997.

———. "A Document Dated 5384 (1624) Concerning a Dispute on Lending Money to Christians in Jerusalem." In *Chapters in the History of the Jewish Community in Jerusalem,* 2:77–96. Jerusalem: Ben-Zvi Institute, 1976.

Beinart, Haim. *Chapters in Judeo-Spanish History.* 2 vols. Jerusalem: Magnes Press, 1998.

———. *The Expulsion of the Jews from Spain.* Jerusalem: Magnes Press, 1994.

Benayahu, Meir. "A Bundle of Letters from Eighteenth- and Nineteenth-Century Jerusalem." *Jerusalem: Quarterly Devoted to the Study of Jerusalem and Its History* 1:2 (1958): 74–88.

———. *Medical Essays of Rabbi Raphael Mordecai Malki.* Jerusalem: Yad ha-Rav Nissim, 1981.

———. *Relations Between Greek and Italian Jewry.* Tel Aviv: Diaspora Research Institute at Tel Aviv University, 1980.

———. *Yosef Behiri.* Jerusalem: Yad ha-Rav Nissim, 1990.

Ben Arhah, Eliezer. *She'elot u-Teshuvot Rabbenu Eliezer ben Arha ztz"l.* Ed. E. Basri. Jerusalem: Machon Yerushalayim, 1978.

Ben Habib, Moses. *She'elot u-Teshuvot Mahara"m Ben Habib.* Jerusalem: Hokhmat Shelomoh Institute, 1999.

Ben Naeh, Yaron. "Jewish Society in the Urban Centers of the Ottoman Empire during the Seventeenth Century (Istanbul, Salonica, Izmir)." Ph.D. dissertation, Hebrew University of Jerusalem, 1999.

———. "*Kehillat Yehudei Istanbul ba-Shanim 1650–1750: Mivneh, Irgun, u-Mosdot al-pi Safrut ha-She'elot u-Teshuvot.*" M.A. thesis, Hebrew University of Jerusalem, 1992.

Bentov, H. "The 'Residents' Jewish Community in Fez from the Sixteenth Century." *East and Maghreb* 5 (1986): 79–108.

Benvenisti, David. "Letters About Emissaries From Eretz Israel in Corfu (1722–1789)." *Sefunot* 15 (1971–81): 41–76.

Benvenisti, David, and Hayyim Mizrahi. "Sources for the History of the Jewish Community of Corfu." *Sefunot* 1 (1956): 303–14.

Bonfil, Robert. "Aspects of the Social and Spiritual Life of the Jews in Venetian Territories at the Beginning of the Sixteenth Century." *Zion* 41 (1976): 68–96.

Bornstein-Makovetsky, Leah. "Jewish Converts to Islam and Christianity in the Ottoman Empire from the Sixteenth to the Eighteenth Centuries." In *Hispano-Jewish Civilization after 1492*, ed. M. Abitbol, Y-T. Assis, and G. Hasan-Rokem, 3–29. Jerusalem: Misgav Yerushalayim, 1997.

Braude, Benjamin. "The Cloth Industry of Salonika in the Mediterranean Economy." *Pe'amim* 15 (1983): 82–95.

Cohen, Rivka. *Constantinople-Salonica-Patras: Communal and Supracommunal Organization of Greek Jewry Under Ottoman Rule (Fifteenth and Sixteenth Centuries)*. Tel Aviv: School of Jewish Studies, Tel Aviv University, 1984.

David, Abraham. "On the End of the Office of *Nagid* in Egypt and the History of Abraham de Castro." *Tarbiz* 41 (1971–72): 325–37.

Dimitrovsky, Haim Z. "Rabbi Yaakov Berab's Academy." *Sefunot* 7 (1963): 41–102.

Gerber, Haim. *Economic and Social Life of the Jews in the Ottoman Empire in the Sixteenth and Seventeenth Centuries*. Jerusalem: Shazar Center, 1982.

———. "The Jews in the Economic Life of the Anatolian City of Bursa in the Seventeenth Century: Notes and Documents." *Sefunot* 16 (N.S. 1) (1980): 235–72.

———. "The Jews of Edirne (Adrianople) in the Sixteenth and Seventeenth Centuries." *Sefunot* 18 (N.S. 3) (1985): 35–51.

Hacker, Joseph. "The Jewish Community of Salonica from the Fifteenth to the Sixteenth Century: A Chapter in the Social History of the Jews in the Ottoman Empire and Their Relations With the Authorities." Ph.D. dissertation, Hebrew University of Jerusalem, 1978.

Ibn Sangi, R. Astruc. *The Responsa of Rabbi Estruc Ibn Sandji*. Ed. Moshe Amar. Ramat Gan: Bar Ilan University Press, 1982.

Kaplan, Yosef. *The Western Sephardi Diaspora*. Tel Aviv: Israel Ministry of Defense, 1994.

Landau, Jacob M., ed. *The Jews in Ottoman Egypt (1517–1914)*. Jerusalem: Misgav Yerushalayim, 1988.

Moyal, Elie. *Rabbi Yaakob Sasportas*. Jerusalem: Mosad ha-Rav Kook, 1992.

Orfali, Moises, and M. A. Motis Doladèr. "An Examination of the Texts of the General Edict of Expulsion." *Pe'amim* 46–47 (Spring 1991): 148–68.

Posen, Raphael Benjamin. "Psychological Towers." *Ha-Aretz*. Accessed online, 18 October 2006. (See also under Reiner, Elchanan.)

Reiner, Elchanan. "An Event Which Occurred in the Holy Congregation of Worms Concerning the Great Earthquake of 1636: An Ashkenazi Love Story, Apparently Buried in a Volume of Responsa from the Seventeenth Century, Between the Daughter of a Wealthy Family and a Butcher's Boy." *Ha-Aretz*. Accessed online, 8 October 2006. (See also under Posen, Raphael Benjamin.)

————. "Response: The Gates of Interpretation Are Not Locked." *Ha-Aretz.* Accessed online, 25 October 2006.

Rivlin, Brachah. "Guidelines Toward a History of the Jewish Family in Greece in the Sixteenth and Seventeenth Centuries." In *Hispano-Jewish Civilization After 1492,* ed. M. Abitbol, Y-T. Assis, and G. Hasan-Rokem, 79–104. Jerusalem: Misgav Yerushalayim, 1997.

Rosanes, Shlomo. *Divrei Yemei Yisra'el Be-Togarmah, al-pi Meqorot Rishonim,* 2 vols. Tel Aviv: Dvir, 1930.

Rozen, Minna, ed. *The Days of the Crescent: Chapters in the History of the Jews in the Ottoman Empire.* Tel Aviv: Tel Aviv University, 1996.

————. *The Jewish Community of Jerusalem in the Seventeenth Century.* Tel Aviv: Tel Aviv University and the Israel Minstry of Defense, 1984.

————. *Safrut ha-Shu"t be-Tur Meqor le-Hayyei ha-Kalkalah shel ha-Yehudim be-Impiriyah ha-Ottomanit be-Me'ah ha-16.* Unpublished ms. N.p., n.d.

Sambari, Joseph b. Isaac. *Sefer Divrei Yosef by Yosef ben Yitzhak Sambari.* Ed. Shimon Shtober. Jerusalem: Ben-Zvi Institute, 1994.

Shalem, Shimon. "The Life and Works of Rabbi Moses Alshech." *Sefunot* 7 (1963): 179–98.

Soloveitchik, Haym. *The Use of Responsa as Historical Source: A Methodological Introduction.* Jerusalem: Hebrew University of Jerusalem Department of History of the Jewish People and Zalman Shazar Center for Jewish History, 1990.

Tishby, Isaiah. *Messianism in the Time of the Expulsion from Spain and Portugal.* Jerusalem: Shazar Center, 1985.

Ya'ari, Abraham. *Sheluhei Eretz Yisra'el.* Jerusalem: Mosad ha-Rav Kook, 1977.

Bibliographies

Bunis, David M., ed. *Sephardic Studies: A Research Bibliography Incorporating Judezmo Language, Literature and Folklore, and Historical Background.* New York: Garland, 1981.

Cohen, Hayyim J., and Zvi Yehuda, eds. *Asian and African Jews in the Middle East, 1860–1971.* Jerusalem: Hebrew University and Ben-Zvi Institute, 1976.

Coppenhagen, J. H., ed. *Menasseh ben Israel: Manuel Dias Soeiro, 1604–1657. A Bibliography.* Jerusalem: Misgav Yerushalayim, 1990.

Gerber, Jane S., ed. *Sephardic Studies in the University.* Madison, N.J.: Associated University Presses, 1995.

Salomon, H. P., ed. *Sephardic and Oriental Jewry: Selected Reading Lists of Books in English.* New York: Jewish Book Council, 1971.

Yahadut ha-Mizrah . . . Reshimah Shimushit. Jerusalem: Ministry of Education and Culture, 1981/2.

Responsa Editions

These are first editions unless otherwise noted. Istanbul is cited as Constantinople in the originals. See Short Biographies of the Hakhamim.

Algazi, Isaac. *She'elot u-Teshuvot*. ed. M. Ben-Shimon. Jerusalem: Machon Yerushalayim, 1982.

Almosnino, Joseph. *Edut be-Yehosef*, vol. 2. Constantinople, 1732.

Alsheikh, Moses. *She'elot u-Teshuvot Mahara"m Alsheikh*. Ed. Y. T. Porges. Bnei Brak: n.p., 1982. Original edition,Venice, 1605.

Amarillo, Solomon. *Kerem Shelomoh*. Saloniki, 1719.

Angel, Barukh. *Sefer She'elot u-Teshuvot*. Saloniki, 1717.

Ayyash, Judah. *Bet Yehudah*. Livorno, 1744.

Ben Arhah, Eliezer. *She'elot u-Teshuvot*. Ed. E. Basri. Jerusalem, 1978.

Ben Habib, Moses. *She'elot u-Teshuvot Mahara"m Ben Habib*. Jerusalem: Hokhmat Shelomoh, 2000.

Benveniste, Joshua. *Sha'ar Yehoshu'a*. Husiatin, 1904.

Berab, Jacob. *She'elot u-Teshuvot Mahar"i Berab*. Jerusalem: n.p., 1958; original edition, Venice, 1663.

Castro, Jacob. *Shu"t Oholei Ya'akov*. Livorno, 1783.

De Boton, Abraham. *Lehem Rav*. Jerusalem: n.p., 1981; original edition, Izmir, 1660.

De Boton, Jacob. *Edut be-Ya'akov*. Saloniki, 1720.

Gavizon, Me'ir. *Responsa*, vol. 2. Ed. E. Schochetman. Jerusalem: Or ha-Mizrah Institute, Machon Yerushalayim, 1985.

Hagiz, Jacob. *She'elot u-Teshuvot Halakhot Ketanot*. Jerusalem: n.p., 1981; original edition, Venice, 1704.

Hagiz, Moses. *Shete ha-Lehem*. Premysl, 1898; original edition, Wandsbek, 1733.

Ha-Levi, Eliyahu. *Zakken Aharon*. Constantinople, 1734.

Ha-Levi, Mordecai. *Sefer Darkhe No'am*. Venice, 1697.

Hayyim Jacob of Safed. *Sama de-Hayye*. Amsterdam, 1739.

Ibn Sangi, Astruc. *She'elot u-Teshuvot*. Ed. M. Amar. Ramat Gan: Bar-Ilan University Press, 1982.

Ibn Tzur, Jacob. *Mishpat u-Tzedakah be-Ya'akov*. Alexandria, 1894.

Ibn Yahya, Tam. *She'elot u-Teshuvot Ohalei Tam*. Ed. J. Tzemah. Jerusalem: Haktav Institute, 1998; originally published as part of *Tamat Yesharim*, Venice, 1620.

Karo, Joseph. *Avqat Rokhel*. Leipzig, 1859; original edition, Saloniki, 1791.

Katzabi, Joseph. *She'elot u-Teshuvot Mahara"m Katzabi*. Constantinople, 1736.

Melamed, Me'ir ben Shemtov. *Mishpat Tzedek*. Saloniki, 1799.

Meldola, David. *Divrei David*. Amsterdam, 1753.

Mizrahi, Israel Me'ir. *She'elot u-Teshuvot*. Constantinople, 1732.

Perahyah, Aaron ha-Kohen. *Perah Matteh Aharon*. Amsterdam, 1703.

Sasportas, Jacob. *She'elot u-Teshuvot Ohel Ya'akov*. Amsterdam, 1737.

INDEX

Abarbanel, Bienvenida, 26
Abarbanel, Isaac, xxv
Aboab, Samuel, lx
Adriatic Sea, xxxv
adultery, 83–87, 136–38, 139–42, 147.
  See also marriage
Africa, xlvi
agunah (grass widow), l, 22, 35, 54, 63,
  66, 67. *See also* widow(s)
Alboraycos, xxi
Aleppo (Aram Tzovah; Halab), xxxvii, 26,
  27, 35
Alexandri, Jacob, 153
Alfandari, Hayyim, lxi
Algazi, Isaac b. Abraham: biography of,
  lvii; *She'elot u-Teshuvot,* #69, 13–14
Algazi case, 8
Algeria, xl, xlii, lxiii, 73
Algiers, xxxix, xl, lviii, 15, 16–17
Alkabetz, Solomon: *Lekhah Dodi,* xxxii
Almohads, xix
Almoravids, xix
Almosnino, Joseph b. Isaac: biography of,
  lvii; *Edut be-Yehosef,* vol. 2, #20,
  143–46
Alsheikh, Moses: biography of, lvii;
  *She'elot u-Teshuvot Mahara"m Al-
  sheikh,* #57, 26–28; *She'elot u-Teshuvot
  Mahara"m Alsheikh,* #118, 29
Amar, Abraham, 63
Amarillo, Solomon b. Joseph: biography
  of, lvii–lviii; *Kerem Shelomoh, H. M.*
  #10, 153–54; *Kerem Shelomoh, H.M.*
  #29, 5–6; *Kerem Shelomoh, H.M.* #31,
  5, 6–7
America, xlvi
Amsterdam, xxxiii, xlii, xliii, xliv–xlv,
  xlvii, lxiii, 22, 102, 103, 109, 139, 156
Andalusia, xviii
Angel, Barukh: biography of, lviii; *Sefer
  She'elot u-Teshuvot,* #51, 64–65
Antwerp, xliii, xliv

apostasy, xiv, xxii, 54, 55, 61, 62, 71, 72,
  105, 152. *See also* conversion
apostles, 117
Arians, xvii
Aristotle, xxi, 93–94
artisans, xxxi, xxxvi, 22
Ashkenazi, Zvi, xxxvi
Ashkenazim, xxxii, xxxv, xxxvi, xxxvii,
  xliv, xlvii, 8, 29, 67, 109, 125, 131
Atruti, Nissim, 36, 37
Augustine, Saint, 3
Austria, xxxv, xxxvi
Averroes (Ibn Rushd), 94
Avicenna (Ibn Sina), 132, 133
Ayyash, Judah b. Isaac: *Bet Yehudah,* lviii;
  Bet Yehudah, H. M #4, 73–76; *Bet
  Yehudah,* H. M #18, 16–17; *Bet Yehu-
  dah,* O. H. #10, 15; biography of, lviii

Baer, Marc, 42
Balkan states, xxxiv–xxxvi, 143
banditry, xli, 77, 78–79
Barbados, xlvi
Basilia, Aviad Sar Shalom, 139
Bayezid II, xxix
Bayonne, xlvi, lxii, 155, 156, 157
Belgrade, xxxiv, xxxv, 143, 153
ben Abuya, Elisha, 95n
Ben Arhah, Eliezer b. Isaac, lviii; *She'elot
  u-Teshuvot,* #13a, 71–72; *She'elot
  u-Teshuvot,* #13:2, 115, 116–17
Ben Attar, Judah, 80, 81
Benayahu, Meir, 26
Benbassa, Esther, xxxv, xxxix
ben Ezra, Abraham, 94
Ben Habib, Moses b. Solomon: biography
  of, lviii; *She'elot u-Teshuvot,* vol. 1,
  #144, 35–37; *She'elot u-Teshuvot,* vol.
  1, #193, 150–52
ben Hassin, Abraham, 81
ben Israel, Menasseh, xlv, 52
ben Ramokh, Meir, 85

ben Samuel, Yohanan, 58
Ben Ullo, Joseph, 81
ben Uzziel Finzi, David, 139
Benveniste, Hayyim, lviii, 42–48, 52
Benveniste, Joshua b. Israel: biography of, lviii; *Sha'ar Yehoshu'a*, E. H. #27, 42–48
Berab, Jacob: biography of, lix; *She'elot u-Teshuvot*, #39, 127–28; *She'elot u-Teshuvot*, #44, 129–30
Bible, 3, 42, 44, 45, 83, 93, 96, 106, 107, 108, 126. *See also* Torah
bigamy, 134–35, 147
Bizini, Samuel, 36–37
blood libel/ritual murder, xxiv, xxxvi, 8–12, 13–14. *See also* murder
Bordeaux, xlvi
Braudel, Fernand, 23
bribery, 13, 29, 30, 72, 78, 79, 117, 153–54
Buber, Martin, 92
Budapest (Bodon), 143, 144
buildings, height of, 64–65
Bursa, xxxii, 29
Burton, Robert, *Anatomy of Melancholy*, 131
business: in Jerusalem, 118; and marriage, 125; and Monson, 74; and Morocco, xlii; and Western Sephardim, xlvii; women in, 26. *See also* commerce; merchants; trade
Byzantine Empire, xxviii, 4

Cairo, lx, 32, 74. *See also* Egypt
Capsali, Elijah, xxix
Capsali, Moses, xxx, lx
Capsali family, xxxiv
caravans, 30
Cardoso, Abraham Miguel, xxxix
Casablanca, xl
Castro, Abraham de, xxxviii, lix
Castro, Jacob, lx, 150, 151, 152; biography of, lix; *Shu"t Oholei Ya'akov*, #22, 38
Catherine of Aragon, xxxiii
Catholic Church, xlii
Catholicism, xviii, xix, xx, xxii, xxiii, xlvii, 99
Catholics, xliii, xliv
Çelebi, xxxviii

Cephalonia, 113
charitable fraternities, 102–5
Charles II, xlv
Cherethites, xxxiv
children, 61, 63, 103–4, 126, 127, 128, 129, 135, 147
Chmielnicki, Bogdan, 66
chocolate, xlvi
Chriqui, Rahamim, 35–36
Christian Europe, xxx
Christianity, lxii; conversion to, 62, 93; in Spain, xvii; and use of nativity medallion, 112–14
Christian physicians, 132, 133
Christians, 61; in Amsterdam, xliv; and blood libel/ritual murder, 8; and charity to poor Jews, 109–11; as concubines, 127, 128; and Corfu, xxxiv; donations from, 92; and forced conversion, 71; marriage to, 3; moneylending to, 23, 24; as musicians, 121; in Muslim Spain, xix; Muslim treatment of, 4; in Ottoman Empire, xxix; and property rights, 6; and Ragusa, xxxvi; relations with, xiv, xv; relations with *conversos*, xxii; in Rhodes, xxxiii; as servants, 3; in Shekhem, 136; in Spain, xxii; and taxation, 11; testimony against, 3; treatment of Jews by, 3, 64; and Venice, xxxiii. *See also* non-Jews
Christian savants, xxxiii, xlv
chuetas, xxi
circumcision, 101, 103, 108, 138
civet cats, 38
code of law. *See* non-Jewish law
Columbus, Christopher, xxv
commerce, xxxii, xxxiii, xxxvii, xl–xli, xliv, 21. *See also* business; trade
concubine, 127–28
Conforte, David, 97
Constantinople (Istanbul), xxxii, xxxviii, liv, lviii, lix, lx, lxi, lxii, 8, 29, 33, 42, 46, 47, 54, 59, 71–72, 98, 131, 132; Sephardim in, xxviii, xxix, xxx–xxxi
contract, 27
conversion: after baptism, 63; to Judaism, 144, 145; multiple, 62; in Portugal, xxvi–xxvii; return to Judaism after, 72, 103; in Rhodes, 71–72; at Second Coming of Jesus, 109; of Shabbatai Zvi,

xxxii; and slavery, 144; in Spain, xviii, xx, xxi, xxv, xxvi. *See also* apostasy

conversos, xiv, 68; and adultery, 139; in Algiers, xl; as *an_sim* (forced ones), 99–101; assimilation by, xxii, xxiv; bequests of, 99–101; and charitable fraternities, 102–5; and Christian charity, 110; and concubine, 127–28; and flight from Iberian penninsula, xlii–xliii; in France, xlvi; and Holy Child of La Guardia trial, xxiv; and Jewish faith, 92; leadership of, 52; and levirate marriage, 97, 98; in Livorno, xxxix, xlvi; and marriage, 99–100; and moneylending, 22; in Morocco, xli; motives of, xxi–xxii; persecution of, xxii; and relations with Christians, xxii; reversion to Judaism by, xliii; and Spanish Inquisition, xxiii–xxiv; as term, xxi; in Tiberias, xxxvii; and travel, 139; in Venice, xxxii–xxxiii; and Western Sephardic Diaspora, xlii–xlvii

coral, xl, xlvi, 21

Cordovero, Moses, xxxvii

Corfu, xxxiii, xxxiv, lxiii, 23, 24–25, 40

Cossacks, 66

courts, non-Jewish, xiv

crafts, xli, 26

credit, 44, 74

Crete, xxxiii, xxxiv, 94

Cromwell, Oliver, xlv

crypto-Judaism, xxiv, xxvii, xlii, xliii, xliv, 127

Culi, Jacob, *Me'Am Lo'ez,* xiv

Curaçāo, xlvi

Curiel, Abraham, 69, 70

currency, value of, 23–25

Dalmatia, 61, 68

Damascus, xxxvii–xxxviii, lix

David, Rabbi, 130

David ha-Reubeni, 53

Davis, Natalie Zemon, 32

death, 22, 33, 36, 54, 58, 59–60, 103, 104, 105, 126, 140, 142. *See also* inheritance

de Boton, Abraham Hiyya b. Moses: biography of, lix; *Lehem Rav,* #13, 23–25

de Boton, Jacob b. Abraham: biography of, lix; *Edut be-Ya'akov,* #31, 147–49

de Boton family, lix

debt, xxv, 5–7, 32–34, 43, 44, 47, 71, 74, 81, 110, 111

de Fano, Judah, 62

de Fonseca, Isaac Aboab, 52

del Medigo family, xxxiv

denunciation/defamation/slander, 77–82, 83, 85, 86, 87

de Robles, Moses, 157–58

dhimmis, xxix

diplomacy, xli

disease, 68, 69, 134

disputations, forced, xx, xxi

divorce, 54–57, 61, 62–63, 67, 74, 77, 79, 97, 125, 126, 138, 140, 150–52, 157

Dury, John, 109, 110

Edirne (Adrianople), xxxi, xxxii, liv, 72

Egypt, xxxviii–xxxix, lix, lx, 32, 33, 38, 45, 46, 47, 51, 54, 67, 73, 96, 98, 131, 132, 133. *See also* Cairo

ejaculation, 131, 132

England, xliii, 8, 110. *See also* London

English traders, xxxi

Esperanza, Gabriel, lx

Ethiopians, 107

Europe, lx; and Corfu, xxxiv; currency values in, 24; Jewish community in, 51; Jews and Christians in, 115; and Spalato, 68

Europe, Western, 139; assimilation and apostasy in, xiv; *conversos* in, xlii, xlvi, 22; *mahamad* in, 51; Polish refugees in, 66; Sephardim of, xlii

European Jews, xxxvii, xlii

Europeans, xxxi, xxxiii

excommunication, 156, 157

exile, 44

expulsion. *See* Portugal; Spain

family, xxviii, xxix, 150, 151, 155

family firm, 21

father(s), 26, 103, 104, 105, 136, 147, 151, 152, 156, 158

Fatimids, xxxviii

Ferdinand, King of Spain, xviii, xxiii, xxiv, xxix

Ferrer, Vicente, xxi

Fez, xl, xli, lx, lxi, 83, 85, 87

finance, xlv, 21, 26

finances, 8–9, 13
fines, xli, 78, 79, 86
fire, 58
fish, strange, 107, 108
Flanders, 127
food, 22, 35, 62, 108, 129, 130, 157
forgery, 33
France, xliii, xlvi, 155
Francos, xxxvii
fraternities, charitable, 102–5
French Jews, xxxii, xl
French traders, xxxi
friars, xx, xxi, xxiii, xxvii

Gabbai, Judah, 29, 30, 31
Galante, Moses, 52
Gavizon, Me'ir: biography of, lix–lx; *Responsa* vol. 2, #43 [=44], 185-86, 115, 117–19
Gaza, xxxvii, lviii
Germany, 8, 9, 67, 109
Gerson, Solomon, 84, 85, 86, 87
ghetto, xxxiii, xxxvi, xlvi
Glückel of Hameln, 26–27
Goa, 53
God, 43, 44, 47, 107, 120, 121
gold, xl, 21, 23, 113
governor, 71, 77, 78, 79, 85, 86, 87
Grana, xxxix
Granada, xxiv
Greece, xxxv, lxi, lxii, 5, 6, 7, 53, 112, 120
Greek myth, 106
Greek Orthodox Church, 112
Greek philosophy, xxi
Greeks, 23
Guerre, Martin, 32, 53

Habsburg Empire, 143
Hadidah, Judah, 85, 86
Hagiz, Jacob b. Samuel, lii, lviii, 92; biography of, lx; *She'elot u-Teshuvot Halakhot Ketanot*, part 1, #240, 107; *She'elot u-Teshuvot Halakhot Ketanot*, part 1, #245, 106–8; *She'elot u-Teshuvot Halakhot Ketanot*, part 1, #249, 106, 108; *She'elot u-Teshuvot Halakhot Ketanot*, part 1, #255, 106, 108; *She'elot u-Teshuvot Halakhot Ketanot*, part 2, #92, 109–11

Hagiz, Moses b. Jacob, lxii; biography of, lx; *Shete ha-Lehem*, #31, 139–42
Hai Ga'on, 94
hakham/hakhamim, xlii, li, 83; as term, liii
ha-Kohen, Solomon, 11, 83, 84–87
ha-Kohen (Maharsha"kh), Solomon, lxi
ha-Levi, Abraham b. Mordecai, lx
ha-Levi, Eliyahu b. Benjamin: biography of, lx; *Zakken Aharon*, #25, 93–95
ha-Levi, Isaac, 75
ha-Levi, Judah, xviii, 94
ha-Levi, Mordecai b. Judah: biography of, lx; *Sefer Darkhe No'am*, E. H. #5, 66–67; *Sefer Darkhe No'am*, E. H. #59, 96–98; *Sefer Darkhe No'am*, Y. D. #26, 131–33
halitzah, 96, 97
halshanah, 71
Hamburg, xlv–xlvi, lxiii, 139
ha-Reubeni, David, 53
Hayyim Jacob b. Jacob David of Safed: biography of, lxi; *Sama de-Hayye*, H. M. #6, 68–70
Hayyim of Imram, 87
Hebron, xxxvii
heresy, xx, xxiii, 91, 93–95. *See also* idolatry
Hillel, 43
Holy Child of La Guardia trial, xxiv, 8
homosexuality, 87, 126, 147, 148
Hormuz, 29, 31

Ibn Abi Zimra, David, 91
Ibn Aderet, Solomon, xx
Ibn Ezra, Joseph, lxii
Ibn Gabirol, 94
Ibn Nagrela, Samuel, xviii
Ibn Sangi, Astruc b. David: biography of, lxi; *She'elot u-Teshuvot*, #28, 8–12
Ibn Tzur, Jacob b. Reuben: biography of, lxi; *Mishpat u-Tzedakah be-Ya'akov*, #116, 77–82; *Mishpat u-Tzedakah be-Ya'akov*, #143, 134–35; *Mishpat u-Tzedakah be-Ya'akov*, #265, 83–87
Ibn Yahya, Tam (Jacob) b. David: biography of, lxi; *She'elot u-Teshuvot Ohalei Tam*, #91, 99–101
identity, 32–34, 53, 66, 67, 155
idolatry, 111, 112, 113, 115, 116–17, 119, 139, 140. *See also* heresy

imprisonment, 79, 81
incest, 136, 137–38
India, xxxvii, xlvi, 53, 54, 55
inflation, 23, 24, 25
inheritance, 6, 33, 99–101, 102, 103–5,
    128. See also death
Inquisition, xxiii–xxiv, xxvii, xlii, xlv,
    xlviii–xlix, 103, 127, 140
insurance, 103
Iraqis, xxxviii
Isabella, Queen of Spain, xviii, xxiii, xxiv,
    xxix
Isabella (daughter of Ferdinand and Isa-
    bella), xxvi
Isfahan, 30
Islam, xix, xxxii
Israel, Isaac, 63
Israel, Jacob, 86
Italian Jews, xxxii, xxxiv, xxxvii, xlvi, lxii
Italy, xxxvi, xxxix, xliii, lxii, 8, 9, 94, 107,
    108
Iyad, David, 63
Izmir (Smyrna), xxxi, xxxii, liv, lxi, 13

Jabli, Samuel, 36, 37
Jacobs, Louis, Theology in the Responsa,
    91
Jerusalem, xxxvii, xxxviii, lviii, lx, lxii,
    106, 109–11, 115, 117, 150
Jeshurun, Isaac, xxxvi, 8
Jesus, xviii, xxiii, 109, 110, 113
Jewish dogma, 91
Jewish elite, 51–52
Jewish law, xxii, xlvii, xlix, l, li, 51, 52, 83,
    91, 96, 150. See also rabbinical court(s);
    witnesses/testimony
Jewish oral law, xxxix
Jewish philosophy, 93, 94
Jewish ritual, 8, 51, 91, 156
João II, King of Portugal, xxvi
Juan of Castile, xx
Judaizers, xxiv, xlii, xliv
Judeo-Arabic culture, xxxix

Kabbalah, xxxi, xxxvii, xxxviii, lxiii, 93,
    115, 120. See also mysticism
Kahu/Kaunos, 36
Kaposi, Hayyim, lx
Karaites, xxxix, 91, 92, 96–98
Karlowitz, peace of, 5

Karo, Joseph b. Ephraim, lvii, 28; Avqat
    Rokhel, #68, 112–14; Bet Yosef, lxi;
    biography of, lxi–lxii; Shulhan Arukh,
    xxxii, li, lviii, lix, lxii
Kastoria, xxxii, 120–22
Katzabi, Joseph b. Nissim: biography of,
    lxii; She'elot u-Teshuvot Mahara"m
    Katzabi, #21, 32
kehillah/kehillot/kahal/kehalim
    (community/communities), xxx, xxxi
kidnapping, 144
Knights Hospitalers, xxxiii
Knights of Malta, xxxix
Kohen, David, 105
Kohen, Isaac, 85, 86
Kol Nidre, 141
Kuti, Raphael, 63
Kyra, Esther, xxx

Lamdan, Ruth, Separate People, 26, 27
Larissa, xxxii
Lavi, Simeon, xxxix
law. See Jewish law; non-Jewish law
lay leaders, 3, 51–52, 77, 78, 79
lazaretto, 68–69
legal scholars, xxxix
Lepanto, 5, 58
letter of agency, 32, 33, 34, 39, 40, 41
Levantine communities, xxxii
Levy, B. Barry, Fixing God's Torah, 91
Livorno, Italy, xxxix, xlvi, liv, lviii, lx, lxii,
    lxiii, 139
London, xxxiii, xliii, xliv, xlv, lxiii, 22,
    109, 139, 140. See also England
Low Countries, 127
Luria, Isaac (AR"I), xxxvii, lxiii

Macedonia, 120
Maghrebi Jews, xxxix
magic, 106
mahamad (lay leaders), xliv, xlv, xlvii,
    51–52
Maimon, Sheikh, 77, 78, 81, 82
Maimonides, Moses, xviii–xix, 75, 93, 94,
    95; Mishneh Torah, li
Majorcan Jews, xl
Malkah, Jacob, 80–81
Malki, Raphael Mordecai, 115, 119; biog-
    raphy of, lxii
Mamluks, xxxviii

Manoel, King of Portugal, xxvi, xxvii
Mantuan rabbinical court, 142
marginal groups, 4, 51, 61, 136
Marrakesh, xl
marranos, xxi. *See also conversos*
marriage, 77, 79; abuse in, 129–30; to additional wife, 74–75; age at, 125; annulment of, 75, 129, 157, 158; and bigamy,
 134–35, 147; and business, 125; and
 charitable fraternities, 104; to Christians, 3; clandestine, 155–58; and *conversos,* 99–100, 128; and convert to
 Judaism, 129–30; as cure, 134, 135;
 dowry for, 157; to former slave, 144,
 145–46; and Karaites, 96–98; levirate,
 96–97; and melancholy, 131–33; number of wives in, 131–32, 134–35; in
 pre-modern world, 125; and public behavior, 120–22; refusal of intercourse
 in, 147, 148, 149; between Sephardim
 and Ashkenazim, 125; and sexual abuse,
 144, 147–49; stages of, 126. *See also*
 adultery; remarriage; sex/sexuality; wife
Martínez, Ferrant, xx, xxi
marvels, 106–8
Mary, mother of Jesus, 113
masturbation, 126, 132
matchmaker, 145–46
Mattuk (Mi-Attuck), Isaac, 30
Medici, xlvi
megorashim, xli
Meknès, xl, 77
Melamed, Me'ir ben Shemtov: biography
 of, lxii; *Mishpat Tzedek,* vol. 3, #4,
 53–57; *Mishpat Tzedek,* vol. 3, #23,
 39–41; *Mishpat Tzedek,* vol. 3, #27,
 61–63; *Mishpat Tzedek,* vol. 3, #35,
 58–60
melancholy, 131–33
Meldola, David b. Raphael: biography of,
 lxii; *Divrei David,* #73-76, 155–58
menstruation, 120, 126, 135, 156
mercantile trade, xlvi, 21–22, 103
mercenary, 61–63
merchandise, 39, 40, 41
merchants, 43; in Amsterdam, xliv; in
 Corfu, 23; and Izmir (Smyrna), xxxi; in
 Livorno, xlvi; and Monson, 74; in Ottoman Empire, xxx; and Spalato, 69, 70;
 travel by, 29. *See also* business; trade

messianism, xix, xxviii, xxxii, xxxix, 53,
 110
Meyerson, Mark, xxin
millenarianism, xxiii, 92, 109, 110
minorities, XXIX
Mishan, Moses, 6
Mizrahi, Eliahu, lxi
Mizrahi, Elijah, xxx, lx, 52
Mizrahi, Israel Meir b. Joseph: biography
 of, lxii–lxiii; *She'elot u-Teshuvot,* O. H.,
 #1, 136–38
Mogador, xl
Mohács, 143
Mohammed, xviii
money changing, xxxiv
moneylending, xxxiv, 21–22, 23–25, 27,
 38, 115–19, 150
Monson, Abraham, 73, 74–75
Morea, lxii
moriscos, xxii
Morocco, xl–xlii, xliii, lix, lxi, 51, 73, 77,
 134
Mortera, Saul Levi, 52
mulays (governors), xli, 77–78, 79; as
 term, liii
murder, 4, 22, 29, 30, 77, 79, 140,
 153–54. *See also* blood libel/ritual
 murder
Muslim authorities, 77, 78, 80
Muslim court(s), 32, 33, 150, 151, 152.
 See also non-Jewish courts
Muslim law, 150
Muslim philosophy, xxi
Muslims: in Algiers, xl; baptized, xxii;
 expulsion of from Portugal, xxvi; and
 forced conversion, 71; and moneylending, 116, 117; and property rights, 7;
 relations with, xiv, xv; in Shekhem, 136;
 and slavery, 145; in Spain, xviii–xix,
 xxii; and Spanish attack on Algiers, 15;
 subordination to, 64; treatment of Christians by, 4; treatment of Jews by, 3, 4,
 64; in Tunis, xl. *See also* non-Jews
Must'arib Jews, xxxvii, xl, 29
mysticism, xx, xxii, xxxi, xxxii, xxxvii,
 xxxix, 115. *See also* kabbalah

Nação, xlvii, 102
nagid, xxxviii, 51, 77–78, 79, 80, 81, 82
Nahmanides, Moses, xx

Nasi (Mendes), Gracia, xxx, xxxvii, 26–27, 127
Nasi (Migues), Joseph, xxxvii
Nasi/Migues family, xxx
Nathan Ashkenazi of Gaza, xxxii
nativity medallion, 112–14
natural philosophy, 106
Navarre, xxv
Netherlands, 109, 110
New Testament, xviii, 96
nickname, 54, 55, 56
Nissim, Rabbenu, 113
nocturnal emission, 134, 135
non-Jewish courts, 4, 13, 14, 144, 145. *See also* Muslim court(s)
non-Jewish law, 3, 129. *See also* Jewish law
non-Jews: adultery with, 136, 137; and blood libel, 13; conversion to Judaism by, 129; fraternization with, 3; law against converting, 129, 130; money-lending to, 21, 23; and property rights, 16, 17; testimony from, liii. *See also* Christians; Muslims
non-Sephardim, 29
North Africa, xiv, xix, xxv, xxvii, xxxix, xlvi, 73, 75, 134
nuevos christianos, xxi

Oral Law tradition, 96
Oran, xxxix, xl, 74
orphans, 21, 51, 115, 119
ostracism, 11, 12
Ottoman court, xxx, 42, 43, 44, 45, 46, 47
Ottoman Empire, 53, 129, 147; and Aleppo, xxxvii; and Algiers, xl; and Belgrade, xxxv; blood libel/ritual murder in, 13–14; and *conversos,* xliii; and Corfu, xxxiv, 23; and Crete, xxxiv; currency values in, 24; and Damascus, xxxviii; and Eastern Sephardic Diaspora, xxvii–xxx; economy of, xxviii, 24; and effect of war on trade, 39; and Egypt, xxxviii–xxxix; Jewish philosophy in, 94; Jews and Christians in, 115; and Lepanto, 5; and North Africa, xxxix; and Palestine, xxxvi–xxxvii; and Patras, 5; Polish refugees in, 66; and Ragusa, xxxvi; and Rhodes, xxxiii; and Spalato,

xxxvi, 68; treatment of Jews in, 4; and Venice, xxxiii; and war with Habsburg Empire, 143
Ottoman-Italian wars, 5
Ottoman Turkey, xxxv, 35, 69, 127, 128
Ottoman Turks, xxviii, 33, 59, 101; and Belgrade, xxxv; envy of, 11; and property rights, 5–6, 7; and Sarajevo, xxxvi

Pact of 'Umar, 4
Palestine, xxxii, xxxvi–xxxvii, lviii, lix, lxi, 92, 107, 115, 136
partnership, 21, 24, 26, 27–28, 46, 47
pasha, 77, 78, 79
Patras, xxxii, 5, 6
penitence, 120–22
Perahyah, Aaron b. Hayyim Abraham ha-Kohen: biography of, lxiii; *Perah Matteh Aharon,* #5, 120–22
Perahyah, Hasdai ha-Kohen, lix
perfume industry, 38
Pernambuco, xlvi
Persia, xxxvii, xlii, 29
Philistines, xxxiv
physicians, xxx, xxxiii, 132, 133
Pico, Joseph, 29, 31
Pinto, Joseph, 119
piracy, XXXI
plague, 68, 69
Poland, 66
Polia, lix
Ponentine communities, xxxii
poor people, xxxvi, 43, 45, 52, 70, 109–11, 117, 136, 145, 151
Portugal, xiv, xxv, xxvi, xlv, lxi, 71, 102, 110, 127
Portuguese Inquisition, xxvii
power of attorney, 32
pregnancy, 136–38, 156
priests, 115
printing, xxix, xlv, xlvi, xlix
professions, 22
property, 5–7, 33, 44; in Algiers, 16–17; and blood libel, 9; communal, 9, 10; confiscation of in Spain, xxv; and great fire of Saloniki, 58; and letter of agency, 39, 40, 41; and Spanish attack on Algiers, 15
prostitution, 132, 156
Protestants, xliv, 92, 109–11

public office, 3
purity of blood statutes, xxii–xxiii, xxiv

quarantine camp, 68–69

Rabbanites, xxxix, 96
rabbinical court(s), 3, 32, 51, 86; and communities, 83; of Constantinople, 71–72; and divorce, 150, 151, 152; and Eastern Sephardic Diaspora, xxix; in Egypt, 133; of Mantua, 142; in Morocco, 78, 80, 82; proceedings of, li; verbatim testimony before, l. *See also* Jewish law; responsa; witnesses/testimony
rabbinic scholars, xxxiv, xxxix
rabbi(s), 22, 79; in Algiers, xl; in Amsterdam, xlv; authority of, 51–52, 77, 78; as *conversos,* xxi; and Damascus, xxxviii; as elite, 52; and historical sources, xlix; integrity of, 83; and Izmir (Smyrna), xxxi; and Jewish philosophy, 95; and Judaizers, xliv; Karaite rejection of, 96; and Morocco, xli, xlii; and Ottoman Empire, xxxii; in Palestine, xxxvii; and priests, 116–17; and private life, 147; proceedings of, li; and responsa, xlix, l, li, lii; in Safed, xxxvii; in Sarajevo, xxxvi; as term, liii; and Torah, 52; in Venice, xxxiii; and Western Sephardim, xlvii
Ragusa (Dubrovnik), xxxiv, xxxvi, liv, 8–12, 70
Ragusa Jewish ghetto, xxxvi
Rama"b (RM"B), 81
Rashi, 116
Reccared, xvii–xviii
Recife, xlvi
remarriage, 22, 31, 37, 54, 55, 58, 60, 66, 96, 97. *See also* marriage
repentence, 140–42
responsa, 91–92; classes of people in, l; creation of, li–lii; defined, xi–xii; division of, liii–liv; life stories in, xii, lii–liii; and pseudo-questions, lii; and rabbis, xlix, l, li, lii; technical phrases in, liii; topics in, xlix; verbatim testimony in, l–li; witnesses in, liii. *See also* rabbinical court(s)
Rhodes, xxxiii–xxxiv, 71–72
robbery, 4, 22, 77, 78–79, 80, 129, 130, 139, 140, 141, 157

Rodriga, Daniel, xxxvi
Rodrigue, Aron, xxxv, xxxix
Romaniotes, xxviii, xxxiv, 29
Roman law, 3
Romano, Joshua, 62, 63
Rosetta, lx
Roth, Cecil, xxin
Russia, xlvi, 66

Sa'adiah Ga'on, 94
Sabbatean movement, xxxix, lx
Sabbath, profanation of, 139, 140, 141
Sadducees, 96
Safed, xxxi, xxxvii, xxxviii, lviii, lix, lx, 115
Safed mystic circle, xxxii
Safi, xl
Sages, liii, 97, 118, 140
Sakankor (fish), 108
Saloniki, xxix, xxx–xxxi, xxxii, lviii, lix, lxi, lxii, lxiii, 23, 54, 58–60, 70, 120, 122
Samaritans, 136
São Tomé, xxvi
Sarajevo, xxxiv, xxxvi, 68, 69–70
Sasportas, Jacob, 100; biography of, lxiii; *She'elot u-Teshuvot Ohel Ya'akov,* #59, 102–5
Sasportas family, xl
Sasson, Aaron, 11
scapegoats, 4
science, 106
Senior (Seneor), Abraham, xxv
Sepharad, xvii
Sephardic Diaspora, Eastern, xxvii–xlii, xlvi, xlvii
Sephardic Diaspora, Western, xxxvi, xlii–xlvii
Sephardim: and assimilation, xiv; community of, 51; Eastern, xxvii–xlii, xlvi, xlvii, 22, 125; historical writing of, xxix; identity of, xiii–xiv; and language, xiii, xiv; living conditions of, xiv; and marriage, 131; marriage with Ashkenazim, 125; and Ottoman Empire, xxvii–xxx; persecution of, xviii; and Spain, xvii; Spanish-Jewish identity of, xix; as term, xxvii; in Venice, xxxii–xxxiii; Western, xxxvi, xlii–xlvii, 22, 52, 125, 139
Serrarius, Petrus, 109

sex/sexuality, 83–87, 126, 131–33, 134–35, 136–38. *See also* marriage
sexual abuse, 144, 145, 146, 147–49
Shabbatai Zvi, xxxi–xxxii, xlii, lxiii, 131
Shalom, Joseph, 100–101
Shapira, Nathan, 109
shaving, 139, 141
Shekhem (Nablus), 136
Shiraz, 30, 31
Shkokim (Uskoks of Senj), 61, 62
Siamese twins, 107–8
Sicilian Jews, xxxviii
silver, 21, 23, 113
sin, 120, 134, 135
Sinai, Moses, 157
slander. *See* denunciation/defamation/slander
slavery, xxv, xxvi, xxxiii, xxxv, 21, 143–46
social class, 125
Society for Dowering Orphans, 102, 103–5
Sofia, lxi
Soloveitchik, Haym, l
Spain, xiv, lxi; attack on Algiers, 15; Catholic, xviii, xix, xx; and charitable fraternities, 102; Christians in, xxii; expulsion from, xxiv–xxvi; invasion of North Africa by, 73, 75; Jewish life in, xvii–xxvii; millenarianism in, xxiii; and Morocco, xli; Muslim, xviii–xix; Muslims in, xxii; and North Africa, xxxix; persecution in, xviii, xix, xx–xxi, 110; travel to, 139, 140; and war with Venice, 39, 40, 61
Spalato (Split), xxxiv, xxxvi, liv, 39, 40, 41, 68–70
Spanish Expulsion, xiii, xxviii, xli, xliv, 93, 94
Spanish Inquisition, xxiii–xxiv, xlii, xlv, 103, 127, 140
Spanish language, xxvii
Spanish/Livornese Jews, xxxix
Spanish Reconquista, xix–xx, xxiv
Spinoza, Baruch, xlvii
Suleiman the Magnificent, xxx, xxxi, lxi
sultan, 72, 143; and Eastern Sephardic Diaspora, xxviii; and Egypt, xxxviii; harem of, xxx, 26; license from, 27; and Morocco, xli, xlii, 77–78; mother of, 42, 46; and property rights, 6, 7; service to,

xxx, 43, 44, 45, 47; and Shabbatai Zvi, xxxii; and slavery, 144–45; and taxation, 64; as term, liii; wife of, 42, 46
sürgün (transfer), xxviii
Sweden, 66, 109
Syria, xxxvii, lix

Taitatzak, Joseph, lvii
Tall Aslan, 35–37
Talmud, xxxix, li, liii, lix, 43, 94, 96
Tangier, xl, 83, 85, 86, 87
Tatars, 66
taxation: and Aleppo, xxxvii; and bloodlibel, 9–12, 14; and Christians, 11; in Hamburg, xlvi; and Izmir (Smyrna), xxxi; in Jerusalem, 117; and Jewish courts, 51; in Morocco, xli; in Ottoman Empire, xxix; and Rhodes, xxxiv; and Spalato, xxxvi, 68, 69, 70; by sultan, 64; in Turkey, 11
testimony. *See* witnesses/testimony
Tétouan, xl, lxi, 73, 74, 75, 86
textiles, xxxi, xxxvii, xl, 33, 38, 40
Thirty Years' War, 109
Tiberias, xxxvii, 53, 54, 55
Tlemcen, xxxix, xl
Toledo, xxii
Torah, xxxix, 43, 74, 143; call up to, 141, 142; and Jewish philosophy, 94, 95; and rabbis, 52; and responsa, 91; study of, xl, 117. *See also* Bible
Torquemada, Thomas, xxv
torture, 85
Tosaphists, 116
toshavim, xli
Touansa, xxxix–xl
trade, 33, 43; and Aleppo, xxxvii; in Algiers, 16; centrality of, 21; and *conversos*, xliii; and Corfu, xxxiv; effect of war on, 39–41; in Egypt, xxxix; and France, xlvi; in gold and silver, 113; and Izmir (Smyrna), xxxi; and Kastoria, 120; in Livorno, xlvi; and moneylending, 23; and Ottoman Empire, xxviii, xxxii; in Ragusa, 9–12; and Rhodes, xxxiv; and Sarajevo, xxxvi; and Spalato, 39, 68, 69; in Tunis, xl; between Turkey and Europe, 9–12; variety of, 21, 38; and Venice, xxxiii, 39; and war, 103. *See also* business; commerce; merchants

trades, variety of, 22
Trani, Joseph, lviii, lxii, 28
travel, 22, 47; and *conversos,* 139; dangers
   of, 126; and Eastern Sephardic Dias-
   pora, xxix; and identity, 53; and mar-
   vels, 106, 107; by merchants, 29; by
   Monson, 74; and poor people, 136, 137;
   and Spalato, 68
Tripoli, xxxix
Tsaga, 113
Tsakarisiánon, 113
Tunis, xxxix–xl

Vakif, 5, 6
Venice, lx, 106; and Amsterdam, xlv; and
   Corfu, 23; and Crete, xxxiv; dancing in,
   120–21; Jewish ghetto in, xxxiii; and
   Lepanto, 5; and moneylending, 23, 24,
   25; and Patras, 5; and Ragusa, xxxvi;
   and Sarajevo, xxxvi; Sephardim in,
   xxxii–xxxiii; and Shkokim, 61, 62; and
   Spalato, xxxvi, 68, 69; and trade, 39,
   40, 41; war of with Spain, 39, 40, 61
Verona, 108
Vienna, 143
violence, 66, 78–79. *See also* war
Visigoths, xvii
Vital, Hayyim, lvii
vizier, 42, 43, 44–47

war, 5, 15, 39–41, 73, 75, 103, 109, 143
wealth, 4, 43, 153

widow(s), 63, 67; abandoned, 29, 31; and
   adultery, 84; in business, 26–27; and
   Jewish courts, 51; moneylending by, 27,
   115, 119; and Polish refugees, 66; remarriage by, 22, 37, 54, 55, 58, 60, 66;
   of Tall Aslan, 35; and testimony, l. *See
   also* women
wife, 29, 54, 72, 73, 74, 75–76, 86, 140.
   See also marriage
witnesses/testimony, liii, 83, 84–85, 86,
   87, 151, 157. *See also* Jewish law; rabbinical court(s)
women, 72; and adultery, 84, 85, 87; in
   business, 26; and childbirth, 126; as concubines, 127–28; and *conversos,*
   99–100; in crafts, 26; and divorce,
   150–52; in finance, 26; and homosexuality, 87; and Karaites, 96–98; moneylending by, 21, 27; in Ottoman court
   circles, xxx, 42, 46; of Patras, 6; private
   lives of, 125; pseudonyms for, liv; and
   public behavior, 120–22; and steel-
   welding, 26–28. *See also* widow(s); wife

Yemen, xlii
yibum, 96–97
Yitzhaki, Abraham, lxii

Zakhariah, Rabbi, 130
Zante (Zakynthos), 8, 39, 40, 41, 61, 62
Zin, Yeshua, 75
Zohar, xx, xxxix, xlii, 93